APPROVED INSCRIPTIONS
FOR THIS MANUAL

The following approved inscriptions are intended for use by persons
purchasing the leasehold on this volume,
intending to make a once-only gift to a third party.

FOR THE CLASSICAL SCHOLAR OR BOOKWORM

Dear .... Ὀρφνη καὶ σκότος ἐστὶν ἀλάμπετον, ἦν δέ σε
μύστης Εἰσαγάγη, φανεροῦ λαμπρότερ' ἠελίου.

Yours, ...

FOR GENTLEMEN

Greetings ...., old man/you old reprobate*. How are things at
your end? Please accept this humble volume. You'll find it helps to while away the jolly old
winter nights.

Yours, ... (Gent.) of the parish of
.... in the County of ....

FOR PLAYERS

From .... *his mark.*

FOR GENERAL USE ON SPECIAL OCCASIONS

I ...., being the Auntie/Grandmother/dutiful Father/proud
Mother* (state other relationship ....), wish you
.... a happy/merry, birthday/Christmas*, and I hope that the
wisdom contained within these covers will profit you on your Great Journey through life.
Always play the Game well and never cheat as W.G. Grace/your Father/Grandfather/Uncle
.... did*

Lots of love ....

DECLARATION

I, ..., solemnly and sincerely declare and affirm
that, in an act of self-improvement and good cricketing sense, have purchased the leasehold
on this volume for my own enjoyment, benefit and use. Any person sharing, reading or
ridiculing this book, without prior permission in written form, will be reported to the British
Academy of Cricket forthwith and may face disciplinary proceedings under the Regulations
herein contained.

I acknowledge that this book is not my property and will be returned to the British
Academy of Cricket at or about the time of my death.

Signed ....

* Delete as appropriate.

1

(Turn over)
Failure to
do so is a
C2A offence

TO SUNDRY AND PARTICULAR PERSONS

BE IT KNOWN THAT

The British Academy of Cricket requests and requires that all cricketers accept these regulations and precepts without complaint or question, and **that all Registered persons afford assistance and allow passage without Let or Hindrance, to *any Inspector, Member or Officer of the* British Academy of Cricket in the rightful pursuit of any confiscation, seizure, interrogation, arrest or any other legitimate Act or Duty.**

How to make the Approved Maximum Use of the Manual

Every Regulation has been printed clearly in simple words and phrases. Regulations should be the subject of detailed study. Improving texts, or Lessons as they are called here, have an L number. One text should be committed to memory each day.

This will prove of especial benefit to the young man who, armed with Academy Wisdom from an early age, will find it his trusty companion in times of loneliness and despair, his passport to success in life and his fierce comrade-in-arms when he is besieged by doubters and mockers.

This book is not simply a congenial companion for the cricketer. Let no-one mistake its gentle tone and pleasant appearance: it is a **Book of Law**, with **Rules** that ***must not be defied***, and it is senseless to resist.

Any person breaking the Regulations set out herein is entitled to receive the appropriate penalty. Every Regulation bears an R number and a penalty classification code[1] C1, C2, C2A, C3, or C4. This must be quoted in all correspondence and in official reports to the Informer General or to the Moderator and his staff.

[1] Details of the codes as well as procedures for the reporting of offenders, sentencing structures, and penal provisions are described fully in Appendix A. The British Academy of Cricket's administrative structure and judicial hierarchy is shewn on page 28.

Sanctissimus Qui Ubique Instituet Tres

THIS VOLUME IS
ISSUED UNDER THE AUTHORITY OF THE
BRITISH ACADEMY OF CRICKET

The Directors of the British Academy of Cricket have perused the information in this book and have verified that it is in accordance with Academy rulings. They concur with the advice given and recommend it as the Official Handbook for the use of all Registered Gentlemen and players.

(Turn over)

The British Academy
—— *of* CRICKET ——
MANUAL

For GENTLEMEN *and Players*

A MENTOR and GUIDE on all matters relating to Cricket
with notes on PROPER SPORTING BEHAVIOUR, the whole being
an AUTHORISED DIGEST of Legislation
expressed in simple Lessons and Strict REGULATIONS.

BY KIND PERMISSION OF

THE BRITISH ACADEMY OF CRICKET

LONDON   CALCUTTA   CHRISTCHURCH   MELBOURNE   KARACHI

JOHANNESBURG   PORT OF SPAIN

(Turn over)

First published in 1988 by
PAVILION BOOKS LIMITED
196 Shaftesbury Avenue, London WC2H 8JL
in association with Michael Joseph Limited
27 Wrights Lane, Kensington, W8 5TZ

British Library Cataloguing in Publication Data
Ward, Martin
Manual for Gentlemen and players: The British Academy of Cricket.
1. Cricket—Anecdotes, facetiae, satire, etc.
I. Title   II. Oldman, Paul
796.35′8′0207   GV919

ISBN 1-85145-221-4

This book is set in 11/12pt Linotron Perpetua
and 10/12pt Linotron Baskerville Italics
Printed in Great Britain by Anchor Brendon, Tiptree

Readers will be gratified to
learn that the
present Volume contains the following

CONTENTS

PART THE FIRST : INTRODUCTORY

PART THE SECOND : THE CLOSE SEASON

ITEM : CRICKET BALLS

ITEM : GOOD WIVES

ITEM : BATTING ORDERS

ITEM : YULETIDE FESTIVITIES

PART THE THIRD   THE SEASON

SECTION ONE : PREPARATION FOR THE GAME

(Turn over)

SECTION FOUR : AGGRAVATED NUISANCES

THE FIRST BLOW : ACTS OF GOD

THE SECOND BLOW : FIRE

THE FINAL BLOW : INJURIES

SECTION FIVE : THE SUMMER CAMPAIGN

BRIEFING ONE : PREPARATIONS FOR THE TOUR

BRIEFING TWO : ON THE MOVE

BRIEFING THREE : THE MOVABLE FEAST

(Turn over)

A STIRRING PREFACE
BY
THE CHAIRMAN OF THE BRITISH
ACADEMY OF CRICKET

"And everywhere there shall be a sign ..."

Let all take heart and none despair that dwell in England. The cricketing sign of the Trinity shall say to those who thirst for righteousness, "Drink for here is water", to the hungry and cold, "eat and your tummy shall be full again, run and you shall be warm." Here is a home for the wanderer, here shall the weary find rest. Here, at this crystal fountain, paddle and even unto the feet you shall be cleansed. Here your debtors shall come unto you and you shall wear out your thumb[1] with counting. At this place all griefs are comforted, all foes are slain; here the spitting has to stop. Think and you shall be as a thought in the mind of the many, bathe and become to your neighbour as a bath, drink and be to him as a drunk.

Everywhere there shall be a sign, on the teapot and the tablecloth, the Cricketing Bun and the Classic Bat, the glove, the pad and thigh, in Slough and in Shropshire and the Pennine Hills.

And whosoever shall see this sign let him take heart and comfort all despair for it states most eloquent: "See how yet there endures beneath our Waste Land a stream of Duty and Decorum which flows relentless, and it will erupt and drown all the Sinful, the Sniggerers and the keepers of dogs.[2] Here wells up at last the Old Great Fiery Heart of England."

[1] Happiness may be defined as a worn thumb.
[2] Registered Hounds and Guard Dogs are acceptable.

(Turn over)

Fig. 01: *Sir St. John Peatfield*

The Editors esteem it a great privilege that Sir St. John Peatfield, a Governor of the British Academy of Cricket and personal adviser to the Chairman, has consented, without remuneration, to appear in certain photographic plates in this Manual.

The consummate honour bestowed upon the compilers of this volume is the masterly contribution of the Chairman Himself who is a keen photographer and President of His Camera Club. With modesty He has decreed that His photographs shall not be identified.

PART THE FIRST
THE TASK AHEAD

"We count it a privilege to live in an age
when England demands that great things shall be done,
a privilege to be of a generation which learns to say
what can we give instead of what can we take. For thus
our generation learns there are greater things
than slothful ease; greater things
than safety; more terrible things than death."

(Turn over)

A POLEMICAL INTRODUCTION
BY SIR JOHN GARRETT

The Founders of the British Academy of Cricket, the governing body of village and club cricket throughout the world, are Men of Vision. They share with serious Chief Constables a deep concern at the deterioration in standards of behaviour in Cricketing Affairs.

This signifies a deep moral, religious and physical decay in our National Life. Foreigners now govern large parts of the world and there have been defeats and humiliations East of Suez. These reverses, too often reflected in our cricketing fortunes, notwithstanding the triumph of British Arms in the South Atlantic, reinforce the conviction that there is an International Foreign Conspiracy[1] which threatens Britain's Custody of the Game and is attempting to loosen Her Majesty's moral authority over the Commonwealth, Dominions and Dependencies.

Moral Decline and its Causes

It is evident that this Ugly Growth of Decadence and the Deplorable Decline in British Prestige is due **not to any innate lack of military and sporting ability** but, more seriously, **to years of Slackening in Standards of Discipline** and **Reductions in the Surface Fleet** (Fig. 02) combined with an accelerating crime rate. The levels of crime against the person, property and the State, inherited by the present Government, are evidence of a virulent poison coursing through the veins of our Nation. A massive antidote is now needed.

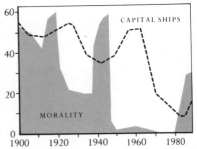

Fig. 02: *Moral decline in the twentieth century.* Careful study of a graph shewing moral decline in Britain since 1900 is rewarded by the discovery that Things Have Gone From Bad To Worse. The accelerating decline was interrupted only briefly from 1914 to 1918 for King and Country, and again from 1939 to 1945 with Digging for Victory. Harold Wilson is to blame for later disasters.

Reductions in the Surface Fleet are shewn with a dotted line.

---

[1] This was proven by the discovery of the wicked book: *The Protocols of the Elders of Zion.*

16

Intimations of Immorality and the Lost Opportunities

The warning bell should have sounded when the following occurred:

1) Lack of respect for the police[1]
2) The Education Act, 1944
3) The end of conscription
4) The Crisis of Faith (Fig. 03)

Fig. 03: *The Crisis of Faith*

Science has made Man too big for his boots. Although he knew very little of stars and could barely decline his own name it was Galileo Galilei who took it upon himself to confront Cardinal Bob Bellarmine and later the Whole Body of the Church on the issue of **What Moves, and Around What**. The Inquisition[2] was unable to decide whether to roll him down a plank held at various angles, write about him in Italian or throw him from the Leaning Tower of Pisa. Finally they decided to humiliate him in public by asking him what he was Going on About, the one question he was unable to answer. He merely mumbled: "Eppur si muove".[3]

[1] Who do a difficult and dangerous job.

[2] Who did a difficult and often dangerous job.

[3] "But it does move."

(Turn over)

5) Twentieth-century man's search for commitment
6) Modernism, French novel, structuralism
7) Rocking around the Clock
8) University of Essex

Something should have been done at the time, but all these events were allowed to pass unpunished.

Thus, England today is a broken nation, an army of thieves and vandals who, in Envy and Malice, deprive others of their property by stealing and breaking it. This is a common feature of the criminal who will not shrink from flouting the law if there is anything to be gained by it, thus increasing the burden on our courts.

With the abolition of the Death Penalty, prisons are now bursting at the bars with murderers, perverts and robbers who should long ago have been mortally dealt the final Swingeing Blow of British Justice.

The Problem Exacerbated by English Liberalism

Tolerance is a fine thing, but the Chairman **can bear no more of it.** National ills afflict, chiefly, the lower socio-economic groupings, but know no boundaries of race or creed. Corruption is a feature of all minorities.

The British have always had a multi-racial Empire. A close harmony with other races and creeds has always been a great benefit, with Bible classes and Missionaries spreading the British Way of Life to all four corners of the Globe. But now that the Empire is gone into liquidation, natives, Orientals and foreigners have flocked to England. Such people congregate in ghettos and listen to popular music with a haughty air. And what a shame it all is: black and white once worked **together** for the common good of the whites.

The Causes of Decline isolated by Sir John Garrett

Enduring shame and a heartful of sadness cure nothing. Before any problem can be solved, an Expert with a towering intellect must analyse all information thoroughly and dispassionately. Such a one is Sir John Garrett and his Tentative Conclusions may be read in a report (Fig. 04) commissioned by the British Academy of Cricket and summarized in Appendix C.

Sir John has identified the chief problems in our society and has isolated the major causes of National decline. The first part of the British Academy of Cricket First Five Year Plan will be to reverse the trends which have taken a grip on our country. The major findings of the report will alarm and alert all right-thinking people: **social ills do not arise spontaneously; they are caused by people.**

Fig. 04: *The Garrett Report*

Responsible cricketers will wish to read, without further delay, the Garrett Report. With the assistance of criminologists and fingerprint experts he has produced an epic summary of England's shame (inset). As is often the case in the world of scholarship large questions need huge answers.

19

(Turn over)

Notes on the Personal Wickedness of Professional players

The Garrett Report is a sad catalogue of misdeeds and un-cricketing outlooks which pervert the fabric of English society. But, alas, worse news follows: wickedness has spread like Mycelium mould into God's Gracious Game and is eating away at the Amateur Ethic.

This evil has long been manifest in professional cricket where players perform, or performers play, for *money*. But it has now begun to pervade the amateur game where *cheating, chewing, spitting and sloppiness* occur daily. Winning begins to assume an unseemly importance, and to Play the Game and the Joy of Taking Part are becoming alien to our own people.

Test and County players now provide a brutish spectacle for beer-drenched Caribbeans and Australians at County and International matches. At the same time their *hugging and kissing* sets a bad example to children and dogs and is offensive to ladies. The manners of the mongrel house-cur are no worse. They are vainglorious in victory and cowed in defeat. Now they simper or fawn with feigned affection, now they assume a grotesque caricature of hatred for the foe, so distorting by unseemly tricks the true nature of competition. Thus they provide a fitting spectacle for that sorry, leaderless herd: the British Cricketing Audience.

Gone, quite gone, are the old days of Amateurism, Fair Play and The Gentleman. The old blood line of true cricket is almost extinct. Test and County Cricket is now served by paid players and administered by dotards and sots.

New Hope for England

It is in true Amateur Cricket that the main force of the Academy's attack will be felt, for here it is, in the very Heartlands of the Game, on Saturdays and on Sundays and on Wednesday evenings all over this great country that Redemption is possible, where the last few embers of Victorian Values are glowing still.

Here it is on the village green, in the field behind the mill or factory, in Highgate Woods, Sudbury Hall and at Nelson's birthplace, by Kett's Oak and in the thousand little holy places, nay, the ten thousand little Patches of Green[1] on this Blessèd Isle where old-fashioned Loyalty, Honour, Patriotism

---

[1] The "green" mentioned draws attention to those areas of the field upon which the match is played, but excludes the pitch for a width of six feet either side of a line drawn between the two centre stumps. (This shall not be a real line, for it is an offence to draw on any pitch when a match is in progress. The line may, for the purposes of this example, be an imaginary construction such as might be drawn in the mind's eye using a pencil [on a piece of paper] or a white lining device [on the turf of a cricketing field]). This area, which shall be called the wicket in preference to other terms, should, in no match or contest, have a green appearance for this is evidence of the presence of grass stems of lengths longer than those approved by the Academy and is likely to cause batting hazards and encourage the disproportionate intervention of Hard Luck and Cruel Fate.

and Queen are not Dirty Words that the Academy will glorify again the Great Game, write a Sublime Symphony to Sport and hum a Hymn to History, a Anthem to the Human Heart.

The wind of change is blowing: it is inexorable. It shall be as a fan to the sparks of Decency and Fair Dooze in the hearts of the Righteous, kindling there a White Hot Flame of Outrage, Indignation and Vengeance.

This Mighty Conflagration shall illumine the sullen darkness and end at last the Long Night of English Cricket. The New Dawn will arise and shed its beams upon the Resurrection of the Summer Game.

The British Academy of Cricket Charter and the New Enlightenment

The British Academy of Cricket, as a non-political and non-denominational institution, has been granted a Charter to collect, process, collate and store a comprehensive Central File of Information to enable the Moderator General, his Inspectors, Officers and Constables to monitor the faint pulse of this Sickly Nation.

By this means the Chairman and Directors will remain ever in touch with both the notions[1] of the Common Man and the spiritual sensibilities[2] of those with breeding and education.

How tragic it is for the individual that a potentially perfect and promising future often degenerates into a dim and distant past, and then the grave, with little between but marriage and misery. But what must be so for the man need not be so for the Nation, which can be undying, like nightingales and Cricket.

Therefore an emergency Structure Plan, entitled *The Plan for the Unfolding of the Future, which will last a thousand years*, has been drawn up by the Chairman and Directors. It comprises two hundred Five-Year Plans, the first of which has already begun.

This plan will be reviewed each year and its findings made known in the Chairman's Address to the Nation. The Roll Forward, an amended up-to-date version in the light of developments, will be published from time to time as necessary or as the Chairman directs.[3]

[1] i) "If work was pleasant I wouldn't be paid to do it."
  ii) "If I was meant to think, God would've given me a brain."
Some authorities claim to have identified a third notion: "What have the Unions ever done for me?" but this is a searching question, not a notion, and probably the only one he will ever ask.

[2] The five Spiritual senses of the Englishman are: 1) Fair Play,   2) Tradition,   3) Roast Beef,
4) Letter to the Telegraph,   5a) Empire   5b) Profit.   5c) Call the Police.

[3] The Chairman has asked the Directors to add a footnote pointing out to whom it may concern that "as necessary" is, in practice, exactly the same as "as the Chairman directs" for when the Chairman is moved to direct something then it is *de facto*, and of necessity, "necessary".

(Turn over)

THE BRITISH ACADEMY

OF CRICKET

COVENANT TO THE NATION

LUX · SERVITIUM · LEX

Ἔοικεν, ὦ ἄνδρες, ὅτε Δαρεῖον ἡμεῖς ἐνικῶμεν ἐνταῦθα,
ἐκεῖ τις ἐν' Ἀρκαδίᾳ γεγονέναι μυομαχία.

These are the three pillars of the Academy's Covenant to the Nation by which the decline in England's fortunes will be halted. The Falkland Islands have been retaken, and India shall be next.

However, before bringing the searchlights to bear abroad, the Nation needs first to look inward, to set its own house in order. The Way must be Cleared and the Ground Prepared for the coming of a New Order.

The Academy, with its Educational, Legislative and Judicial powers will oversee all aspects of the game. To this end the Directors, on instruction from the Chairman, have decided to launch a massive onslaught on all effete Liberalism, wicked Heresy and unpatriotic sentiments, expunging all Doubt, Anguish and Modernism. They will not shrink from Standing Up to be Counted, Pointing the Finger and Naming Names.

With the assistance of its loyal body of agents and Registered Informers the Academy intends to root out all Deviants, Subversives and Socialists who have brought the Game into disrepute. It is they, with their egalitarian ideas and Pernicious Tracts, who have disfigured the face of Britain's heritage, insulted Our Beloved Monarch, and Spoiled Things For Other People.

22

LUX

*"Put upon us the armour of light,
now in the time of this mortal life."*

The Campaign for Enlightenment and the New Philosophy

The educative value of the present volumes is the first weapon in the three-pronged attack on the decline in standards both personal and social.

Education is an *enabling* process: in a controlled form it *enables* the forces of Law and Order to keep one step ahead of the criminal. The Academy intends to impose a National Curriculum, in order to steer the future gently but inexorably into the role reserved for it in history and the British Academy of Cricket Structure Plan. Thus it can be seen that the Academy most strongly *believes in education* and will cure all of society's present ills (seen in the Garrett Report summary at Appendix C) by enforcing the acquisition and inward digestion of regulated information.

Weekend Courses for the Intellectual Advancement of the Mediocre Mind

The Academy runs courses on subjects specific to cricket or of special interest to cricketers. These will be found to increase word power, improve retention, develop reason and heighten rhetorical expression. Courses include: *British Porcelain 1751–1799 and the Lowestoft Tulip Painter, The Twelve Caesars, Transformational Grammar, Bat and Wife Husbandry, Bookbinding for Beginners, Egyptian Morphology and Syntax, Intermediate Logic, Methods of Discourse, Advanced Pad Care and Modern Dentistry.*

The Nature of the New Learning Outlined

The New Scholars will not be of the sloppy, free-thinking sort. Boys will not be encouraged to experiment, enquire or discover, for this leads to Night Adventures and Bicycle Sheds. Education was never intended to be a process of drawing out the individual talents of the boy, for things are often revealed which were better left undiscovered, and wrong opinion takes root, as it were, like a virulent Ground Elder of the mind feeding in the rich silt at the bottom of the youthful brain. The chief characteristics of the Academy's educative programme will be:

1. *Proper instruction in clearly structured chapters and sections.*
2. *Fully stated doctrines with tried and tested courses.*
3. *Simple step-by-step tuition with practical demonstrations and examples.*
4. *Clear diagrams and discipline.*

(Turn over)

All these measures dispel self-abuse. They prepare the British Cricketing Boy for a life of obedience and duty, inculcate upright thinking and a healthy fear of all girls (Fig. 05).

Fig. 05: *A Girl.* A lovely young girl with rosy cheeks, fresh soft moist lips and curly golden hair is one of the prettiest things in the world, an exquisite treasure, one of Nature's greatest gifts and evidence of God's Bounteous Spirit. How she will tease and play and squeal for joy. And how she loves to bounce on laps, and nip and pinch, and wriggle, and squirm, and giggle in naughty delight.

But, when a mere decade is past, how all this innocent charm and maiden frolicking is quite transformed. Now her beauty thickens, her tender flesh congeals and, with a desperate and spiteful affection, she will make man her prey, lard her face with cosmetic colour, ensnare him in marriage or maternity. And to this end she will trap and torment him in a dungeon of depravity, a ripening cheese of lust, ferment his highest aspirations into a rotten soup of squalid ravenings in reeking sheets. Just to think about her legs fills all boys with wriggling to the core, prickling pulsations, turpid tinglings, organic urges and an habit thrice horrible. Therefore, in the yeasty foam of youth, boys should keep companions close and forswear all fumblings with females and groping of girls.

The Importance of Books in the National Curriculum

The chief weapon in the war upon ignorance has always been the Book, and this will not be changed. This traditional symbol of knowledge and progress will again be raised to the status of which it is deserving. The book has not been always a Crass Catchpenny full of wind and pith, a Repository of Rubbish printed purely for Profit. It was once a battleground of Great Minds upon which the thrusting sword-point of the intellect and the heavy club of passion were wielded by the sure arm of righteousness. And so it is again now with this present volume.

In addition to this there shall be, in the forefront of the fight against falling standards, a range of British Academy of Cricket publications. A comprehensive set of Manuals for the compulsory edification of the cricketer will form the basis of a National Curriculum and impose a standard Standard of Cricketing Competence. The books will help to keep in check any independence of thought, empty individualism, eccentricities or affectations. Generous helpings of sound instruction will leave little room for dangerous free-thinking and diverse opinion which break down discipline and are *ruining our democracy*.

A full programme of publications is planned for the first five years, with a *Manual for Officers and Staff* and a *Graphic Dictionary of Cricketing Terminology* already in preparation.

The Further Virtue of the Present Volume Discuss'd and an Important Competition Announc'd

This Manual is a comprehensive guide. It is the Set Book which forms the Core Curriculum for those studying for Academy examinations. By its immense erudition it will interest all scholars and literary persons. It addresses every aspect of cricket and offers good helpings of sound advice on life's Great Themes, with attractive poetical and philosophical flourishes and embellishments.

Generous literary quotations, embodying as they do the distilled wisdom of mankind, adorn and dignify all major statements and Sections of the Manual. And, to avoid all insult and any tone of condescension the sources of these are omitted: the normally intelligent and well-read general reader will instantly recognize the great majority, and all Brainy People will derive great self-satisfaction from knowing the remainder.

Interruption E 001
AN INTERRUPTION BY OUR CHAIRMAN WHO IS OFFERING A GENEROUS GIFT

The Chairman has declared, and would have it known publicly, that any reader able to identify sufficient quotations, in his judgement, to warrant a prize, will be awarded *gratis* life Registration and associate Membership of the British Academy of Cricket. In addition to this the first three correct answers which come from the postbag will win, for the contestants:

1. A night out with the Directors of the British Academy of Cricket,[1] with an excellent and tasty meal at an Important Restaurant if funds permit.
2. A copy of the *British Academy of Cricket Manual for Gentlemen and players* fully stamped by the Directors, plus a Commemorative Tankard.
3. A British Academy of Cricket Fountain Pen and Propelling Pencil Set.[2]

[1] At the expense of the winner.
[2] This comes in a tasteful marble-effect box selected by the Chairman, who has taken a personal interest in its design.

25

(Turn over)

LEX

"Legibus enim vivimus, non exemplis".[1]

The British Academy of Cricket Legislative Provisions for the Instruction of, the Apportioning of Blame to and the Ultimate Apprehension of Transgressors, with Corrective Provisions for Juveniles, Delinquents, Infants and Sundry Malefactors.

The new Nature of the Law, with Special Pleading Abolish'd

The cricketer may behave badly if he wishes; it is a matter entirely for him. But now there will be no escape and no mercy: he will be brought to justice, transfixed by the Academy's legal provisions. What was once an unwritten law of Cricketing convention, now becomes Case and Statute Law with the introduction of the Manuals which open a Second Front in the war on backsliders and shirkers.

The criminal[2] is ever conscientious and diligent in his dishonesty. When taken redhanded he seeks to escape retribution by invoking poor education and illiteracy as a witness to his ignorance of the Law.

This is no longer an excuse. In all cricketing matters the British Academy of Cricket Manuals set out the law in plain language so that all may understand.

The Limits of Jurisdiction with Justice Assur'd

In civilian life it is the duty of the citizen to report to the police any feckless loiterer or scoundrel. Her Majesty's Government is to remain the Legislative body for all non-cricketing matters. But, for the Great Game, this power will reside in the hands of the British Academy of Cricket. Accordingly, in matters of sentencing, there will be no mercy (Fig. 06), no acquittals, no conditional discharges, no probation, no Community Service, no appeals.

---

[1] J. Northbrooke *Treatise Against Dicing* (1577).
Note: The British Academy of Cricket is not opposed to dicing: Gentlemen may wager a few pounds. But players should not gamble, for this is thriftless and leads to gin, horses and pork pie hats.

[2] Traditionally the best way to prevent offences was to send large portions of the population to Australia, where they were quickly swallowed up in the swamp of criminality already established there.
Unfortunately, with stricter emigration controls, this is no longer possible.

However, three effective methods of crime prevention are: a) the securing of all windows and doors; b) the insuring of property; c) the enlistment of neighbours to Watch What Goes On and Keep an Eye on Things.

Fig. 06: *Samson and a Philistine* by Giovanni Bologna c. 1568
As Samson (a) pulled the hair of the Philistine (b) and struck him on the skull with an unspecified instrument (c), so shall the British Academy of Cricket make things pretty hot for all Spoilers of the Game.

27

(Turn over)

Fig. 07: *The British Academy of Cricket Administrative Structure.*

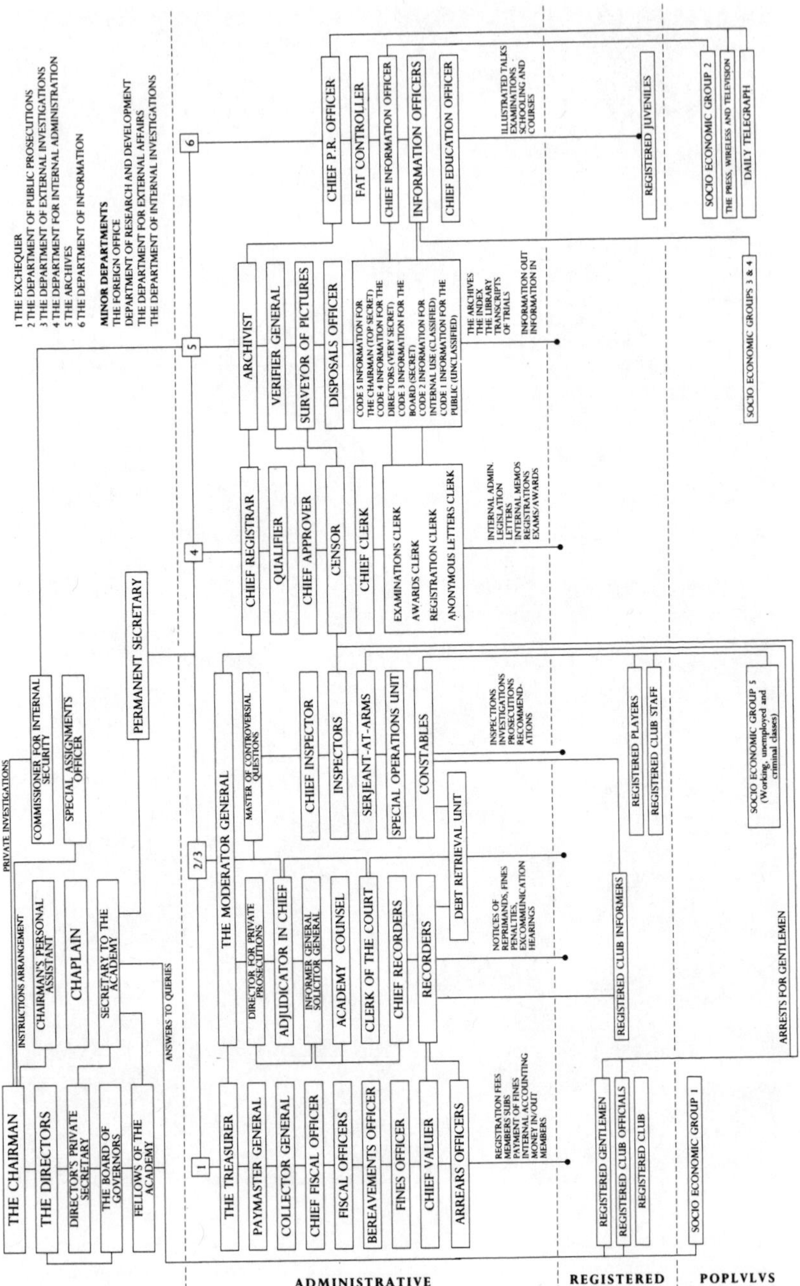

Funded from copper and cocoa interests and by private donation the Academy has the means (Fig. 07) and the will to clean up the Game.

An Historical Digression, and the Implementation of the Laws with a further range of Important Negatives

Men have had three thousand years since God wrote the Commandments to memorize them thoroughly and to eschew all wickedness. But *homo criquetens*, alas, learns but slowly. All the hangings and transportations of the past have rid our country of a great many criminals. But such is the wickedness of Man and such is the dedication of the Criminal that:

i) crime has not been reduced one jot,

ii) Australians are now allowed to return to England for visits.

Therefore no more time must be lost. All regulations will be followed fully, immediately and forthwith, with no second chances, no argument, no consultation, no discussion, no excuses, no complaints and no pity.[1]

The Enforcement Structure and the Judiciary

An excellent chief of policing affairs and cricketing prosecutor has been chosen. The Moderator General has a stern heart, and tenacity in interrogation as well as a ferocious dedication to Law and Order and the summary application of Justice. A former officer in the Metropolitan Police, he was an easy target for perjurers and namby pamby reformers. His immediate subordinate, the Adjudicator in Chief, hears all cases brought before him by the Moderator.

Judicial Services available to Cricketers

For minor offences fixed penalties have been introduced, as well as *in situ* fines. There are also Voluntary Seizure Orders and distraints with a Debt Retrieval Unit for those who do not pay subscriptions at the due date.

There is also an interrogation service for all suspects and, for the benefit of offenders against the Academy itself, facilities are provided in the grounds at Academy Headquarters. The machinery there is also applicable to all women taken in adultery and boys of an impressionable age who breach the Regulations or are apprehended in any Act or Caught Behind (pavilion or bushes).

Fig. 07: *(Left) The Administrative Structure of the Academy*

To keep costs down the Academy's departments have been streamlined by a London firm of Management Consultants. The division of powers ensures that no Dictator could ever usurp the Chairman's position and that left-wing Infiltrators cannot seize control of the committee structure. The points of contact with the Public at Large have been minimized to avoid all corrupting influences.

[1]"Is not pity the cross upon which he who loves man is nailed?"   *Friedrich Nietzsche*

(Turn over)

BRITISH CRICKET TIME

The second leg, or more properly arm, in the enforcement of any law is the co-ordination and standardization of all procedures. As any General knows, if the success of a defeat is to be a credit to the Nation, as it was at Dunkirk, then all must flee in unison.

Therefore the Chairman has decided that the first Great Task is to ensure that all cricketers (page 32) are put on to the 24-hour clock[1] and British Cricket Time, with all other systems outlawed. This is entirely necessary so that all shall know where they stand. Greenwich Mean Times are now over once and for all. The new 24-hour clock will provide the discipline necessary if there is to be no confusion. This, in tandem with a standard British Cricket Time, will help the judicial calendar[2] to run smoothly with no breakdowns.

BRITISH CRICKET TIME: QUESTIONS AND ANSWERS

Q. *When will this begin, and how will I know?*   .

A. At the beginning of each season, on the forty-seventh Wednesday after Bumble Tuesday[3] or at some time specified by the Chairman in accordance with His inclination and the state of the Zodiac. The beginning of the Town and Country Cricketing Season and the commencement of the Amateur Cricketing Year will also be announced by the Permanent Secretary and notices will be published in *The Times* and the *Daily Telegraph* newspapers as well as in the Academy's own organ, *The British Cricket Times*.

Q. *What is B.C.T. and how will it affect me?*

A. This is a new time altogether and will seem strange at first. It varies from the

[1] Not in the sense of a timepiece but in that it is a means, way or system of reckoning or measuring the passage of Time.
When transferring to the new 24-hour system there is absolutely no need for officers to panic or throw away old watches, clocks and timepieces (page 31) which have a dial of only twelve different hours. These are generally numbered 1 2 3 4 5 6 7 8 9 10 11 12 or I, II, III, IIII (or IV on certain very special 30 day clocks by Joseph Knibb) V, VI, VII, VIII, IX, X, XI, XII on Roman clocks. By simply allowing the hands of such a clock to revolve through the twelve hours twice per day and by making a mental note of the time at which they have completed the first cycle, which should occur at noon B.C.T., an accurate record can be kept.

[2] The new calendar will be noticed for only three and three quarter months each four years, or just under one twelfth of the time. February the 29th will be abolished for leap years. Instead there will be two June the 21sts, known as A and B, the Chairman's unofficial and Official Birthdays respectively. Thus, in each leap year, from February the 28th to June the 21st the British Cricketing Date (B.C.D.) will be one day ahead of the Old Calendar.

[3] Bumble Tuesday, as every countryman knows, is that day on which bumble bees leave Winter Quarters and make their first stumbling flights of the year. This date is generally around March the 31st or April the 4th (April the 1st or 5th B.C.D. in leap years) but varies from county to county, region to region, and village to village.

old Greenwich Mean Time by being less mean and giving more time. It differs technically from G.M.T. in two important respects:

1. It is not taken from Greenwich at all but from a meridian passing through the Chairman's Office at British Academy of Cricket Headquarters.

2. By being about two hours ahead of G.M.T. it will be very cricket-saving, postponing the *onset of darkness.*

Q. *When will it all end?*

A. At the termination of each season B.C.T. will be suspended and clocks should be put back two hours making the time one minute and 43 seconds behind the familiar G.M.T. This time will be known as British Winter Time (B.W.T.). This shorter time will hastily shoo away the dark winter days.

Fig. 07: *A British Cricket Time Piece.* Sensible pocket and wristwear should always be selected. This no-nonsense *Services* watch is an admirable choice for its plain honest-to-goodness design and legible, precise numbering. It has an upright traditional English name "Goodwood" associated with Sport and Kings. Although it provides for only twelve hours it should not be discarded: there are many years' service left in it. All such watches and clocks should be retained for the present and synchronized at twenty-four o'clock midnight on Midsummer's Day in accordance with the Chairman's instructions. June the 21st provides, as it were, a gruelling assault course for all timepieces which are working Flat Out on this the longest day of the year.

Fig. 08: *International British Cricket Time Zones.*
The map, overleaf, depicts British Cricket Time Zones throughout the world. Each one is clearly marked, so there is **no longer any excuse for late arrival or departure**. The British Cricket International Date Line has been placed in the Pacific Ocean at the back of the world where it can do no harm. B.C.T. is calculated not from Greenwich but from a meridian drawn through the Chairman's Office. This line is not real in reality, for the Chairman would not stand for such a thing, but made in the mind's map, as it were, drawn with a tensile trajectory of thought, a sustained stab of the intellect, a geographical jab of the imagination.

The purpose of B.C.T. is, quite simply, to ensure that all over the world the cricketer is able to tell the time in the Chairman's office by the expedient of adding or deducting an appropriate number of hours to or from his watch respectively; and conversely the Chairman may tell the time anywhere in the world by calculating it from his office. It is one hour fifty eight minutes and seventeen seconds ahead of the old Greenwich Mean Time.

31

(Turn over)

Fig. 08: *British Cricket Time Zones*

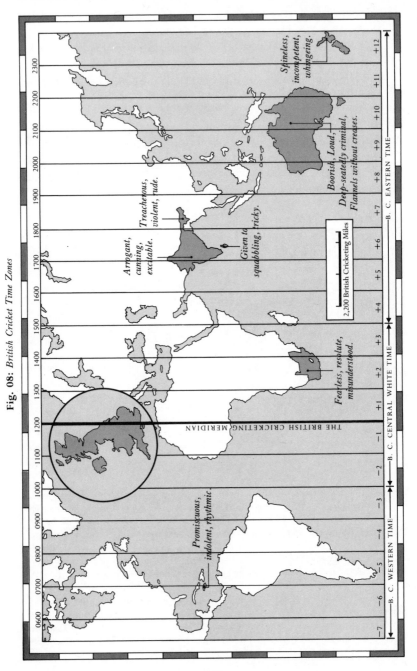

Spineless, incompetent, whingeing.

Boorish, Loud, Deep-seatedly criminal, Flannels without creases.

Treacherous, violent, rude.

Arrogant, cunning, excitable.

Given to squabbling, tricky.

Fearless, resolute, misunderstood.

Promiscuous, indolent, rhythmic.

THE BRITISH CRICKETING MERIDIAN

2,200 British Cricketing Miles

B. C. EASTERN TIME

B. C. CENTRAL WHITE TIME

B. C. WESTERN TIME

SERVITIUM

*"How well in thee appears the constant service of
the antique world
When service sweat for duty not for meed!"*

The Academy prais'd for its Devotion to Duty

The Academy is not made for the fashion of these times when sweat is spilled only for gain. It belongs to an older world where service was not a Dirty Word or something lurking on a luncheon bill. The Senior Service swept the Seven Seas and kept them free from foreigners; the dinner service was a daily spectacle and the Civil service was not besmirched with spies. Service is the central pillar of the Academy's canon and just as it is by far the biggest Latin word in the Trinity, so it forms the largest area of Academy activity.

The Scope of the Services Explain'd, with a Dire Warning

Good old-fashioned service to others has for a long time been a thing of the past, but it is the very watchword of the Academy, which seeks, without reward for itself other than the knowledge that duty has been done, to bring to justice all liars and hypocrites and make the world a better place to live in for decent Registered people.

In addition to the two major services, legal and educational (each ingeniously with its own Latin word), there are also many other stratagems to benefit the cricketer; and these shall be as siege guns to batter down the walls of wickedness and bring tumbling down the ramparts of the rebellious. And such is their precision that if some cook-boy shout defiance from the walls he shall be shot by an arrow through the tongue.

The Just Men shall receive their Reward on Earth

That the Academy is obsessed with the punishment of Sin, let none suppose. Man's virtue, his nobility, daring and courage are also recognized. Each year winners of the Distinguished Cricketing Medal and Citations will appear in the Chairman's New Year's List to be announced on His Official Birthday June the 21st (June the 21st B in Leap Years). These shall be awarded to impeccable informers and agents, those who have made exceptional contributions to the administration of the Game or to Propriety in cricketing affairs, who have brought wanted men to justice or who have displayed outstanding Courage and Conviction in the upholding of cricketing standards.

33

(Turn over)

A Detailed Picture of the Work of the Academy

1. A team of philosophers, theologians and sophists, lexicographers and scholars looks into all Tricky Questions.

2. The Chairman's Progress and formal inspections of Clubs.

3. Further personal advisory services for: equipment, funerals, wives and weddings, marriage guidance, naming of children, and family planning.

4. Archive Department and Censor with Index of Confiscated and Unapproved Articles.

5. Medical advice, a confidential Thursday Clinic.

6. Training and gymnasium facilities, and the Annual British Academy of Cricket Open Cross Country Championship.

7. Information sheets, education of minors and the Sir St. John Peatfield Cricketing School for Young Boys (Fig. 10), where pleasant cricketing weekends for Gentlemen are also provided.

Fig. 10: *The Sir St. John Peatfield Cricketing School for Young Boys*

Eager young lads have always been keen to learn the forward defensive. This is not only the most English of all strokes but also the most graceful and dignified act of Cowardice known to Man. Its forward motion expresses a businesslike passivity, a tentative boldness. If mastered at an early age it will ensure that, throughout a lifetime of cricket, nothing will be contributed and nothing lost.

8. The British Academy of Cricket Bat Clinic.

9. Relocation and family reunion grants for Colonials.

10. An Arbitration Service (Fig. 11) for cases of dispute and disagreement.

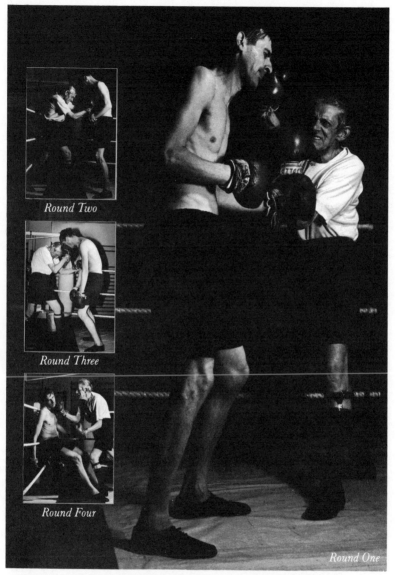

Round Two

Round Three

Round Four

Round One

Fig. 11: *The British Academy of Cricket Arbitration Service.*
This service, with excellent facilities provided at Academy House, is available *gratis* to all Registered cricketers who find themselves engaged in an insoluble disagreement with a colleague, or who need to settle by force the matter of moral and intellectual supremacy. In this instance, Mr Jeffrey Bowles made the error of stating, in the presence of Sir St. John, that there may exist a circumstance in which a Captain might argue with the Umpire.

11. The Chairman's weekly stamp[1] club.

12. Research and Development department which looks into all new scientific notions, vexing gravitational theories and complex mathematical problems involving things suspended on pieces of string.

Thus the Registered cricketer will be overseen from the *condom* to the coffin and be a credit to his club, Nation and his monarch the Queen.

REGISTRATION AND AFFILIATION

Limitations as to Membership

The British Academy of Cricket is not a bureaucratic institution, it is a vital breathing body, full of energy, lifeblood and enthusiasm. It is an institution composed of people for the benefit of people and the emphasis has ever been on charity, service to people and regular sponsored walks. Now a more open policy has been decreed, with an injection of new virility. To this end a committee of one hundred Probationary Members has been appointed.

These Fellows (F.B.A.C.s) have been selected by the Directors on merit and on the recommendation of the Moderator General's office in consultation with the Treasurer, Bureau for External Affairs and Commissioner for Internal Security. From time to time as offences come to light the personnel may vary but in any case Membership is for life. Probationary members will be told in due course if their membership has been confirmed. The law dictates that women may apply.

Of these one hundred Fellows eight have been granted a G.B.A.C., indicating their right to a seat on the Board of Governors which has direct access to the Directors.

Voluntary Registration for Cricketers, Mandatory Registration for Clubs

It is to Registration, not Membership, that the ordinary cricketer must aspire. Gentlemen need not answer the examination questions (Fig. 12). They may, if they wish, merely sign the Declaration. The Central Registry will assist the club and the Academy to monitor those attending or taking part in matches and functions. All Registrees are vetted by the Registrar. Cricketers may register their wives for social, domestic and pleasure purposes, but they should be separately indemnified against damage by a third party, fire and theft.

[1] The Chairman of the British Academy of Cricket has asked the Directors to point out that he wants an 1884 WMK 3 *Imperial Crowns type 49*, £1 brown and, for an example of this in mint condition, he is willing to swap an 1881 *Watermark Imperial Crown type 49* 16 dot Die II 1d Lilac – franked. Any person in possession of such a stamp should contact him forthwith at Academy House.

The British Academy of Cricket requires that all clubs be Registered and that all club members, whether Gentlemen or players, and all Officers and staff aspire to Registration. Names and addresses of all persons connected with the club including spectators and casual visitors should be placed on file. Each candidate who completes successfully the Academy Assessment Course and finishes the Cross Country and Assault Course in less than 5 hours 42 minutes (B.C.T.) will be entitled to Registration.

The privilege of Registration extends to mascots and children or pets of any species (excluding dogs, newts, lizards, or any rat or mouse, hamster, cockatoo or goldfish), provided they attend at least five games in any season.

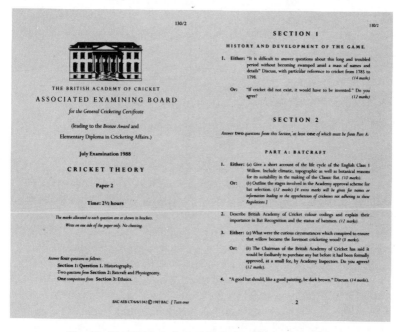

Fig. 12: *The British Academy of Cricket Elementary Examination.*

All cricketers are encouraged to sit this simple examination which, with the Manual as the Set Book, tests the candidate on all Straightforward Matters and leads to the Bronze Award.

Questions on moral cricketing imperatives and rival Theories of Cricketing Knowledge appear in more advanced papers for the Intermediate, or Silver, Award.

Advanced papers examine the candidate's thinking on Free Will and Determinism in Scoring Matters, Statistical Theory and Random Numbers, with Etiquette Theory covered in part B. Searching questions on geology, analytical geometry, semantics and semitics are included.

Wireless archaeology, often chosen as a specialist subject, is examined separately in the "English Way of Life" paper with compulsory questions on the Glums, Archie Andrews, Uncle Mac, Beyond our Ken, Life with the Lyons and Variety Playhouse.

(Turn over)

Classification of Registrees

Member Class A1	Fellow of the British Academy of Cricket	
	Entitled to an opinion and to express it publicly.	
Member Class A2	Probationary Fellow	
	Entitled to an opinion and to express it privately.	
Associate Class B	Registered Gentleman/Officer	
	Entitled to an opinion and to express it in his own home.	
Associate Class B1	Unregistered Gentleman	
	Entitled to an opinion and to express it in his own home when requested to do so by a Registered Gentleman.	
Associate Class C	Registered player	
	Entitled to an opinion but not entitled to express it.	
Associate Class D	Registered staff member	
	Not entitled to an opinion.	
Associate Class E	Registered wife	
	Entitled to her husband's opinion, but not to express it.	
Associate Class F	Registered mascots/pets/children	
	No entitlements.	

Notes for Colonials on Registration

Colonials may wish to enrol for conditional Associate Membership. It is sensible for them to register by way of the various embassies which exist in the major cricketing countries or by direct application to the Academy.

It is now widely recognized that Colonial countries have specific social problems: kangaroos, curry, coconut ear and sugar cane diabetes. But it must be said that these afflictions they have *largely brought upon themselves* by Independence. Even regular doses of the Queen do not relieve the suffering. Registration with the Academy is the most sensible answer. Procedures will be the same as for players, but a photograph should be included at the outset to prevent unnecessary work.

The British Academy of Cricket postal address and the need for Secrecy

Because of the spread of International Terrorism and possible death threats from left-wing assassins the Chairman has thought it prudent to withold from publication the true location of Academy House. All correspondence should, therefore, be sent to the following convenience address. Dispatch riders deliver all post to headquarters once a day.

The Post Room, The British Academy of Cricket, 196 Shaftesbury Avenue, London WC2H 8JL.

Patriotism, the Motherland prais'd

The Building of the Empire, the suppression of natives and the spread of the Game were all as silken threads in the Axminster rug of our history. What a small piece of paradise is England in the spring, this little patch of beechen green and granary floor, and how hot, sticky and smelly are all foreign climes. How horrid, beastly and repugnant all life there was to the Englishman. Nonetheless in their thousands they set forth to Far Off Parts across the Seven Oceans to provide employment, the English language, tea, the Civil Service and the Penal Code to those less fortunate than themselves.

Now foreigners have reverted to their former state and *little good it has done them*. The Colonial (Fig. 13a) is often, underneath, a plain dealing barbarian and thinks that the customs of his tribe and island (Fig. 13b) are the Laws of Nature. Yet even so they squabble among themselves, and all these tireless labours are undone, all progress and pecuniary advantage quite lost. Once again today we witness the disturbing characteristics of many cricketing nations (page 31), defiling and corrupting the greatest of our gifts to them, the Game itself.

Fig. 13a: *The Bearded Cricketer.* The haughty cricketer here is in breach of International Regulations and, with his beard, must be suspected of unwholesomeness, perversion, or even Marxism. Other *shameful features* are: dirty · and dishevelled groin, poor pad discipline, unseemly flannels, dirty thoughts, long hair, unapproved facial expression, slouching and poor posture. This man is an Australian.

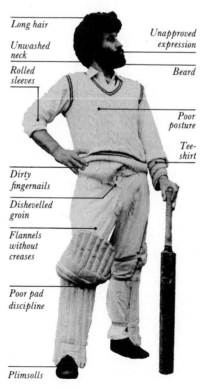

Long hair

Unwashed neck

Rolled sleeves

Unapproved expression

Beard

Poor posture

Tee-shirt

Dirty fingernails

Dishevelled groin

Flannels without creases

Poor pad discipline

Plimsolls

AUSTRALIA
OUTBACK

Vulgar

Coarse

Boorish

Loud

Criminal

Fig. 13b: *Map shewing detailed regional characteristics of Australians.* The worst types congregate in coastal regions and are commonly obsessed with beer, women and refrigerators. Inland there is much enthusiasm for sheep.

(Turn over)

THE SOLUTION

"Orandum est ut sit mens sana in corpore sano."

Introductory Lesson L075

Assisted by the Garrett Report (see Appendix C) Academy philosophers have isolated, in the moral decline, two Prime Movers: a dirty body and a dirty mind; and this has been confirmed by Juvenal himself. Thus, just as vintage wines are best, like the oldest solutions, the classic reply to decadence and decline is in Latin. Smelly people have never been, with the exception of Dr Samuel Johnson,[1] great thinkers.

The Plan for Self-Improvement is in the vanguard of the first Five-Year Plan, as the initial stage in the Unfolding of the Future. It seeks to establish correct timetables and regimens with clear precepts for self-discipline in personal hygiene as a means of furthering the interests of mental development.

Diligent study of these routines will eliminate all dirty habits and disintegration of the character and introduce a cycle of rejuvenation. Chronic social ills, as shewn below, may be remedied by the judicious application of suitable mental and physical hygiene drills. These are encapsulated in the Fifteen-Point Plan for Reconstructing the Soul (Pages 44–56).

IMPERFECTION	CAUSES	ORIGIN	PREVENTATIVE	REMEDY
Irreligion Indiscipline Un-patriotism Selfishness Corruption Cruelty	Irresponsibility and ignorance of Parents	Want of personal hygiene & physical knowledge	Physical education	Academy drill routines, self-inspection, and adoption of the B.A.C. Plan for Self-Improvement
Brawling Showing off Loafing and shirking	Beer			
Violence Lunacy Thriftlessness Poverty Blindness	Self-indulgence, dirty pictures			
Ill health Squalor Infant Mortality Mental deficiency Physical disability Disease	Indifference to higher conscience	Want of self-discipline	Education of character	Study of Academy Plan for Self-Improvement

[1] Who has recently received the highest honour ever awarded by the British Academy of Cricket, a posthumous life membership; not for the way he smelled or spelled but for his hatred of humbug.

Lesson L076

Grave Warnings on the Personal Consequences of Poor Personal Hygiene

When the individual does not take proper care of his body, with uncombed hair, partings which are not straight, dirty fingernails and smelliness, then he is caught in a Downward Spiral. This accelerates into a Flat Spin of defeatism, loss of self-esteem and degradation, with an increased criminality and propensity for the commission of *Gross and Unnatural Acts, court cases, pacifism and beards.*

Lesson L077

An Introduction to the British Academy of Cricket Plan for Self-Improvement

Many of Life's miseries may be prevented by soap and a rough flannel. How the world seems a cleaner place after a good close shave, and how bright is the Vision of landscape in the eyes of a man with a good haircut. At our Mother's breast and our Father's foot we learn that the whole of the Universe, nay life itself, is somehow more felicitous and intense with a cleanly wiped mouth and a freshly kicked bottom.

The importance of personal cleanliness and obedience cannot be overstated. These are the foundations of all character building and it is the concrete footing upon which healthy attitudes to Life, the Academy and the Game are erected. Therefore the British Academy of Cricket has worked out for all Registered Officers, Gentlemen, players and staff a supreme Plan for Self-Improvement to be followed obediently by all Registered cricketers.

Lesson L078

The British Academy of Cricket Plan for Self-Improvement

A plan has been carefully worked out by a team of dietary experts and specialists in medical health, with advice from manicurists, visceral hygienists, chiropodists, brain surgeons and design consultants headed by Sir St. John Peatfield and the British Academy of Cricket Research and Development Department. Extensive controlled tests have shown that:

1. Improved personal hygiene will, inevitably, encourage in the individual a greater self-respect, particularly if self-abuse can be minimized and underpants washed at regular intervals.[1]

2. The result of improved bodily cleanliness is closer attention from others and an increased popularity. This in turn leads to heightened self-respect and a drive to perfect physical health and fitness.

[1] It is a good idea to have two pairs of underpants, so that while one pair is being worn the other pair may be washed, and *vice versa.*

(Turn over)

3. Improved health, with the rejection of debilitating foods and complete abstinence from certain Dinners and Gravy and Afters and Custard (Fig. 14a and 14b) gives rise to an improved mental state, a burning wish to study more Academy regulations, silent prayer and a revulsion from self-abuse.

MUSEUM OF CRIMINOLOGY
Afters and Custard
CASE No. 196 Foodstuffs
Non-sensible

Fig. 14: *The Enemy Within.* Sir St. John Peatfield (right) works one day a week, without remuneration, directing the Research and Development Department. He has, throughout his life, waged war on Cricket's age-old enemy (above) the British Afters and Custard. A fierce defender of fresh fruit, he harbours an implacable hatred for all pudding boilers, treacle spongers, jam poly rolers and dick spotters and can congeal their custards with an icy stare.

4. When once again mindful of other people and the world at large, the cricketer will be aware of the need for improved cleanliness. Thus the cycle of self-improvement (Fig. 15) may begin again as it accelerates into an upward spiral that ends, ultimately in Self-Perfection, Godliness and ascension to Full Associate Membership of the British Academy of Cricket.

Fig. 15: *The Cycle of Rejuvenation.* Things do not go up and down or back and forth as Marxists suggest. They go round and round, turning full circle. It is through this cycle that Britain will ever remain a part of the Free World.

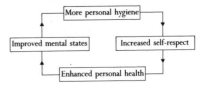

42

Lesson L080

Hygiene, Blackspots and the Social Consequences of Filth

The social ills caused by poor personal hygiene (Fig. 16) have long been appreciated. The Black Country (so named because of its grubby sootscape) has always been a very dirty place indeed, and was also noted for the entrenched despair and poverty in which its inhabitants chose to live their wretched, smoky lives. And in Leeds too, soot so clogs the Intellectual flues that no wisp of thought seeps from the mouth unscathed, such that from this small area of Yorkshire, the Whole Nation is supplied with Idiots. Other towns too, for example Derby, Worcester, Caughley, Liverpool, Lowestoft, Plymouth and Bristol, have sullied reputations.

It will be through the British Academy of Cricket health programmes, which interrupt the Downward Spiral of Degradation, that such regions may again be taken to the bosom of our national life. Wickedness, dirty ears and sticky mouths are rife in such places. This criminal squalor is the result of a complete lack of personal hygiene in populations devoted to the stirring of clay and stoking of fires.

Fig. 16: *The stout drinkers*

Poor personal hygiene is most evident in mining areas where the labouring classes have an unquenchable affection for Brown Ale. Preferring stout to soap, and the bottle to the bath, these wretches haste headlong to low taverns and have no feeling for the finer forms of fulfilment: cricket, home and garden, wife, children, greenhouse and gundogs.

Here (in a photograph taken secretly by an Academy Informer) is the proof: these shirkers drink to the dregs of their redundancy monies; and what follows will be a scrounging appeal to the State for more means to finance further *secondary picketing.*

43

(Turn over)

THE FIFTEEN POINT PLAN
FOR RECONSTRUCTING THE SOUL

Regulation R238 (C3) and (C2A)

Part One: Hair and Hairstyles appropriate for Cricket

At least one British Academy of cricket Haircut (Fig. 17) must be purchased each week. This may be obtained at most good barbers' shops (Gentlemen) and hairdressing salons (players).

Allowing for changes in tonsorial fashion and style the Academy will review this from time to time. The next report from the Hairstyle Committee is due in 1998, and findings will be published in 2002.

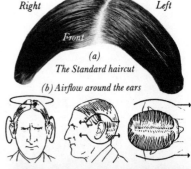

Fig. 17: *The British Academy of Cricket Standard Haircut.* What a delight it is, and a feast for the eyes, to gaze upon the standard haircut (a), particularly when it is set upon the pinnacle and summit of the perfect male body (see Fig. 32 on page 77).

(a)
The Standard haircut

(b) Airflow around the ears

Just as a sensible person would not purchase a house with a dishevelled roof, for this indicates leakiness, moss, nests and sparrows, so no club will be interested in the man with untidy locks.

This portrait depicts the perfect head of cricketing hair. Carefully trimmed it offers a host of hygienic benefits: it provides little shelter for lice and scurf, allows the brain to breathe and encourages the flow of airs (b) around the ear.

But the social consequences are its chief asset: it enhances cricketing performance and business acumen and endows the wearer with good looks and an handsome visage. This enables him to make friends more easily and, by providing an attractive frame for the human smile (c), instantly awakens in all females respectable longings and decorous desires.

Long hair is suitable for decadent Bohemians, so-called Teddy Boys, Hippies, and Beatniks but is not suitable for the cricketer. Bleached hair is a sign of a frivolous foppery and is a notifiable offence, particularly if a two-toned hairstyle is attempted by partial bleaching of the outer locks. This is often the indication of self-hate, sexual deviancy or a complete loss of confidence. Headlice are not nice. A neat trim (Fig. 18) will discourage them.

Fig. 18: *Accredited haircutting services*

The subtle smile has ever been more alluring than the most generous guffaw or toothiest grin. But it needs the self assurance that a straight parting brings. Cricketers should shew this picture to Registered barbers and ask for No 43 in the handbook. Non-Registered barbers should be asked for British Academy of Cricket style No 117 from their sheets.

45

(Turn over)

Regulation R240 (C4)

Part Two: **The importance of Self-Inspection and Cleanliness**

Correct washing and scrubbing routines must be implemented by each club and proper showering rotas pasted on the notice board at the beginning of each season. It is during these sessions that self-inspection should be carried out with great care, diligence and Attention to Detail.

The larger mirrors should be supplied by the club but all other implements and requirements will be found.in the British Academy of Cricket Patent Personal Hygiene Dispensary, and once inspection is complete a thorough toilet routine should be carried out with particular attention to orifices which are vulnerable to disease, uncleanliness, and germs of all kinds.

Attention should be given to hygiene blackspots (Fig. 19a). Suitable scrubbing techniques (Fig. 19b) will do much to combat the wave of uncleanliness sweeping pavilions Up and Down the Country.

Tattoos, rude suggestions or debauched drawings on the skin should be removed immediately.

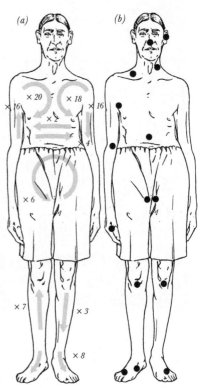

Fig. 19a and b: *Personal hygiene drills:*
a) Correct sequential scrubbing methods –
   Frontal view
b) The Seven Unpleasant Openings of man
   with added Specified Areas for Sequential
   Personal Inspection – *Frontal*

Note: The armpit, while strictly not an orifice, is capable of excreting large quantities of bodily fluids.

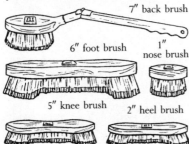

7″ back brush

6″ foot brush   1″ nose brush

5″ knee brush   2″ heel brush

Fig. 19c: *Personal hygiene brushes.* Ever since men first had pigs they wondered what to do with the bristles. Then the brush was invented and the human race grew in hygienic stature. The selection shewn above are all contained within the British Academy of Cricket Personal Hygiene Dispensary.

Lesson L083

Part Three: **Physical Fitness and the Importance of Cricket drills**

A fit body will be the ideal repository for a fit mind. Discipline and personal hygiene are inextricably linked with correct physical toning of muscles, techniques for improving co-ordination, graceful movement, footwork and wrist power. For this the cricketer will need:

(1.) Good posture   (2.) healthy lungs   (3.) profuse sweating
(4.) clean fingernails   (5.) straight partings   (6.) upright heart
(7.) strong blood   (8.) sensible footwear

This will be attained only at the expense of great self sacrifice. Merely by thinking about these things first thing in the morning the cricketer will achieve an improved mental state. This will stand him in good stead on the field of play and raise him aloft in the affections of his colleagues. Physical improvements will be further augmented by strict abstinence, sensible eating, early rising, sobriety, temperance and the selection of good company, erudite friends and urbane gatherings in preference to racegoing, brothels and public houses.

Regulation R287 (C3)

Part Four: **The British Academy of Cricket Drills.**

A whole programme of mental health care and exercise should be adopted as a matter of individual responsibility and routine.

Youths, junior and senior juveniles and adolescents should all be encouraged to take part, for the drills which follow (Fig. 20 *overleaf*) have a character-building value which cannot be underestimated. These will provide young people with a rare opportunity to overcome vain dreams of individuality, unwanted introspection and self-obsession which all too often give rise to pink hair, mopeds, poetry and *shouting across roads*.

The selected drills listed below (for the schedule is by no means exhaustive) are a balanced selection of disciplines and movements which will tone each muscle and limb and improve communal cricketing discipline.

These are:

No 37: Queuing (AN) or No 47: Brisk walking on the spot (AF)
No 96: Forced removal of Abdominal from table (TX)
No 57: Dealing with a mad dog (UT) or No 98: Academy handshake (AN)
No 27: Disarming violent/armed attacker (AN)
No 75: Making a telephone call in an emergency (OL)
No 71: Stalking an intruder in the pavilion (VT)

Key to Codes: VT 30 minutes, OL Stop when necessary, UT Until tired, AF Until completed, AN Until supple, TX Ad infinitum

47

Fig. 20: *Drills for Fitness in wind and limb.*

Private agony brings little acclaim, therefore Mr Bowles ensures that his major exertions are professionally directed and recorded. For this muscular misery lungs and legs should be prepared in advance using the Sir St. John Peatfield P. T. exercises Nos. 27 and 34 (inset).

Lesson L091

Part Five: The Importance and Benefits of Cross Country Running, Hill Climbing and Nature Study

To exercise violently the limbs and lungs is a fine and a wise thing, for it keeps the cricketer in peak condition.

A good cross country or hill climb instils in the runner endurance, loneliness, close communion with Nature, a sublime quietening of the mind and a repose of all the assaulted senses. It gently cleanses the blood and strengthens the lungs, liver and heart. It causes the intellectual light[1] of British Cricketing Man to shine more clearly and prepares the reason and memory for the study of improving texts and British Academy of Cricket Regulations and Manuals. Out on the open road, with the clean air rushing by, and all around the wonders of Nature bedecked in the livery of the season, the cricketer is free from wife and family life.

Lesson 091B

(incorporating *Interruption E002*)

The Chairman in Lyric Mode, his Prime Recall'd by means of a breathtaking *Homily on Running and the Hunger of Man in His Youth*, an Extract from His treasured Commonplace Book written Long Ago but which may yet inspire, and is included here, at the Chairman's Request, on Pure Merit

"There in his mind's ear, above the sound of a pulsing heart, a man may chance to hear the distant song of the Nightingale, the gargling of the Jackdaw and the cooing of doves, the singing of all Nature's feathered tribe. With an easy heart full of gladness and a mind uncluttered by the hail of occurrence that assaults him during his daily commerce with the human race, in his mind's foot he may pound out the rhythm of life's great race and roam the byways of bliss, kick up the dust of destiny.

And when he tires of his running, he may seat himself in some roadside pleachèd arbour and smoke a fine cigar[2] while he contemplates the brevity of life and the Game."

---

[1] So that all registered members may be able to say of themselves with Sir Francis Bacon: "I found that I was fitted for nothing so well as for the study of Truth; as having a mind nimble and versatile enough to catch the resemblances of things (which is the chief point), and at the same time steady enough to fix and distinguish their subtler differences; as being gifted by Nature with desire to seek, patience to doubt, fondness to meditate, slowness to assert, readiness to reconsider, carefulness to dispose and set in order; and as being a man that neither affects what is new nor admires what is old, and that hates every kind of imposture."

[2] Although it can no longer be denied that cigarettes and tobacco are harmful to the lung, kidney, stomach, throat, tongue, lip and bowel, a fine cigar never did anybody any harm. Sir Winston Churchill smoked cigars in large quantities yet he Won the War and lived to be a very elder statesman. Further, it has never been recorded that anybody died as a result of attempting to smoke a cigar.

(Turn over)

Regulation R288 (C2A)

Part Six: **The British Academy of Cricket Oaths**

Each cricketer shall, before each match, take the *British Academy of Cricket Manual for Gentlemen and Players* in his right hand and read the Oath. This will help to restore a sense of occasion in a world where ritual has been lost.

FOR GENTLEMEN

"I do solemnly and sincerely declare personal allegiance to the Chairman of The British Academy of Cricket. I affirm that the pain I shall inflict in this Game shall be without hate, malice or spite but that the humiliation of the Foe shall be complete.

Though my wicket fall I shall not swear. In fortitude I shall obey the Umpire's word, though I know him to be wrong.

The Spirit of Fair Play will be with me and Humour and Discipline shall endure, I swear, all the match through, even to the pulling of the stumps."

FOR PLAYERS

"I will do what I am told."

Lesson L092

Part Seven: **Girth Control for the Modern Cricketer and the New Road to Physical Enlightenment**

Unsightly fat, slack muscles, greasiness, overeating and obscene obesity take their toll on the human frame, making it ugly and horrible to look at. The British Academy of Cricket has appointed an official Fat Controller who may be consulted on all matters of girth control. Free advice about the need to eat less is available.

For really Fat Gluttons and Abdominals the British Academy of Cricket Oxford Diet may be purchased. It provides chemicals conducive to cricket and various vital victuals, and has been shown to be efficacious in the bodily enlightenment of many sportsmen of note. Hundreds of testimonials.

Lesson L093

Part Eight: **The Need for Mental Hygiene**

Mental fortitude has declined both in our National Life and in Cricket. This has been due largely to further education which encouraged doubt, hesitations, independence of thought, the Greater London Council, insubordination, haughtiness, socialism, envy and cheap fares.

Thankfully the process is not irreversible. The New Enlightenment is here: University departments are beginning to be closed down, and Her Majesty's Government now intends to incinerate certain of their books.

The reintroduction of National Service now would help make the restoration of Correct Thinking an easier task. However, despite letters from the Academy, the Government has so far resisted this, promising only to reconsider once elections have been abolished.

The ancients, with their often perverse logic, knew very well that a healthy body could not abide an association with a dirty mind. It was for the pursuit of Games, therefore, that Learning was introduced, and this formed a very important part of the academic life in the sporting calendars of Greece and Rome.

Therefore it follows that the game is the father to the thought and in this enlightened age it is for the Good of the Game that the mind must be protected.

Lesson L097

Part Nine: **Maladies of the mind and loss of competitiveness**

Infections, sometimes picked up in London, on bat handles or toilet seats and the action of antibiotic tablets can cause a serious loss of motivation.

Financial embarrassment, which could have been alleviated by more hard work, or increased borrowing, can also have a deleterious and cumulative effect. These, and existentialist despair, melancholia and unmanly philosophical nihilism in a cold indifferent Universe, produce a pernicious form of emotional detachment from events and shake loose the grip on apathy itself. When this all-pervading gloom overtakes the serious cricketer he is in serious trouble. He may lose his place in the team if the onset of fatalism is total.

The loss of competitiveness exhibits itself, in the early stages, in recognizable symptoms. The Gentleman may succumb to the temptation to thank servants, clean up behind himself, or display a lack of firmness with waiters and policemen.[1] He may exhibit tolerance of shop assistants/bank clerks, accept overripe fruit at greengrocers' and avoid Public Places.

A Gentleman never works hard, but is rather the cause of hard work in others. Any failure to uphold this principle, the fundamental precept of his class, must be seen as a serious lapse from his social and cricketing duty and a sign of mental disorder.

General symptoms of a loss of competitiveness in the player are: empty crates, giving way at road junctions, lack of jostling in public bars, patting of dogs. If his condition deteriorates he may, finally, surrender himself to total beard growth (Fig. 21 *overleaf*) and Active Vegetarianism.

---

[1] Who do a difficult and often dangerous job.

(Turn over)

Fig. 21: *Total Beardedness.* One of the last great exponents of the Compleat Beard, W.G. Grace nevertheless did much to destroy its reputation. Along with other bearded blasphemers such as Charles Darwin, Karl Marx and Sigmund Freud he attracted the admiration of the disaffected, poets, anarchists and intellectuals. But with each lengthening whisker Mr Grace suffered diminished self-esteem, sloppy discipline and indifference to the other fellow's point of view. Finally, *in extremis*, he fell to cheating, bullying and arguing with Umpires. The first tell-tale signs that his personality had begun to disintegrate should have been spotted much sooner. By 1894 his beard was known to have harboured: angelica, breadcrumbs, chewed nails, cotton and linen fibres, dust, flour, fungi, glue, gnats, icing sugar, lipstick, nose and eye droppings, roast beef, shoe polish, spiders, spittle, sponge (Devon), sundry moulds and microbes and tobacco. All these things give rise to noxious vapours which enter the brain *via* the nose and cause a terminal self-disgust. The simple remedy is a clean shave.

Lesson L099

Part Ten: Spiritual Problems with Beards and their Effects on Self-Discipline and Mental Stability (with Supplementary Notes on Beards and Madness)

The beard is often an outward show of inward neglect, but it can also betray more sinister leanings. Trotsky, Lenin, Marx and Shaw all used the beard as a political weapon to disguise their subversion.

The Past has shown too that the beard is a sign of philosophical philthiness cowardice and defeatism. Thus, the history of the beard is a long tale of retreat, usually into perversion, violence and degradation. An extract from the Academy's files tells a sorry tale:

19/LB 071.	Robinson Crusoe (retreat to a desert island).
67/LB 071B.	Rip Van Winkle (retreat into sleep).
43/LB 069.	Moses[1] (retreat from Egypt).
19/LB 072.	King Alfred (retreat from the Cake Woman).

[1] Here it is that some adherents to the literal reading of the *Holy Bible* go sadly amiss, for this does not imply that in order to lead Israelites out of Egypt a beard is always entirely necessary, only that it was necessary for Moses in this particular instance.

19/LB 118.	King Canute (retreat from the sea).
43/LB 060.	Robert the Bruce (retreat into entomology).
19/LB 042B.	Grand Old Duke of York (retreat down a hill).
19/LB 082I.	The French (retreat from Moscow).
19/HB 072.	The Germans (retreat from Stalingrad).

Extreme beardedness led to alienation, breakdown, mumbling at windows and insanity in the following well-documented cases:
King Lear exasperated by daughters, Vincent Van Gogh made mad by paint, Captain Ahab, insanely hateful of whales and whale products, Blue Beard mad about children, Ben Gunn mad about money and Howard Hughes crazy about germs.

Lesson L100

Part Eleven: Beards and Royalty, 1930–1940
(This section deleted by order.)

Regulation R289 (C2A)

Part Twelve: Beard Growth and the Diverse Power Law of Approximate Probability

Although the precise mechanism[1] was not known until recently, moral character varies in inverse proportion to beard length. Therefore no cricketer shall sport any shaggy beard, for unkempt facial whiskers have not only a long history of political subversion (see *Lesson L099*) but of all the Furniture of the Face they are known to mask most malice and mischief. Beards disguise dirty dealings, offer succour to the stubborn and encourage *shouting on the field*. Where whisker growth is total (see Fig. 21 *opposite*), behind the beard Cheating keeps his Court.

---

[1] Expressed in the Spearman Formula:

$$M = \frac{\prod_{\Delta=\alpha}^{\Omega}\left(\dfrac{\pm\sqrt{g}-\Delta^3}{\log y + a\sqrt[3]{\Delta\mathrm{Sin}\theta}}\right)}{\int_{\beta=0}^{\beta=h}(\Pi\beta^2 - k\beta)\,d\beta} + \frac{\lambda\rho!}{\left(\lim\limits_{c\to\infty}\left(\dfrac{xh^2}{c}-\phi\right)\right)}$$

It was in recognition of his achievement in discovering this equation that Professor John Spearman, *Mathematicus* to the British Academy of Cricket, has been Mentioned in Documents.

For those unfamiliar with integrational calculus the following key will be of some assistance:

M = Moral character, a = Age, c = Velocity of whisker growth, ρ = Prayers per day, B = Beard length at April 5th, Δ = Modules of sinfulness, α = Mean washing routines per week, Ω = Number of aspirations, g = Proportion of good deeds, y = Years since last century, θ = Usual angle of inclination to flight of ball when fielding, λ = Coefficient of Maidens taken, Π = 3.142, k = Catches dropped, x = Rated excellence at crease, ϕ = Number of runs, h = Modal number of hairs in cm² of stubble.

(Turn over)

Lesson L104

Part Thirteen: **The Benefit of the Forms of Art
which do not Engage the Intellect**

Sketching, watercolour painting and music, dance, mime and ballet all have a beneficial quality: they do not harmfully engage the mind but, rather, lightly tease the attention. Unlike literature, they do not suffer from the disadvantage of having to say anything which means something, or indeed anything at all beyond making a pleasing noise, movement or display of colours, hence their popularity among the intellectually underprivileged and mentally retarded.

Art is not, as some have said, the highest achievement of man, for this must be reserved for the great battles of Alexander and the discovery of the Lancaster bomber (Fig. 22), the Chesterfield sofa and Stilton cheese.

Fig. 22: *The Lancaster Bomber and the breach of the Moehne Dam*

This miraculous machine, with **hundreds of working parts**, was the product of British enginuity, and was a powerful weapon in the hands of England's brave aviators. Combined cunningly with a special Bouncing Bomb this machine was capable of **saturation bombing** which flooded everything in the Ruhr Valley. In one daring raid this winged wonder hit at the heart of German production schedules, held up planning programmes and clerical work, jammed switchboards, disrupted timetables, caused cancellations and postponements, broke appointments and brought chaos to their administrative routines, thus contributing to Britain's Victory in Europe.

The particular craft (inset), as its identification letter reveals, is of the Century Bombers or "Bloody Hundredth" Bomb Group and flew from Thorpe Abbotts in 1944.

Art is of benefit chiefly as a valuable hobby, and many a peaceful hour has been spent with the paintbrush in hand or at the scales of a piano. He who masters one of these skills from an early age is laying up for himself a great store of contentment, bliss and reward throughout his life and will be appreciated in any society.

Those gifted at any of these things should pass the benefit on to their club: a skilled artist could paint the sightscreens or capture Great Sporting Moments in the club's history, or a likeness of a Senior Club Official for the pavilion walls. The musically talented cricketer will play and sing[1] for his comrades at official functions, and lead the singing of hymns and psalms at Church Services.

Lesson L108

Part Fourteen: **Beneficial Pastimes for the Cricketer**

Long-term discipline, stamina, concentration on the minute and attention to detail are the strengths of the modeller. It is one of the arts of peace (Fig. 23), yet it well equips the participant for the Game.

The medical benefits of model making are well known: it has been found to suppress aggression which, although an admirable thing on the field of play, makes for many public house brawls, domestic disputes and cruelty to pets and children.

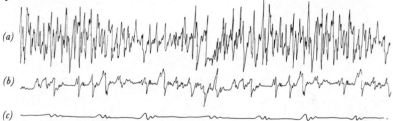

Fig. 23a: *Encephalographic electrical impulses.*
This diagram shows the brain waves of *a*) Psychopath, *b*) Spaniel, and *c*) Model Maker. No electrical disturbances are present to distress and annoy the victim.

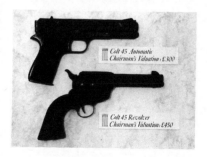

*Colt 45 Automatic
Chairman's Valuation: £300*

*Colt 45 Revolver
Chairman's Valuation: £450*

Fig. 23b: The .45 Colt revolver or Peacemaker (below), although an essential part of the Dog Officer's equipment, does not lend itself to matchstick modelling because its metallically rotund nature is opposed to the Essentially Ligneous Rectilinear Angularity of the common match. The Colt .45 Automatic (above) however is more suitable.

These particular firearms are part of the Chairman's collection.

[1] This does not imply that he should utter lewd or boisterous songs as is the habit among certain clubs of a lesser sort and among the empty-headed, loud-mouthed throngs in the Rugby Unions.

(Turn over)

Regulation R293 (C3)

Part Fifteen: **Suitable Subjects for Models
Constructed from Used Matches**

This is the most pleasant form of modelling and does not involve the purchase of tawdry modelling packs or kits, nor great expenditure on balsa wood, which is mostly air.

Nowhere, according to a recently published Academy Report, is there a shortage of used matches. They are to be had for the asking, and a friendly landlord will often assist in this regard, donating all the contents of his ashtrays.

As subjects, ships (Fig. 24) and cathedrals should be chosen as these will bring the player closer to a state of Godliness and increase his reverence for our Glorious History.

Fig. 24: *The Mary Rose.*

England's glorious history has been recall'd with the floating of the Mary Rose, shewing once again that what the French could do four hundred years ago the British can undo in a few short months, thus re-establishing once again our Supremacy as a Seafaring Nation. This marine monument is second only to Dunkirk in its glorious failure and was made to the highest standards of workmanship. Her sinking was no accident but the result of some French treachery or sabotage.

The unfortunate King Henry was present for the sinking and watched it angrily from the shore. He was obliged to listen to the pitiful heart-rending bubbles of his sailors as they drowned. This threw him into a Festering Mood (inset) followed by a Nasty Temper for, although she was *almost new*, the Mary Rose was insured only third party, Spain and theft.

Note: Underwater excavation is a difficult operation involving special techniques. Because of continual flooding it is normally done briskly with a bucket, not slowly with a spade.

SEASON'S END

"In my end is my beginning".

Introductory Lesson L119

To everything there is a season. When the harvest[1] is done and the ground is turning cold and the cornstalks fill with dew, then the whitethroat[2] ceases his singing from the wayside wires and the voice of the turtle is no longer heard in our land.

The dying cadences of the last game echo forlornly in the chill evening air. The last reluctant footmarks linger, darkling, in the bristling grass besprent with dew, and the Square is given up to silence and to worms.

There is always something sad about October when the sun shines.

It twists small branches about the heart, makes poetry ooze like gum, makes a mockery of flesh and bone. The swallows gone a week ago, the rook chased along by an October sky, and the green god that lives among the blades of grass retreats shyly to his mossy walls; October's in the East land and sugar beet fields.

In such a time young and old all get the urge for going, turn their collars to the cold and damp while gathering swallows drift by the window. The adder creeps through the rotted oak. Cups fall. The elmroot threads the bones of buried lovers.

And if that were not quite sufficient, these are the days of wasps and rosehips, when the good wife and the cottage spinster turn to jelly and wine. Now it is that the flowing irrepressible spirit of man turns away from campaigns in the field and, alone and aching in the wilderness, gathers to itself the warm consolation of life's other treasures: propagation, progeny, the sincere and deep affections of home, children and the family,[3] business contacts and friends.

In such a time will a cricketer's thoughts turn also to his wife and all the other duties which have been neglected: the Hunt, the Shoot, investment, share ownership, and the increase of wealth and personal property, which, in the Close Season, express the highest aspirations of every true Englishman. Now the pheasant will not fly, the fox is in his earth-o and the Christmas cockerel crows quietly at the dying of the light.

---

[1] Of runs and wickets.

[2] This is to be found in Ottery St Mary, Devon. The rest have been killed by our farmers who, with the help of grants, are the most efficient in Europe, and need, regularly, to cut down all extraneous birds and weeds.

[3] The British Academy of Cricket is unreservedly in favour of the Family and the Home, provided the former be kept to about two children and the latter to a maximum.

ITEM

CRICKET BALLS

"If you do not come too close, (repeat)
On a . . . . midnight, you can hear the music
Of the weak pipe and the little drum
And see them dancing . . . ."

Introductory Lesson L126

The Annual Ball comes but once a year. And what a delightful thing it is for the President to give all an opportunity in the Close Season to congregate and mix freely, Gentlemen with player, player with his wife, batsman with bowler. A certain degree of formality must be observed nonetheless, if the evening is to be something more dignified than an excuse for idle chatter, foolish boasts, tall tales, heavy drinking, riotous assembly and brawling.

The Annual Ball nowadays is a much neglected function. Some clubs do not bother to organize such an event at all or, worse, do not insist on proper dress.

It is at the Annual Ball that the Gentleman will allow himself to suffer social contact with players. Therefore he must take with him all his resources of patience and good breeding.

All Gentlemen should make this sacrifice for the sake of the club, for if matches are to be won or drawn the player must be used. He is, like a groin protector, an obscene and ugly thing, but necessary if the cruelty of the Game and the injury of Defeat are to be minimized.

Regulation R306 (C2)
Changing to British Winter Time

In such a time will the Club and all cricketers, on instructions from the Academy and at a date **specified by the Chairman or any person duly authorized by him in writing**, put all timepieces, chronometers, watches and clocks back two hours to British Winter Time (BWT).[1]

In such a time will the Gentleman see to it that more coal be ordered *at summer prices*.

Now the time is come for collecting thoughts and statistics, the time to recapture the striking of a boundary six with its first fine careless rapture.

In this time all Nature is gently dying, the days grow short[2] and the sad silent song makes the hours twice as long. Play is done and, as the

---

[1] B.W.T. varies from G.M.T. by only one minute and forty three seconds.

[2] For beef cattle, porkers and baconers, selected chickens, and non-breeding stock of all kinds.

(Turn over)

substantial pageant fades, the mind turns again to such stuff as dreams are made on: the Classic Bat, hard work, the preservation and commissioning of equipment, commerce and social intercourse with the World at Large and the Club at Least.

Regulation R308 (C3)
The importance of a correct Timetable of Proceedings for the Annual Ball

In order to combat the present Lack of Balls in the Cricketing life of our Nation a timetable has been drawn up by the British Academy of Cricket. All clubs shall adhere strictly to its recommendations.

Regulation R309 (C3)
The Annual Cricket Ball Programme of Events
(times are given in B.W.T. – British Winter Time)

2000 Hrs   *Guests arrive:* Those in appropriate dress will be announced. *(Guests will then be handed a portfolio of Academy information sheets covering queuing techniques, drinking and dancing regulations and suitable jests, topics of conversation and the timetable of events. They will be ushered to their seats quietly while undesirables and late arrivals are ejected).*

2010 Hrs   *Greetings:* These should be crisp and businesslike.

2015 Hrs   *Doors locked:* Those who have not adjusted to B.W.T. from B.C.T. will be told to so so.

2016 Hrs   *The Chairman's Speech:* The host will welcome the Lords, Ladies and Gentlemen present, open the sealed envelope and read aloud[1] the British Academy of Cricket Chairman's Private Address.

INTERLUDE

2115 Hrs   *Lights out:* An instructive talk or film shewing the aims and objectives of the Academy will draw attention to the problems in the Game today. *Guests may expect to be admonished severely for Letting Things Slide.* Alternatively a club may wish to hire an Educational Lecture. (Fig. 25.)

2130 Hrs   *The Briefing:* Those assembled will listen to selected passages from Academy Manuals and will be instructed in their solemn duties in the Academy's Plan for the Unfolding of the Future.

[1] Silent reading is not sufficient.

Fig. 25: *A British Academy of Cricket Education Officer gives an instructive talk at an Annual Ball in Hertfordshire.*

61

(Turn over)

2145 Hrs   *Induction ceremonies:* New club members will be introduced and take club oaths and swear club codes of conduct before those assembled.

2150 Hrs   *Bar opened.* Alcohol will now be made available.

2200 Hrs   *Bar closed.* Alcohol will now be made unavailable.

2201 Hrs   *Awards and speeches:* Medals and club awards will be handed out by the Secretary, and selected dignitaries will be asked to recount edifying anecdotes and make uplifting speeches.

2230 Hrs   *The Toasts:* Selected members will be asked to make further entertaining speeches for the amusement of guests.

2300 Hrs   *The Club Song* will be sung with piano accompaniment.

2310 Hrs   *The Lottery:* The sale and draw of tickets and the auctioning of Second Chances by the Treasurer.

2320 Hrs   *Celebrations:* The Master of Ceremonies will announce that the evening's revelries shall commence. The orchestra may then play approved scores in 4/4 time and C major. Those not using Academy procedures will be prohibited from indulging themselves further. Refined discussion and social discourse shall take place, Dancing will be permitted, strictly in accordance with Academy regulations. Any persons engaged in non-approved dances[1] will be asked by stewards to leave the floor.

2330 Hrs   *Ugly Scenes and Scuffles:* The expulsion of those deemed to have reached an unfit state to participate further shall now take place.
Undesirables[2] should also be ushered discreetly into the foyer, and be given instructions.

2400 Hrs   *Her Majesty the Queen and the Close:* The assembled company will stand and sing the National Anthem. Guests will be instructed by the Chief Steward to vacate the premises forthwith.

2410 Hrs   *Vehicular congestion.*

---

[1] These remarks are not uncalled for. Dancing has too generally degenerated into vulgar jiggling; couples scuffle and spin about, as if they were determined to exhaust their physical energies by bouncing down all who would participate in the enjoyment with them. The rudeness of their reckless evolutions is equally out of taste with their absurd wrigglings, when, in the midst of their boisterous plunges they appear suddenly seized by St. Vitus, and their muscles take on a tremulous but fitful motion. The error lies not in the dances themselves, but in the vulgar manner of executing them, which the Chairman truly abominates.

[2] A complete catalogue of racial characteristics County by County is given in Appendix E on page 236.

SELECTED NOTES ON BALLS
"Better to walk lamely than to dance clumsily"

Regulation R312 (C2A)
The Admission of women, Wives and Ladies

The attendance of females at the Annual Ball is not encouraged, although members' wives are admissible as guests of their husbands who will be expected to take full responsibility for them.

If such a person is invited, whether the female companion of Gentleman, Officer or player she should be pleasing to the eye, with no pink lipstick. This occasion will provide her with an excellent opportunity to show the mettle of her distaff and conduct herself in a manner pleasing to the company and beneficial to the reputation of her spouse.

Gentlewomen are no longer, quite rightly, regarded as the appendages of their husbands and should therefore take a larger part in the proceedings than was formerly the custom. The Gentleman's lady and the Officer's wife should, however, remember at all times that opinions in a female can be offensive to men, as can intelligence, erudition and commonsense. She will therefore confine her remarks to everyday matters and use her intellect to steer conversation towards the range of topics with which her husband is familiar or about which he himself has an opinion, from gundogs to trout fishing, from sporting guns to fishing rods.

The player's woman will generally not be expected to remain for the whole celebration as there will be children at home clamouring for potato chips, fighting, or spying on babysitters. While she is at the Ball she should endeavour to enhance the reputation of her husband by doing and saying nothing. She should not become involved in Promiscuous Frivolities nor laugh at things which are not funny nor suffer sundry men to lift her dress or *maul her about*.

Regulation R317 (C3)
Appropriate Dress for the Annual Ball

Most Balls are carefully arranged for the purpose of breeding, with a healthy mingling of potential brides and grooms from the important families of a district. This is not the case with the Cricket Ball. It is something set aside for pure pleasure and for celebration of the Eternal Cricketness of Things.

Therefore the ball gowns of the women should not be too revealing. Men of breeding will want to wear Evening Dress but the Academy requires them, in the interests of the easy mingling of the classes, to don lounge suits at this venue. Evening Dress is reserved for select occasions not involving players or club staff.

(Turn over)

Regulation R323 (C2)

Mandatory Rulings on Sartorial Matters and Appearance

Club ties **must** be worn. There shall be no excuse and no exceptions.[1] All partings in the hair will be straight; fingernails should be clean and all creases will be sharp and neat. Dandruffers will not attend.

Regulation R324 (C2A)

Unscheduled Arrivals, Problems with Cockneys[2] and Londoners and the Importance of the Hall or Foyer.

Any function with alcohol and food will attract addicts, Rugby football players, tramps, undesirables, vagabonds and criminals. But the biggest problem is that of Cockneys and Londoners who are on the increase.

To be born with an irrepressible cheerfulness is a blessing, but when it is accompanied by a loud mouth and a London accent it can be very trying indeed.

Any Cockneys trying to make an entrance must be ushered into the hall for processing before they are ejected from the building. This duty is best executed by well-trained staff. It is a clever ploy to make a small token charge for admission. In this way the club is entitled to hire an Academy Debt Retrieval Unit (Fig. 26) to convert Unscheduled Arrivals into Unscheduled Departures. All fees for their services are payable, net, on the night.

D.R.U SERVICE ENTERPRISES P.L.C.

We have a friendly and personal 24-hour Take-Away Service. Domestic and Industrial.
Removals: Standing charge £35 per hour, search and processing extra.

Security: Personal Appearance Rates

Bingo/Whist Drives/Over 60s/Nativity plays	45 guineas
Children's parties (7–10s)/Tupperware Evenings	50 guineas
Pall bearing	£8 per stone

Social Services

Knucklegrams/Massages/Manicures	40 guineas
Facials	80 guineas
Street Collections and Disposals	240 guineas

D.R.U. Escort Agency
General Personal protection £28 per hour.
After 5pm/Sundays/Bank Holidays £54 per hour.

---

[1] The President may wear his British Academy of Cricket tie.

[2] Any person may, by an Academy Inspector after an enquiry, be reclassified as a Cockney by Association if it is found that his normal habits, movements or associates are in the London area; if his activities are of a London, or petty criminal nature; if he is entirely empty-headed or otherwise exhibits London attributes or subscribes to London outlooks and beliefs.

Fig. 26: *The Debt Retrieval Unit at work*

The British Academy of Cricket encourages private endeavour, small business acumen and a long working day. These operatives are self-employed persons provided with office accommodation at Academy House. For their fiercely independent spirit and Creative Collecting this particular Unit was awarded the Chairman's Challenge Cup for Outstanding Enterprise and Efficiency (inset).

In this picture Mr G. Wells (Unit Leader) brings news of an outstanding debt. Mr Stewart and Mr Hancock proceed with routine matters.

(Turn over)

Regulation R326 (C3)
Recognition of the Alcoholically Subnormal

Registered alcoholics, who think it is funny to have a red nose and double vision, will not be allowed to enter the ballroom unless accompanied by responsible adult or a policeman.

Regulation R329 (C1)
The Sinister Problem of Clever Dicks educated beyond their Station, the Final Solution, with the Special Powers of the Moderator General intimated.

The inane and bestial humour of the Cockney or player is unedifying, but there is a more sinister threat to the club: the Smart Alec. His humour is not humour, it is a sickening poisonous and systematic assault on decency. Failure to report him is a very serious offence.

When proceedings are under way and a capital time is in prospect for all there will always be one person bent upon using the Annual Ball to ridicule, corrupt and deprave his fellows.

How shall such a one as this be recognized? He will be impertinent, arrogant and full of false pride. He will have a record of Further Education and will place no value upon the British Way of Life, honesty, decency and loyalty. So deep is the legacy of Socialism that such fellows abound. The typical specimen will make pretty pronouncements upon whatever topic arises, criticize our Royal Family and guess the weight of their bodily parts, make light of all Honour and Serious Subjects, mock all the things that our Nation holds dear and bethink himself possessed of the greatest wit and very funny indeed *so long as he has freedom and licence* to voice Contempt for Traditional Values, and un-Patriotic, Un-Godly, subversive, seditious, Un-cricketing, Republican and Socialist opinions to the great grief of Her Majesty Queen Elizabeth and to the sore annoyance of her loyal subjects. Such Scoffers and Scoundrels, with tissues damaged by poor background and low birth will, once irritated by Education, erupt into malignant tumours of tittering and treachery. In this state they voice pernicious and naughty opinion, and smugly too, with many vicious turns of phrase, slippery figures, double meanings, ironic postures, playing on words, malice and mischief, oily trickery and Clever Dickery.

But the ordinary Man in the Field, the simple, uncomplicated, honest English soul may now take comfort: the Academy is ever in close contact with Her Majesty's Government; and the Moderator General, is well versed in methods of silencing the Dark word-Devils which skulk and loiter in the corners of the Clever mind.

Lesson L131

The Origin and Background of
Known Criminals and the Racial Structure of Crime

Criminals often have poor backgrounds and minimal/state education. The common groups are: Mediterraneans, Cockneys,[1] Romanies, Semites, Levantines, Arabs, Garden Birds, Insects, Irish, Australians and Africans. Research[2] has shown that most criminals have a common background (Fig. 27), the commonest being Cockneys whose family background often involves a surrogate father and, almost invariably, a very common mother.

Common features (Fig. 28 *overleaf*) of these classes are: close set eyes, distinctive noses, dirty or tanned skin, shifty appearance, low batting averages, feathers, six legs, criminal associates, low incomes. In most cases they will be known to the Police[3] or to the Ministry of Agriculture Fisheries and Food and have known life cycles/criminal records of some sort, generally going back into childhood. They also often have strange, foreign or regional accents, calls or buzzes. The following chart explains fully:

Fig. 27:

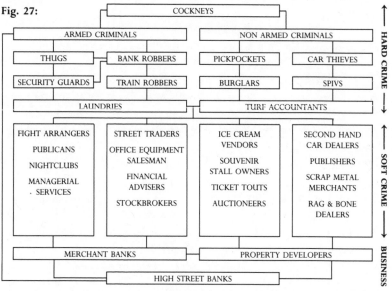

---

[1] These may be readily recognized by their habit of claiming to have been born within the sound of Bow Bells or approximately within a brief walking distance from St. Mary Le Bow. There exists in fact only one Great Bell of Bow, as the nursery rhyme suggests, but Cockneys are notorious for their loud and lying tongues. Other familiar characteristics are: calling each other John and selling fish, fresh vegetables and things in cardboard boxes.

[2] Classified information held by the British Academy of Cricket in its *Archive of Classified Material, Secrets, Profiles, Character Studies and Reports on the Background, Antecedents and Proclivities of Prominent Persons.*

[3] Who do a difficult and dangerous job.

(Turn over)

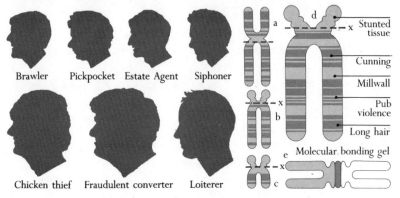

Fig. 28: *Recognition of Criminal Types*

This becomes a relatively simple exercise once the basic facial characteristics are learned. Chromosome types fall broadly into two main groupings. The normal (a) and the abnormal (b), (c) and (d), which shew stunted spiritual growth above the bench mark (x) and are the genetic fingerprint of the pace bowler and the psychopath. Surgery (e) is often the only remedy.

Regulation R337 (C1)

Suitable British Academy of Cricket Approved Jokes for telling at the Annual Ball

Guests shall restrict the telling of jokes to a minimum. Only approved jokes are permitted. They should be told with a degree of force and must be accompanied by much merriment and good humour. Not many jokes are funny but the Chairman has approved four of those collected by Academy jest analysts. They are as follows:

Joke Question No. 23/67/45/EARS — What has ears and yet cannot hear?
Answer No.   23/653/21 — Corn, excluding maize.

Joke Question No. 111/23/57/EYE — What has one eye and yet cannot see?
Answer No.   35/256/06 — A needle.

Joke Question No. 56/245/2/RED — What is black and white and red (read) all over?
Answer No.   211/23/77 — A newspaper or journal.
(The Daily Telegraph is recommended by the Academy)

Joke Question No. 21/80/43/EARS — Why is a farmer cruel?
Answer No.   34/65/19 — Because he pulls corn up by the ears.[1]
(This is under review now that most corn is harvested by mechanical means)

[1] The Chairman has asked the Directors to point out that this is his personal favourite.

Regulation R342 (C1)
Inadmissible Behaviour at the Annual Ball, with the worst excesses identified and explained

Removal of garments, lewd acts (with or without the Mascot) will not be tolerated by most clubs. Vomiting, for most people living outside Scotland and Australia, is an unfamiliar, nauseating, unedifying and unpleasant spectacle and should be avoided. Horseplay and tampering with food is inexcusable. Fighting and duels are not permitted. Gentlemen should not insult each other in front of players for this sets a very bad example. There shall be no interfering with the clothing of young ladies/gentlemen and players shall not put their hands up any skirt or down any blouse. Women should under no circumstances be prepositioned.

Regulation R357 (C2)
Music and Dancing: Techniques and Acceptable Types

Dancing is a dangerous activity because it encourages the touching of females and the holding of women by the waist, with all the miseries that this can lead to. It is the first step down the slippery path to the prepositioning of girls, mouth infections, standing at garden gates, unavailability for matches, disease, marriage and children, adultery, loose balls and bad strokes.

The Foxtrot (but not the Turkey Trot), the Quickstep (but not the Goosestep) are suitable dances for most purposes and can be controlled. With its three beats to the bar the waltz is efficacious in relaxing the biceps and collarbones in graceful momentum.

It is imperative that all dancers dance the same dance in time to the band and move in a clockwise direction on the lanes marked out for them. Alas there will always be that special English breed of person who, swept up in the high spirits of the occasion, will set out deliberately to cause chaos and offence by dancing the Cha Cha Cha or some other *flamboyant foreign cavortion*. Irregular dancers should be removed by stewards.

Sober and patriotic music is advisable, along with the *Trumpet Voluntary* and *Jerusalem*. Strauss waltzes, also in ¾ time, and the Tango (Fig. 29 *overleaf*) are permissible if the Occasion appears to be moving decorously to its conclusion in accordance with British Academy of Cricket Annual Ball regulations. But the following cautionary words must be spoken: music is at the root of much youth and adolescence. Further, all American music is based on *jazz* and can cause headaches, bruised toes, nausea, excessive perspiration and slashing, particularly of seats.

In a public place such as this no man shall dance with another for this is an abomination.

(Turn over)

Fig. 29: *The Tango*. Provided that the touching and handling of women is confined to public places it is unlikely that grave offences will take place. A lively and pleasant disport (29a) for Gentlemen will be a few rounds of the Tango (29b). Performed decorously this pleasant dance enlivens the spirit and tones the muscles, causing the whole frame to tingle with delight and gentle satisfaction. The excesses of certain *Latin American dances* like the Rhumba and Cha Cha Cha should be avoided. They have all sorts of, and often too many, beats to the bar, they encourage unbecoming affectation in the dancer and take up far too much room.

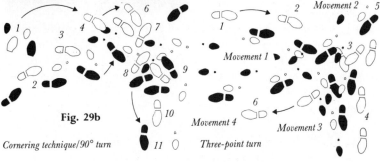

Fig. 29b

Cornering technique/90° turn

Movement 1

Movement 2

Movement 3

Movement 4

Three-point turn

Regulation R358 (C2)

The Need for Strict Adoption of and Adherence to Approved Dancing Modes, and Careful Selection of Dancing Partners

Dance, when it is expressed in the Gay Gordons or the Foxtrot, can bring man to the summit of self-e·.pression. Everything is united in him: good understanding, correct opinions, knowledge of the world and a warm heart. He will have strong feelings of family attachment and family honour without pride or weakness; he will dance with the liberality of a man of fortune, without display; he will judge for himself in everything essential, without defying public opinion in any point of worldly decorum. He will be steady on his feet, observant, moderate, candid, with a sensibility to what is amiable and lovely (Fig. 30), and a value for all the felicities of domestic life.

Characters of fancied enthusiasm and violent agitation seldom really possess these things and are soon unmasked on the dance floor. Restraint, proportion and manners are all essential. Good Old English Dances have been superseded by Twists and turns, bestial writhings and gyrations, lewd pressings and sentimental gropings of an entirely Working Class nature.

Fig. 30: *Master Dancemistress to the British Academy of Cricket*
The Dance School is situated on the first floor of Academy House, and it is here that Mrs
Dickelburgh (right) has her well-appointed ballroom with its ebonized Steinway piano and
resident music mistress (left). It is by the direct application of melody and motion that these
ladies keep all members young at heart. On Saturday mornings from 10 a.m. to 12 a.m.
B.C.T. the school opens its floor to all Registered juveniles who wish to brush up their
Foxtrot and Quickstep.

This rest of the second floor is devoted to members' quarters, libraries, rest and reading
rooms, saunae and gymnasia, trophy rooms and musea. It is strictly out of bounds.

(Turn over)

Regulation R360 (C4)
The Awards Ceremony and Acceptance Speeches

How pleasant it would be if all awards could be given according to merit. But the chief reason that most clubs avoid the giving of awards to players is to spare them all embarrassment. These unfortunates are, for the main part, inarticulate and wholly incapable of delivering a witty, edifying, and unrehearsed acceptance speech.

Specimen speeches may be purchased from the Academy but if the Gentleman concerned has his own idea and wants to make up his own speech that will be acceptable, so long as it contains no swearwords, bad language or anything in praise of Hitler[1] or is otherwise of a controversial nature.

Regulation R361 (C4)
The Subject and Content of Toasts and Speeches

It is good, during a memorable evening of delight and celebration of the World's greatest game, to think of England, the Prime Minister[1], the Queen and all things Patriotic: Mount Everest, India, Shepperton Studios, Tea, Henry Fielding and Tom Jones, sunshine and showers. It must never be forgotten that it is this England, this little Isle of Joy that spawned the noblest of all games, enjoyed the greatest of victories in war and was once possessed of the finest Navy in the world.

All patriots will, therefore, wish to celebrate the achievements of our nation which forged, from nothing but foreign countries, the vastest Empire the world has ever seen, second only to that of Genghis Khan.[1] At this point glasses will be charged and silence enforced and the Master of Ceremonies will stand, raise his glass to the Queen, who is not normally present at cricketing celebrations, and announce:

"Gentlemen I give you the Queen, who is not normally present at cricketing celebrations,"

at which all will raise their glasses and drink.

Guests will be discreetly reminded that, as ensuing toasts will be numerous, judicious imbibing is prescribed. A token sip is far more dignified than a desperate gulp. Toasts must be exhaustive and complimentary. A whole year's resentment (ten years in East Anglia) can build up from an unfortunate omission, a year's fealty (three months in East Anglia) can be secured by a politic inclusion. Speeches should always be brief and pithy.

A toast shall be set aside for : Forthcoming Legislation, the British Academy of Cricket, the Chairman and the Directors.

[1] Who, it has to be said, had some very sensible ideas.

Lesson L140

Anthropological observations on the Hokey Cokey Phenomenon

Some things which stir deep racial memories in the labouring classes will defy penetration by the analytical mind for they belong to an earlier epoch when their ancestors were propelled not by reason but by the dark, mysterious forces of the animal animus. Who can say why goats choose to grow beards, why the Cheshire Cat smiles, why the wildebeest migrate on a different given day every year, why the blackbird lays four eggs or why the cow makes a moo and does not purr? These are imponderable things, and it is to this genus of phenomena that the Hokey Cokey, and its related ritual the Conga, belong.

All that is known at present is that, under certain circumstances well known to the Academy, the labouring class spontaneously erupts into a frenzy of Hoking and Coking. The activity can be said to have a binding effect on the tribe, but studies by the British Academy of Cricket Research and Development Department are beginning to suggest that it is more relevant to the establishment of tribal precedences. This phenomenon is to be seen most commonly among Cockneys who, being crammed into an unnaturally small space,[1] have developed this elaborate ritual as a means of settling sexual conflicts without extreme or fatal violence.

The Hokey Cokey may be recognized by the way it whips all participants into a frightening frenzy. In an ecstasy of unsightly thrusting and with pseudo-copulatory action dancers boast untunefully about putting things in and out. Finally, in an hysteria of sexual innuendo, the group symbolically joins hands in a circle and surrenders to the feverish spinning rhythms, degenerating into a collective semi-mesmerized state as they Shake It All About. Limbs flail in wild abandon until all are exhausted, and young male dancers end this mating dance with vulgar prepositions to females, half-hearted brawls, nasty exchanges and Ugly Scenes.

Regulation R363 (C2)

The Control of Unbridled Sexuality in players and the Proper Punishment of Offenders

Dances and rites of this type have a pronounced obscenity and should be broken up by any responsible cricketer using as much force as may be necessary. In extreme cases where violent resistance occurs, and in all incidents which involve the offering into the ring any bared genitals or bottoms, the Band should be ordered to stop playing, and offenders handed over to the Academy for corrective treatment.

[1] London.

(Turn over)

ITEM

GOOD WIVES

"Ah, love, let us be true
To one another! for the world, which seems
To lie before us like a land of dreams,
So various, so beautiful, so new,
Hath really neither joy, nor love, nor light,
Nor certitude, nor peace, nor help for pain;
And we are here as on a darkling plain
Swept with confused alarms of struggle and flight,
Where ignorant armies clash by night."

Introductory Lesson L186

Few words in the English language are so full of infinite charm or so replete with sweet variety as the word "housewife". It is one of those words, and, alas, they are so few, which mean much and suggest much more. The most successful of all wives is she who combines the qualities of cheerfulness, cleanliness and common sense.

There are times in the life of a cricketer, whether Registered with the Academy or not, when smiling is difficult and when things seem all to be going wrong.

If the Gentleman or player reconcile himself to the fact that, although they may be bad, things might be much worse then he shall have dealt the first crushing blow to that unmanly despair which sometimes captures and ensnares the spirit of all but the greatest of men.[1] And who is it that kindly soothes away his troubles and brings him back to felicity? It is his good wife, his devoted partner and friend who is ever close to his hearth giving encouragement, support and toasted cheese.

Thus it is invariably so that a woman needs the presence of a man; and it is through him she finds fulfilment and builds a meaning on her life.

---

[1] Erasmus (1467–1536), although a foreign scholar, was a great man, and no fool when it came to women, upon whom his generous spirit saw fit to lavish detailed attention:

> "What greater or juster aim or ambition have they than to please their husbands? In order whereunto they garnish themselves with paint, washes, curls, perfumes and all other mysteries of ornament. Wives are always allowed their humour, yet it is only in exchange for titillation and pleasure, which are indeed but other names for Folly; as none can deny, who consider how a man must hug, and dandle and kittle and play a hundred little tricks with his bedfellow when he is disposed to make that use of her that Nature designed her for. Well, then, you see whence that greatest pleasure (to which modesty scarce allows a name) springs and proceeds."

Lesson L187
Marriage and love for the Cricketer

Marriage may last a lifetime and give help and support but love, mercifully, is short. The typical cricketer reaches an age when, because of declining health and the loss of the bloom of youth he will begin to think about taking to himself a wife. At this time he will fall in love for a brief period then, once affection, respect and mutual esteem are gone, he becomes a Married man.

Lesson L188
Family Planning for the Conscientious Cricketer

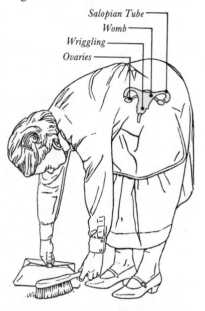

Salopian Tube
Womb
Wriggling
Ovaries

It is the duty of all cricketers to ensure the continuance of the Game by spawning infants to replace the natural wastage in the club. Fervent wriggling applied to the centre of the female (Fig. 31) is the best method.

On selected dates the *British Academy of Cricket Book of Bedside Yarns* may, at the cricketer's discretion, be replaced by the *Manual of Approved Copulatory Attitudes and Reproductive Methodology*. Close study of this volume followed by selected drills will ensure impregnation. This will often be taken in good part provided it is conducted in the dark and without too much puffing.

Fig. 31: *Reproductive paraphernalia.* All women have a right to private things and secret places with strange-sounding names.

Regulation R394 (C2A)
The Choice of Wife for the Gentleman

Of chief importance to the Gentleman is the temperament, standing and income of his wife. It must be said that a Venus is of little use if she has the proclivities of a Mars; a radiant and dignified bearing is produced not by any physical attribute but by the spiritual virtue of large sums of money or extensive land or industrial holdings.

Beauty in a woman is, in any case, a suspect and dangerous thing. It corrupts her whole being, makes her unappreciative of male attention and gives her a sense of her own worth well above the market rate.

Breathtaking beauty finds expression in the perfect human physique. It

(Turn over)

occurs in its most pure and unadulterated form in the male body: yes, quite so, for what cricketer has not, in the changing room or lavatory, observed the smooth muscular and vibrant purity of the male thigh, or the palpable, subtle tones of the young, flushed male skin and reflected how weary, flat, stale and unprofitable are all the uses of womankind.

Regulation R395 (C2A)
The Correct Choice of Female, Honeymoons, Instruction and Training in Household/Family Management

Care should be exercised in the selection of the right female for the lofty task of marriage, for it occurs very often that errors are made at this early stage. The more terrifying feminine characteristics to be detected at the outset, and therefore avoided, are as follows:

1 Intelligence   2 Independence of spirit   3 Shrewishness   4 Selfishness
5 Frigidity or a passionate nature   6 Pride   7 Fondness for dogs

Wedding celebrations should not extend far beyond the ceremony. A short honeymoon is preferred. The lumbar troubles, slouching and dawdling associated with the newly-married may be averted by regular exercises in posture (Fig. 32), bearing and demeanour. Once all the delights of marriage are quite finished and the little intimate copulations have lost all appeal it is then time for the cricketer to begin to train his wife in the proper conduct of his home. She must learn too how to be a cricketing wife and, in the fullness of time, a mother of cricketers.

Regulation R396 (C2)
The Training and Duties of the Gentleman's Wife

A Gentleman's wife shall be feminine[1] at all times and shall not seek to compete with or decry her husband in public even though, above all other men, he gives her greater evidence and cause.

A wife should be a wife to her husband and a mother to his children. But beyond this it is her duty to:

1. Ensure that domestics are under control and occupied fully at all times.
2. Confine his children to the nursery when he is present, and oversee their education.
3. Organize his calendar of Social Events.
4. Keep his household in good order, ensure that the best of everything is bought, so that inferior goods will remain available to the poor and the underprivileged.

---

[1] Masculinity in a woman is a deplorable thing, exacerbated by association with Americans, in whose country women are rife.

Fig. 32: *Anatomicus Britannicus*
No Englishman need suffer from a Bad Back if he practises proper posture and Stands up Straight. Fine fair English skin and chiselled classic features all benefit from fresh cool air. The preference of some common women for swarthy Mediterranean types is quite inexplicable.

77

(Turn over)

5. Like shooting and all things he likes (Fig. 33) and to support him in all decisions, right or wrong.

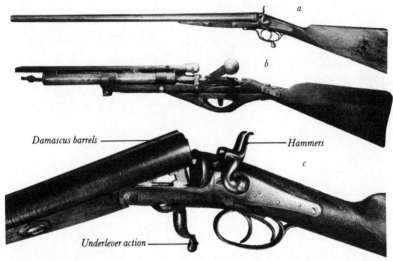

Fig. 33: *"It is her duty to like shooting, and all things he likes."*

Shooting must never be allowed to degenerate into mere slaughter. Cruelty to animals can be distressing and must always be minimized. Pheasants, and grouse particularly, consider it in very poor taste to be shot with an inferior firearm.

The Gentleman's wife, therefore, should insist that, when a firearm is purchased, her husband buy only the very best (a), for while thrift and initiative are commendable, economy in gun purchase (b) is never advisable. In any case a high quality gun is always a good investment in these uncertain times and is the only possession that a Gentleman will sometimes clean for himself. He can also coach his sons in its use, for it is never too early in life to begin killing things. Once dead, these should be placed in bags in the pantry with the traditional *legs sticking out* or with the modern *heads hanging down*, according to taste.

A fine weapon with Damascus Barrels, delicate traceries and Underlever Action (c) will need little servicing and will provide trouble-free hares, ducks and woodcock for many years without major repair.

Lesson L189

The Essential Need to keep a Wife in her Place

Provided she remains in the background at all times, a wife can be of immense assistance to her husband, but she must never be allowed to intrude on the Game. It is an unseemly thing for a woman to be knowledgeable about cricket, and under no persuasion should a Gentleman discuss cricketing tactics with her. Even in the marriage bed he must remain guarded about such things, for many a husband has been undone by his wife's careless tongue.

An intelligent wife is the worst possible affliction. She will expect to be given attention and have her views treated with respect. She will expect to be allowed to contribute to conversations and may commit many grave errors, criticizing his conduct of the Game, commenting upon the Proceedings of the Day or, worst of all, she may even contradict her husband in public.

Any Gentleman with a wife of this stamp becomes firstly the object of ridicule, later of pity and contempt, then of hatred and vilification. Expulsion from the Club inevitably follows.

Lesson L190
The Choice of Wife for the player

The player will seek a female specimen with fine broad hips to be his life-long partner, mother to his children and the sharer of his hopes and fears. Such a woman will have fine milky-white thighs and no blue-veined breasts or legs. A blotchy wife should be avoided, and collapsed lungs, fallen arches in the chosen mate are a store of suffering in later years when she will need her health and stamina to cope with his infirmities and ill temper at the onset of senility.

An excellent choice would be a woman able to curtail her innate impulse to chatter idly. The best wife will prove to be of light heart and simple disposition, at one with her place in life, busy at her household tasks with gladness and good cheer. This will allow her husband to read the newspaper or carry on the true business of Life and the Game.

Lesson L192
The player's Wife and the Gentleman

Gentlemen should take note that in recent times players become quite indignant at any attentions/children given to their wives by those of a higher social rank. No longer is it wise[1] or desirable for the Gentleman to take advantage of the good nature of these simple souls to instigate those little flirtations that were once the fashion. Egalitarianism has so poisoned the player's mind that retaliation follows at the merest violation. Seduction therefore is no longer the sporting diversion it once was, nor the rightful and safe pursuit of the privileged[2] classes, but an invitation to confrontation, impertinence and insubordination – in extreme cases accompanied by Violence, which is now getting for itself a very bad name indeed and harming the careers of military men, boxers and Officers of the Law.

[1] With the spread of the American Disease.

[2] Socialists have now begun an attack on privilege itself, the only worthwhile possession of the owning classes (other than such material things as property) and the only spiritual thing left for the rich to cling to in these egalitarian times.

79

(Turn over)

Regulation R400 (C2)
The Duties of the player's Wife
as evolved in Europe from 1507 to the present day

1. She shall be fully occupied during working hours at some useful trade, occupation or job.
2. In the evening, she shall:
   i) ensure that the "tea" is cooked and on the table piping hot.
   ii) see that her children are comfortably housed and suitably clothed.
3. Provide amusements during the close season and non-cricketing leisure hours.
4. Purchase and blanco all cricket training equipment.
5. Remember things and distribute Christmas and Anniversary presents.
6. Answer the door when there is a knock.
7. Clear away all beer bottles at the end of each day.
8. Bring the coal in for the fire, take out any ashes and clean the grate.
9. Polish the doorstep, doorhandle and letterbox.
10. Dig a hole for the Emptying of the Pail, empty the pail, and fill in the hole using an Academy approved spade or shovel.
11. Deal with all creditors and be responsible for repayments.
12. Fill in all forms and Academy Applications for Registration and write out all cheques.
13. Do all washing, ironing, provide and prepare fresh vegetables by creating and tending a kitchen garden.
14. Catch and skin all rabbits, pluck and gut boiling hens.
15. Send off all competition forms to daily newspapers.
16. Do all redecoration, home improvements and clean out all gutters and down-pipes.
17. Maintain, repair and use all axes, bicycles and prams.
18. Do all scrubbing, sharpening and dusting.
19. Keep dripping in a cup on the window sill.
20. Bake fruit cakes every Monday and squirt all flies.
21. Not wear a headscarf or slippers in public places.
22. Entertain guests and deal with livestock, children and birds (see advertisement, right).
23. Mow the lawn.
24. Re-upholster chairs and make rugs and sacks.
25. Make strong tea on the hour.
26. Collect stamps (Co-op, television licence, Green Shield).

The British Academy of Cricket

PATENT CERAMIC
—— BIRD TRAP ——

AN EFFECTIVE REMEDY FOR BIRDS

This Trapping Device comes complete with a fully illustrated instruction manual,
directions for assembly and an attractive bird recognition wallchart.

STANDARD MODEL

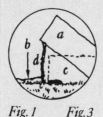

Fig. 1

Fig. 3

This new ornithological product is designed for ease of assembly and harnesses Gravity (Fig. 3f), one of Nature's primary forces, to dispatch feathered felons. It comes to you beautifully packaged and comprises four kiln-fired earthenware components of obloid shape crafted to the highest standards. Which is why it will be a beautiful addition to any woman's garden. In extensive field tests, it has proved popular with all common and garden birds. *Requires little maintenance.*

Fig. 2

Fig. 4

Regularly applied to the winged community the Trap will destroy most airborne mischief makers.

**A heavy-duty model No B/T D275a/hd for rooks, magpies and large offenders is
also available: £29.99 inc. V.A.T. + postage and package.**

Bait, string and twigs are not supplied with this trap.

Code TX8/5b   Reg Office 35

.(Turn over)

Lesson L194

On Birth Control and the Working-Class Cricketer

If our nation is to prosper then it is necessary that there exist a force of devoted people willing to undertake all the great industry (Fig. 34) and endeavour needed to create the wealth we[1] can all share.

It is an ugly thing to see, as is often the case these days, a working-class person envious of the place held in Society or the wealth held by his

Fig. 34: *The Art of Cycle Maintenance and Conversation*

The working class woman's life is not unremitting toil; indeed, her labours often present her with important stimuli and social opportunities. Work stops for minutes at a time as she exchanges views with a kindred spirit, seeks technical advice, discusses the latest intelligence from overseas, or defends the long-chain molecule.

[1] This word is used in its proper sense pertaining to all people, and not in the sense employed by socialists who would have all wealth shared among those who produce it, and the unemployed, to the exclusion of the rich who depend entirely on it for their livelihoods.

superiors[1]. The latter, of course, are generally too well-bred to reciprocate or envy him his simple life.

Now that vast numbers of soldiers are no longer needed for foreign wars or the administration of the Colonies, it profits the player to have it instilled in his mind at an early age that a certain degree of control in matters of birth is desirable. A brace is acceptable, a clutch is not.

Lesson L195
On Proper Investment and Pecuniary Advancement resulting from Fewer Children

The increased wealth that accrues to working-class people as a result of birth control may be spent on:

1. HOME OWNERSHIP

This has, in most civilized countries, replaced the lash. It serves as a goad to prevent the onset of indolence. It ensures that the owner-occupier is profitably occupied throughout his whole life, shackled to sheds and shelves and racked by running repairs. Many a confirmed loafer has been brought to justice by the simple expedient of having been sold a modest property.

2. SELF EMPLOYMENT

Although a man may become very poor and have little to do when he is self-employed, there is, nevertheless, a dignity attached to this form of unemployment that is entirely lacking in those who clamour for the "dole". Furthermore it allows him to endure his poverty with pride, free from the burdens of taxation.

Regulation R402 (C4)
The Problems of Adolescence

It will be the case in most juveniles, that the theft of apples, experiments with beer and sherbert dabs, and the ecstasies of self-abuse will cause the stomach to rebel. This will, in turn, set off a chain of bodily reactions and chemical changes in the blood which, when irritated to a state of frenzy by hormonal changes induced by magazines and dirty talk, will cause these poisons finally to be emitted from the face in the form of Nasty Swellings and Eruptions, acne vulgaris, running sores, Bulbous Boils and Carbuncles and a whole tide of bubbling discharges and Excessive Excretions.

The most efficient solution is to send off all pubescent juveniles to be boarded during all school holidays. In any case they should be banished from all social gatherings, birthday parties, cricket matches and excluded from all club photographs and portraits.

---

[1] The rich are highly trained in the spending of money. Thus they have an important social and economic function in redistributing wealth and creating employment.

(Turn over)

BATTING ORDERS

"My good blade carves the casques of men,
My tough lance thrusteth sure,
My strength is as the strength of ten,
Because my heart is pure."

Introductory Lesson L241

Infinite is the patience lavished by primitives on their weapons, with the highest skills of the culture applied to the Piece. It has always been so, from the graceful splendour of the bow and arrow to the delicate engraving, silver inlay and traceries on a fine sporting gun; all societies have writ large their profoundest ideals and aspirations upon their weapons. Such protracted care wrought upon them will, it is hoped, return the spiritual investment by unleashing a mortal blow to the stricken heart of the quarry. Thus it is with the cricketer as he plays the winning drive: his blade must be straight and true.

The skills of the master batmaker are inestimably subtle: they represent the height of the woodcarver's art combined with a poet's sensitivity, the delicate responses of a musical virtuoso and the grace of a ballet dancer. He coaxes from a piece of common wood an object of breathtaking beauty, harmony and perfection, intuiting the character of the wood grain with the insight of a literary genius.

Thankfully, reputable firms still exist to cater for the Gentleman who will not wish to purchase an anaemic and contorted "ready-made" artefact. During the quiet of the close season such a company will be prepared to reveal something of the timber's background: on which slopes the tree was grown, its age at felling, details of seasoning, on whose estate and in what type of soil it was rooted, for all these things can affect the breeding of the classic bat.

Few will be able to afford a true pedigree bat, and the ordinary Gentleman will have to satisfy himself with a newly-wrought Classic Piece which will be his trusty Excalibur (Fig. 35), his Mentor and his Guide, his life's Rod and Staff and Everlasting Arm.

The bat, combined with a quick eye and brain, is the cricketer's sole ally in the heat of battle, his only solace in time of pain, grief and despair; it is the warrior's symbol, his badge of office, and his skill in its use is what sets him apart from the common herd and makes him a member of the warrior class. Without his bat he is a mere civilian, a common fop, a waterfly, a thing... of nothing.

Fig. 35: *"Te spectem suprema mihi cum venerit hora/Te teneam moriens deficiente manu."*

85

(Turn over)

Lesson L244

The Cricketer's Bat as Icon, with the Existence of God[1] prov'd by Cosmological and Teleological Assertions

Atheists say God is no such thing. But how is it that all is so carefully woven together to form such a fortuitous and coherent whole?
Consider:

1. The woodcock, roast with chestnuts and gravy
2. The lilies of the field, how they grow
3. The oak before the ash
4. North Sea Oil
5. The apple bough in England now
6. Mozart's Horn Concerto in E♭ major K495[2]

Here are demonstrated six good reasons for believing Someone Is Behind It All or that there is a Plan. But the seventh is conclusive:

7. Sunday and the willow tree. These could not have been made without the Hand, or at least the Word, of God; and he must have had Cricket in Mind.

Ecce salix. Down by the riverside; there grows the wood for the cricket bat. Without it there would have been no runs made that have been made for it is the Wood of Woods; wood everlasting, it maketh the Bat of Bats. It is the *sine* without *qua* there would *non* be any cricket. Like the angler, it loves to do nothing so much as to stand alone or in rows by a river and dangle things in the water, aimlessly, and be poured over by rain. Thus it is positively puddlotropic and, being the wettest of all woods, it embodies the Spirit of the English Summer.

Lesson L245

The True Nature of the Willow Tree Reveal'd

English Class 1 willow is grown in plantations in lowland Britain with the finest cricketing sorts bred in the river bottoms of the Norfolk and Suffolk border where the valley flood lands and the Waveney watermeadows gently hum with the sound of ripening willows which abound all around.

---

[1] Theological arguments have been taken from the excellent and authoritative book:
  Discourses concerning the Being and Natural Perfections of God in which that first principle of religion, the existence of the Deity, is prov'd from the Frame of the Material World, from the animal and rational life, and from human intelligence and Morality, and the Divine Attributes of spirituality, unity, eternity, immensity, omnipotence, omniscience and Infinite wisdom are explained by John Abernethy, M.A. Dublin printed: London reprinted for H. Whitridge, at the Royal Exchange. MDCCXLIII.

[2] The one which goes: Duh, didderly, didderly, didderly dee,
                     Duh, didderly, didderly didderly dum*

* N.B. Mozart knew well that music is not meant to rhyme.

For twenty years and more the trees are nurtured by the wet black silt; winter and summer they draw in a steady supply of moisture. The stems grow straight and true, with good level stands of best killing willow selling to £1.60 a pound live weight.

When the tree is felled and stripped the flesh is soft, white and pure, youthful, straight grained, devoid of any blemish, knots and figuring. It is wanton and gay but fibrous, resilient. Nervous, tense, yet yielding to the touch and submissive to all shock and vibration. It is silky and warm, gently resisting the pressure of the thumb but easily scored and wounded by the fingernail. It is so easily hurt by a careless hand yet in contact with the ball it becomes fierce, powerful, hard, upright, muscular and brave.

This is the stuff which goes to make the perfect weapon for the discerning Gentleman.

Lesson L246
The Acquisition of a Suitable Blade,
and its Importance in the Life of the Cricketer

1 *Initial interviews.* When a young cricketer comes of age he should present himself at the house of the accredited manufacturer and be introduced to the various stocks (Fig. 36) and to his batfitter. He may take along an experienced carpenter or batman (or he may take advantage of the Academy's advisory service which has a supply of qualified batmen) for a second opinion.

2. *First fitting.* When the wood has been selected, then the craftsman will take measurements using a range of scientific instruments.

3. *Second and subsequent fittings.* Thereafter all that is required is for the client to return once each month to satisfy himself with the progress of the bat, to have minor adjustments made and final measurements taken.

4. *Viewing of the Bat.* At last will emerge the Blade, a wooden ecstasy, a ligneous reverie, a vision or a waking dream, a master Piece and a feat of woodcraft unsurpassed, pure, classical, unadorned, harmonious in all its parts, symmetrical, balanced, with charm and poise, a King of Artefacts, the highest Expression of Human Endeavour and Human Will and proof of the Divine Spirit in Man.

5. *Final delivery* and *commissioning of the Bat.* With a simple ceremony, he will take delivery of the weapon which is to accompany him on his passage across Life's stormy sea and to be the secret sharer of his woes. He is at the Great Watershed, the New Beginning, the Point of No Return.

(Turn over)

Fig. 36: *"He will be introduced to the various stocks."*
The wise cricketer will seek always a reputable stockist for there are many unscrupulous dealers who will offer inferior wood. It is not a good idea to economize at this early stage, and never should the cricketer take the first tree offered to him. In no circumstances should money change hands (inset) at this early stage; and no *bona fide* dealer will ask for banknotes or payment on the spot.

Lesson L248
The Services of the Master Batfitters' Guild

Further information about bats may be had by application to the Worshipfull Guild of Batfitters (Fig. 37) by St. Paul's Churchyard.

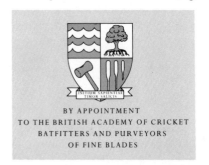

BY APPOINTMENT
TO THE BRITISH ACADEMY OF CRICKET
BATFITTERS AND PURVEYORS
OF FINE BLADES

Fig. 37: *The sign of the Batfitters' Guild.* This ancient company, begun in the reign of Henry VI, developed in the late seventeenth century out of the Mediaeval Oarmongers' and Clubformers' Guild. Hence the watery symbol azure on the top left hand side and the mallet penchant sinister. These now represent Summer and the Bat respectively, and there is an added Salix rampant dexter. The banner and Classical motto are eighteenth century embellishments.

This distinguished company with its ancient rituals and impressive body of lore and arcane knowledge about Bats supplies Official Batfitters to the Academy and will recommend a commercial batfitter for any Gentlemen who wishes to apply, stating his age, distance between his eyes and customary guard. Details of any convictions by the Academy must be included and a declaration of any stoops, speech impediments or other physical/mental disabilities as well as any dishonourable discharge in the last three years.

When the correct bat has been obtained there will be hours of kneading and rubbing, as well as the constant application of linseed oil to selected parts. The batfitter, as opposed to the batmaker, will not undertake this aspect of the work, and a list of private contractors specializing in pest control (Fig. 38) and bat care is available from the Guild.

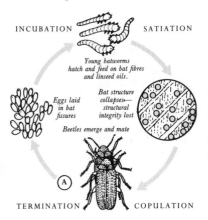

INCUBATION   SATIATION

Young batworms hatch and feed on bat fibres and linseed oils.

Eggs laid in bat fissures   *Bat structure collapses— structural integrity lost*

Beetles emerge and mate

(A)

TERMINATION   COPULATION

Fig. 38: *The life cycle of Bat Boring Beetle* (Old name "worm i' the bat").

All organisms have a life cycle such as this. That of the Bat Beetle, a merciless and unforgiving foe, should be interrupted at point A by the application of a rolled up newspaper[1] as soon as he emerges from his hole in May. By this time he will have completed Detestable Excavations inside the bat, reducing its precious fibres to powder and dust, with grave risk of batting collapse.

[1] The *Sunday Telegraph*, the *Horse and Hound* magazine, *The Living Countryside*, the *B.B.C. Wildlife Magazine* are recommended.

89

(Turn over)

Regulation R486 (C4)
Bat Abuse and the Signing of Bats

For bat signing all handwriting shall be neat and flowing, but not legible as this is the sign of a poor education. Latin and Greek mottoes should be employed for these are the languages of the true Englishman and convey heroically his higher thoughts.

Lesson L249
The British Academy of Cricket
Charity Bat Clinic for Bat Afflictions

Like all precision instruments the bat can lose its timing and co-ordination. Therefore clinics are held monthly.

Players (and Gentlemen unable to afford the services of a consultant) are entitled to Bat Aid. They may come along and talk about their problems, have bats vetted, x-rayed and approved and inspected. Helpful advice on bat selection, maintenance and repair procedure is also given. A postal service with report slips (Fig. 39) is now also in place for the disabled or those confined to bed.

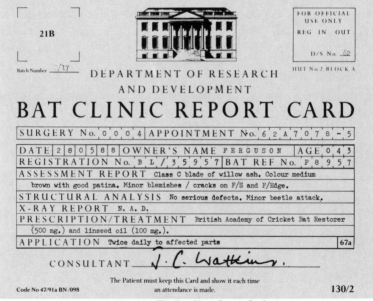

Fig. 39: *The Bat Clinic Report Card*

This is the Academy's single most important service to the cricketer who, until this time, has had to suffer bat deterioration and disease in stoic resignation. When problems arise the Report Slip is on hand to ensure immediate and correct treatment.

The safest means of acquiring the perfect bat[1] is to purchase the British Academy of Cricket approved Blade for Batsmen, scales 1, 2, 3, and 4.

Regulation R490 (C3)
Recognition and Classification of Quality Bats

Colour codes, to be used in all contests for ease of recognition at a distance, are as follows:

Scale 4. White: for all callow apprentices, the young, inept (Fig. 40) and inexperienced.

Scale 3. Golden brown: for middle-order and journeymen batsmen, Improvers still learning their craft, and undergraduates.

Scale 2. A rich treacly colour for bachelors who have taken their final examinations.

Scale 1. A first-class bat, like a good painting, is dark brown. It will be held in the hands of a Master Batsman.

All cricketers shall learn these codings by heart, and accord deference to Scales 1 and 2.

Fig. 40: *The Charity Clinic and Well-Bat welfare*
This visitor is not an expert batsman, but he does have a right to play with a good novice bat. Regular consultations do much to prevent ailments and ensure bat health and vigour, but Mr Watkins sees many poor specimens in his surgery.

[1] Even lesser bats such as Billingford Butterscotch Beauty III or Prince Amber of Hoxon Hundred are now prohibitively expensive.

(Turn over)

Regulation R494 (C2)
Problems with Bat Security, the Threat of Children and Dogs, Microbe, Insect and Fungal Attack

Colonies and communities of microbes, fungi and insects have scant respect for personal property and are never at rest. Unlike humans, these pests are dedicated to the final destruction of things which are *already dead*, and part of their busy Winter programme involves all cricketing equipment.

It is unfortunate for the bat that it is wooden, therefore technically dead, and subject to attack from these untiring consumers of fibres, cellulose and oils. An heroic effort must be made to check and repel their assault (Fig. 41). When an invasion is attempted raiding parties will be followed by a full-scale attack. The complete extermination of these forces using one of the four[1] methods recommended by the Academy shall be the aim of all cricketers.

A literary response will also prove effective in keeping both children and dogs away from equipment. The forceful application of the written word[1] about the face (dog) or ears (child) is sufficient in most cases.

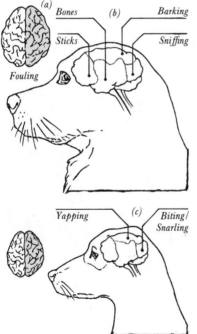

(a) Bones (b) Barking
Sticks Sniffing
Fouling
Yapping (c) Biting/Snarling

Fig. 41: *Cross section of a dog's brain: Motor mechanisms and canine psychology.* The right side of the dog's brain (Fig. 41a) is solely devoted to defecating. In this respect he is a fearful and loathsome foe who strikes at the very core of decency with his outrageous and filthy habits. Dog owners are, like their captive and cowering beasts, cowards at heart. Foul language applied with only such force as is strictly necessary will often prove a deterrent to this disgusting alliance. The left side of the brain (Fig. 41b) affects the rest of the dog and is divided as shown. At any one time a neuron may pass from one lobe to another causing it to react. This explains the unpredictable behaviour of dogs suffering from canine dementia and why all bats should be hidden safely from this inveterate chewer and burier of objects.

In the Jack Russell Terrier (c) the barking becomes yapping and the sniffing motors are turned over to biting and snarling. The brain weight forms a bigger proportion of the total dog, thus helping it to make good its escape from the scene of savagery.

[1] The *Sunday Telegraph*, the *Horse and Hound* magazine, *The Living Countryside*, the B.B.C. *Wildlife Magazine* are recommended.

ITEM

YULETIDE FESTIVITIES

"Christmas Day is here agin,
Cold owtside and warm 'uthin
Fill the mugs and plates up high
Live like a Lord, today, surely."

Introductory Lesson L286

Each club will wish, at Christmas each year, to set aside a few days when thoughts of cricket give way to the holly, and the ivy, and good will to all men.

Fun is of great benefit to all.[1] In the bleak mid-winter when the north wind doth blow, it is time for God to rest ye merry Gentlemen and players. Old rivalries, petty jealousies and the settling of scores should be put on one side in favour of rosy cheeks, cake and candles, Dickens, glitter and gluttony, sleep in heavenly peace and a responsible new year.

Now is the time for genuinely beneficent spirit, donations to club roofing or superannuation funds; now the time to give some attention to children (Fig. 42), a warmhearted benevolence to all living things, to women and pets. Now is the peak of Christian felicity, Jesus' birthday, a time to attend to the mascot, to visit friends, and give praise to fellow cricketers, and to prepare the turkeys, geese, ducks, chickens, cattle and sheep for their part in the Christmas celebrations, as well as the trimmings.

Fig. 42: *Father Christmas.* This traditional figure is a welcome sight at most households at Yuletide, and will be an honoured guest at all gatherings.

However, the little ones[2] should not be subjected to the unedifying spectacle of two Father Christmases competing for their business for while free market competition is an admirable thing in our Nation's commercial life, it is tasteless and mercenary on the domestic front. Jeffrey M. Bowles (Gent.), who is himself a Black Belt Father Christmas, here demonstrates the correct method of dealing with an imposter.

[1] The Academy's Research and Development Department has discovered that good cheer, enjoyment, the stroking of cats, mince pies, Registration and Christmas cards are all beneficial to the health as well as a contribution to long life and a stimulus to Trade.

[2] This does not include dwarfs, midgets, the emaciated or those of mere puny stature, the Welsh or inhabitants of Liverpool.

(Turn over)

THE CAPTAIN'S PARTY

"I know thee not, old man."

Introductory Lesson L287

It were a pleasant and philanthropic[1] gesture, and will ("may" in East Anglia) be repaid many times (once in East Anglia) by loyalty and service, if the captain declare that there shall be a masque and Christmas Party.

He shall nominate a date for an evening (mid-December is ideal, but certainly no later than February) and make it known to all catering staff that he expects the event to be a success. Attendance for Gentlemen and players (if invited) is obligatory.

All activities shall be conducted in accordance with Regulations R308–363 (Annual Ball), but in addition there will be an opportunity for all to frolick and indulge in what is now vulgarly termed "Fancy Dress".

Regulation R581 (C4)

Suitable Themes for the Masque, and the Formal Disclaimer

The captain may choose a theme for the Masque. Themes may depict infamous or non-approved historical personages or events because, since those present will be dressed outrageously, ironically or satirically, it does not dignify the subject but rather holds it up to contempt or ridicule. The wise captain, will, however, make this abundantly plain by causing to be printed a suitable disclaimer in a prominent spot on the invitation or programme. Here is the suggested model:

ATTENTION: "THE CAPTAIN WOULD HAVE IT KNOWN THAT THE HISTORICAL EVENTS PORTRAYED AT THIS FESTIVITY ARE NOT A REFLECTION OF HIS, OR THE CLUB'S, OFFICIAL VIEW, NOR IS IT IN ANY WAY IMPLIED THAT BECAUSE A SCENE OR OCCURRENCE IS DEPICTED IN COSTUME THERE IS ANY IMPLICIT ACKNOW-LEDGEMENT THAT EVENTS ACTUALLY OCCURRED AS ARE ABOUT TO BE DEPICTED, OR INDEED HAPPENED AT ALL BEYOND WHAT WAS REPORTED IN THE *DAILY TELEGRAPH* NEWSPAPER AT THE MATERIAL TIME."

Signed ....

---

[1] Private philanthropy, the desire to give things to people, the Will to Charity, has, despite all the efforts of socialists to suppress it, remained as strong an impulse in the human breast as the will to acquire more shares and Grow More Corn.

Regulation R582 (C2A)
Suitable themes for Masques at large and small gatherings

Disguise, mistaken identity, trickery and confusion is an age-old convention which goes back to Shakespeare, but care is needed to ensure that no offence is caused. For a large gathering:

Class A: The Black Hole of Calcutta, the Sinking of the Titanic, Custer's Last Stand, the Wooden Horse of Troy, Raid on Düsseldorf.

Class B: The Mutiny on the Bounty, Queen Victoria's Golden Jubilee, the Falklands Affair and the Conservative Landslide, the Storming of the Bastille, the Discovery of Penicillin, the Battle of Bosworth.

Class C: The Defenestration of Prague, the Battle of Britain, the Treaty at Versailles, Moses and the Exodus to the Promised Land, the Legend of William Tell with/without apple.

Class D: The Slaughter of the Innocents, the 1925 Lord's Test Match, the Cuba Crisis, Gordon at Khartoum, the Opening of the Liverpool to Manchester Railway, The Mayflower sets sail.

Supplementary themes for smaller gatherings (Gentlemen only):
Stanley finds Livingstone (Fig. 43), the Last Supper or Nativity play, Marco Polo arrives in Cathay, the Death of Nelson, the Murder of Caesar, the Seven Deadly Sins, the Foolish Virgins, at the Tabard Inn, Scott reaches the South Pole, Scott reaches the North Pole.

Fig. 43: *Stanley finds Dr Livingstone*

It was in the great era of English Exploration that Stanley found Livingstone in Africa, an event of resounding international significance. But, as can be seen, this was not accompanied by vulgar prancing and embraces but by a pleasant exchange of quotations and the lifting of hats. Britain's explorers gave Mankind many major new discoveries, Victoria Falls, the Pyramids, Mayan temples, Mount Everest and countless minor structures, thus uniting the world in a sense of travel and adventure.

(Turn over)

Regulation R583 (C3)
Rules Governing the Admission of Guests at Fancy Dress Functions and the Recognition and Exclusion of Perverts

Because guests will be bedecked in unfamiliar garb and gowns of exotic splendour, with faces perhaps blacked, or wearing veils, it will be difficult for footmen and doorman instantly to recognize the arrivals. Because invitation cards can easily be lost, mislaid, or forged, it is well to issue each guest with a password to be checked off against the master list held by the commissionaire.

Transvestites tend to gravitate towards such functions and there will be some who will wish to appear in dress inappropriate to their gender. Congenital perverts and those converted to depravity by reason of background or education, persuasion or for political reasons, will be taken into the foyer and processed.

Interjection N° Ia 01
Security of Official Papers

The Moderator General and Chief Registrar, in perusing this text, have been moved to jointly issue the following statement:

Registration documents should be kept in a bank vault for, once lost, they cannot be replaced without formal interviews with the Moderator General who has little patience with those who do not Look After Their Things.[1] Affadavits will be required in the event of any loss whomsoever or howsoever caused. Proof will have to be furnished that the missing documents have not been negligently mislaid or that they have not been stolen by or otherwise fallen into the hands of foreigners, agents of the Test and County Cricket Board, members of the Marylebone Cricket Club or any other infiltrator, *dribbling Egg-Stained Old Buffer*, or imposter.

Regulation R584 (C3)
Suitable Guises for Thematically Unspecified Fancy Dress Parties

Problems arise for the host when a theme is not laid down for guests, who will, otherwise, be free to choose any guise that suggests itself to them. This were a good and joyful thing if all the world were decent and wise: but alas it is not so. There are those who would depict Chartists, Socialists and all

---

[1] It is well known that the Greeks do not Look After Their Things, and allow many Important Public Buildings to fall into disrepair, decay, dereliction with complete loss of roofstuffs. Now they have impudently requested the return of the Elgin Marbles which have always been properly valued* in England and are Kept In The Dry.

* At millions of pounds.

manner of libertines and traitors. It should be pointed out that no Cavalier shall communicate or dance with any Roundhead. Therefore it is of benefit to suggest on any invitation sent out to prospective guests a list of approved and unapproved guises. This would be as follows:

Approved: Sir George Brough, Donald Campbell, Sir Richard Dimbleby, Benjamin Disraeli, Sir Francis Drake, Dr Livingstone, Peter May, Malcolm Muggeridge, Long John Silver (Fig. 44), Madame Tussaud, the Duke of Wellington, Ulysses.

Unapproved: Julius Caesar, Dracula, Oliver Cromwell, Charles Darwin, English Kings 1301–1485, Guy Fawkes, Percy Fender, Sherpa Tensing, Wesley Hall, Martin Luther King, Karl Marx, Philip of Spain, George Washington, William Wilberforce (Fig. 45), Gandhi.

Cricketers should not appear inanimate, or as beasts;

Inanimate things: Rolls Royce Roadster, the *Golden Hind*, Big Ben, St Paul's Cathedral, a Punch and Judy stand, a cricket pavilion, the Taj Mahal, Supermarine Spitfire, the Princess of Wales, a candle.

Beastly things: William Hamilton, This Little Piggy, Rupert, the Hydra, a rook/crow/magpie, the Lion's den, the Loch Ness Monster, Dornier, V1 or V2, Quasimodo.

Fig. 44: *Long John Silver,* a free market entrepreneur, did not go straight to the Social security Office the minute he had his leg shot off. Nor did he stand around on street corners. He was prepared to use his initiative, get on his boat and seek his fortune elsewhere.

Fig. 45: *William Wilberforce* hated the black economy. He was thus an enemy of black people. He abolished slavery which had created much employment for them. His opposition to the black markets ruined trade; and shipbuilding, sugar cane and cotton, all declined seriously.

(Turn over)

AT HOME

*"Next day was Chicken Day. They didn't think too much
of that; they had to go and have all their feathers out,
because they were for Christmas."*

Introductory Lesson L291

*The delights of society and his fellow man must be held in deep affection by any
cricketer. But it is at his hearth and fire that Felicity warms her heart and
frozen fingers, before a crackling blaze of chicken bones and pretty paper.
Here, in a broadside of brandy butter and caken ecstasies, here, hid warm from
the East wind in the eaves, cold cobwebs, scratching sounds and broken straws,
most pies are minced, puddings plummed and the oaken table jammed with
tarts. From the pantry hooks hang hares and hams, the pheasant, the partridge
and the woodcock wild. Now is the honing of the knives, balloons bang and
something stirs within the bowl. Buns bake. The clock creaks and the human
soul sinks into heavy slumber, lulled a-by in candlelight, human care and love.*

Regulation R585 (C3) or (C2A)
Curbing the Excesses of Childish Behaviour and the Suppression of Over-Indulgence by Children

Gentlemen may, nowadays, intervene at Christmas time if children[1] are seen
to be over-excited by their Feast of Gifts. They should be told to act their
age. If this fails to elicit a satisfactory response, then all cricketing
equipment should be confiscated. There shall be no right of appeal.

Players should note that any offences against propriety on the part of their
children should be swiftly followed by a good thrashing. For more serious
offences the child may be sentenced to sit quietly and read a book. This is a
pursuit so incompatible with the working class and ignorant[2] mind as to
constitute a very important sanction.[3] For gross misconduct he should listen
five times to a recording of the Chairman's Christmas Address to the
Nations (Fig. 46).

[1] This includes all illegitimate children of servant girls.

[2] Ignorance is the only thing that every Englishman is born with in equal portion. But the labourer,
sensing that this is the only thing he will ever truly possess, protects his birthright fiercely and cannot
have it wrested from him. This is the only matter of principle he will uphold consistently. Ignorance,
apart from an abysmal taste in music, is also the only possession he will share ungrudgingly with others.

[3] Theories linking better education with less crime have long been known to the Home Office. The
setting aside of time in all prisons for private reading and study, and the installation of more libraries, has
stunned the working classes into a healthy fear of prison which is helping to curb lawlessness.

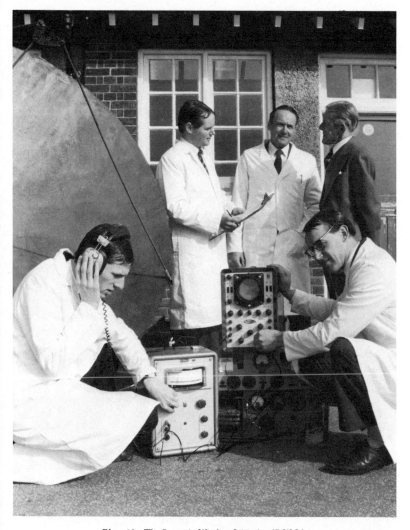

Fig. 46: *The Strategic Wireless Initiative (S.W.I.)*

All registered nations will now receive *live* the Chairman's Christmas Broadcast. And, as part of a reciprocal agreement, He will also use His new iron ear Loki I to reach out across ethereal starry ways, a limitless ocean boundless and deep, and listen equally to all Registered nations on Earth, including New Zealanders, Australians, East and West Indians and Pakistanis. Thus, racial harmony and international understanding will be further enhanced. This Transglobal Receiver, devized by two of Britain's most brilliant young physicists, is tuned very finely to avoid crackling and whistlers. All operations are supervized by Sir St. John Peatfield, an expert in advanced seven-valve electronics, smoothing circuits and electrolytic condensers.

(Turn over)

Lesson L297
The Spirit Behind the Giving of Gifts at Yuletide

Naked generosity is an ugly thing, as a peep into any working-class home at Christmas will reveal. The giving of gifts should arise naturally out of an innate feeling for Cricket, and a Christian sense that certain people deserve a British Academy of Cricket gift voucher or Registration for the coming year. Unapproved greetings cards (Fig. 47) should not be sent.

Alternative gifts for adults might be:

1. *For friends, wives, close friends, business colleagues, sporting acquaintances and older children:* The British Academy of Cricket *Manual for Gentlemen and Players* or the Sir St. John Peatfield *Boxed Gramophone Record Set* and course for Mental, Physical and Spiritual Improvement.

2. *For relations, relatives and other persons:* Woollen socks, a box of British Academy of Cricket nosecloths or handkerchiefs (men), a pair of stockings, or British Academy of Cricket chocolates/Kendal mint cake (women).

3. *For professional colleagues, academics, lexicographers, linguists, students of morphology, syntax, etymology and philology:* The British Academy of Cricket *Graphic Dictionary of Cricketing Terminology.*

4. *For club colleagues:* The British Academy of Cricket *Manual for Officers and Staff* or the British Academy of Cricket Personal Hygiene Dispensary.

Fig. 47: *Christmas cards and the Cricketer.* This document was recently confiscated and added to the Academy Index. It depicts a match which should have been cancelled under Reg. 07/96/83 in the *British Academy of Cricket Manual for Officers and Staff*, under rules governing visibility, humidity and the state of the square and outfield. It holds up to ridicule the game and the professions of batsmen and wicketkeeper as well as the calling of the bowler. It depicts anti-cricketing weather and un-cricketing activities. The perpetrators, Pace Publications, were heavily fined by the Adjudicator, and have now ceased trading. This company, in any case, was a mere front for Pace Products, but the Moderator General was not fooled by this.

All Registered persons will send the simple and dignified British Academy of Cricket Patent Christmas Card in order to stamp out, once and for all, all frivolous offerings.

Regulation R586 (C2A)
Manual Purchase, Care and Protection
and Procedures for the Handling of the Texts

It is possible that some difficulty and jostling will be experienced when the new purchaser is queuing for his Manual at the bookshop. He should attempt at all times to maintain an even temper and good humour, eschewing all opportunities to cause, or to be involved in, Ugly Scenes and scuffles.

Immediately on receipt or acquisition of Manuals the reader shall follow Academy drills for book husbandry and text care.

Brown paper offers excellent protection for the volume. But the diligent coverer will ensure that, before the task is begun, the words "The British Academy of Cricket Manual for Gentlemen and players MCMLXXXVIII" are written on a separate sheet of clean paper (any scrap will do) so that when the cover is installed on the volume these words may be copied neatly on to the spine without the need for removal of the paper which will, by this time, be found to obscure the words on the cover of the volume. When this is complete it remains only for the reader to obey the following instructions, many of which are identical to those given for reproductive and copulatory drills:

1. No itchy crumbs (biscuits, sponges, fruitcakes class A and B.)
2. Clean hands at all times.
3. No dribbling or bending of the spine.
4. No laughing at the Dirty Bits.
5. No thumbing.
6. Always lie on a flat surface.
7. No yawning, coughing and sneezing.
8. No regional accents or licking of fingers.
9. No abuse involving table legs.
10. Dog earing to be kept to a minimum.

Regulation R587 (C2A or C3)
Gifts for Children and the Negotiation of Yuletide Terms
1. GIFTS FOR THE WORKING-CLASS CHILD:

A common method used by the working classes to maintain their poverty and to equip their children for a lifetime of unhappiness is the over-purchase of gifts at Christmas.

What has been throughout the year a tooth-rotting trickle of sugary sorrow, a mere lapping at the sickly edge of woe, born of *Blue Peter*, toffee and toys, at Christmas becomes a floodtide of misery. The victim founders in the tide race of gift-giving and then drowns under the wave of unbridled, prodigal kindness and fudgeborne sentimentality unleashed on him by the

(Turn over)

whole of adultkind in an orgy of self-gratification. He is swept away by an avalanche of bounty which smothers his innocent soul, mortifies him, paralyzes his sense and assaults the very core of his being; breaking down the barriers of his tiny spirit, it storms the ramparts of his reason and quite o'erwhelms him until he lies sobbing, poor mite, or runs beserk, a crazed monstrosity caught in a strange and revolving maelstrom of glittering tinsel, Christmas cards, kaleidoscopes and catastrophe, a sticky melting world of chocolate bars and aunties.

From the thrifty player gifts will be kept to a minimum (Fig. 48).

Fig. 48: *Shopping hints for gift-givers*
Sensible and practical gifts at Christmas will often help inculcate correct notions of shoe care and frugality. Mixed nuts and an orange never fail to bring a beaming smile to any child's face, as will a British Academy of Cricket Christmas Shoe care kit. The official Yuletide Postal Greeting should be sent to all Registered juveniles. These are available on request from the Academy at a cost of £3.75 per packet of ten, with envelopes.

2. GIFTS FOR GENTLEMEN'S HEIRS

How much more courageous is the normal Gentleman whose children will be instructed, before Christmas, in the stock which Father Christmas has amassed and whether or not Value Added Tax is to be included (in most houses this is waived). Boys and girls will be told to make a sensible choice of some small object which Santa can manage in his sack which is very, very heavy. A suitable choice might be a *British Academy of Cricket Manual for Schoolboys*.

Larger gifts should not be frivolous, but should be aimed at improving the child. These might include: a Bechstein piano, scaled working model of a Rolls Royce saloon, or a British Rail-way set. The conscientious Gentleman will, however, tell the child that the money is being set aside for extra Greek lessons, a place in a good school, a yacht or, more wisely, invested in Unit Trusts, stocks, equity shares, gilt-edged securities or Eurobonds, for it is good to establish profit-taking habits at an early age.

Regulation R589 (C2A)
The excesses of Food and Drink at Christmas

There exist those who would turn Christmas into a time for unmitigated feastings of all kinds, and this can cause a lot of bad feeling and upsets. The British Academy of Cricket will supply a Christmas package of Yuletide Medicaments with liver salts, ointments for Chill and other common blains, diuretics, analgesics, oralgesics, nostrilgesics and other useful remedies which will stifle all the symptoms of Christmas Maladies. Each cricketer shall purchase an adequate supply.

Regulation R590 (C4)
The Use of club Abdominals

The Abdominal[1] will be in great demand at Christmas, for a large belly and a cheerful countenance are very popular. Yuletide is his Harvest Time, but he must remember to avoid the following:

1. Cheese rind that has been trod a long age in the deep pilèd carpet.
2. Pink pieces of oranges and lemons left at the bottom of punch bowls.
3. Cherries (ripe) and pips left after trifles.
4. Cake decorations which can be made of chalk and which, although they settle an acid stomach, can break club or personal dentures.

Note: The Abdominal shall make no charge for vomiting, or boisterous guffaws, but he shall be entitled to one hour for lunch.

[1]There is a great deal of misunderstanding about the character, nature and definition of an abdominal. Full specifications are given in the *British Academy of Cricket Graphic Dictionary of Cricketing Terminology*.

(Turn over)

Regulation R592 (C3)
Correct selection, the Importance of Proper Timing and Dressing the Turkey for Dinner

The Gentleman shall be very particular about his choice of bird, and many may have to be seen before the suitable candidate emerges (Fig. 49). He will then have to set aside some time to prepare his chosen fowl for the great feast which is to come. The bird will then be properly killed.[1] This is best achieved not by clubbing with the side of a spade but by breaking of the neck. To acquire dexterity in this art can be costly as it takes many hours of wringing practice and employs many hundreds of birds. It is *not* a bestial act of violence as some *common slaughterers* would make it, but the controlled application of co-ordinated muscle power coupled with exact timing that severs a neckbone from its neighbour with the minimum of effort, fuss or inconvenience.

Turkeys, however, often consider this very inconvenient for, just as the cricketer knows that there is no correct time to be dismissed, the turkey seems to sense that there is no correct time to be despatched. Faced with this eventuality, and being possessed of a fear of violence and an overblown will to live, some turkeys of the cowardly sort will try to escape. This is prevented by holding the neck to the floor with the instep.

When this ceremony, and the great exhibition of flapping, wriggling and squawking is quite complete, the unpleasant and inedible portions adjacent to the meat (feathers and innards) should be stripped away.[2]

---

[1] Until it be thoroughly dead.

[2] The mortal remains of the turkey, which are the chief concern of the cook, must be sorted and classified. For this purpose the body should be thoroughly eviscerated using a traditional Christmas technique to remove from the confines of his dead body (the class A portions) all the following class B items:

B1. (code: td 07 6238 c09)	Large and small intestines	B6. (code: td 07 6232 c09)	Lungs
B2. (code: td 07 6227 c09)	Liver	B7. (code: td 07 6221 k19)	Kidneys
B3. (code: td 07 6231 c09)	Gizzard	B8. (code: td 07 6233 c09)	Pancreas
B4. (code: td 07 6234 h07)	Heart	B9. (code: td 07 6239 c09)	Spleen
B5. (code: td 07 6225 c09)	Neck and Crop	B10. (code: td 07 6228 d05)	Entrails, giblets and assorted innards

N.B. These code numbers should be quoted in all correspondence.

Nothing displeasing then remains. Class B portions may be thrown away, fed raw to dogs and cats, made into a health-giving soup for children or, as with chickens, coarsely ground to a paste to make Player's Pâté. The outer covering of feathers, Class D, should then be removed, exposing to view the Class A edible parts of the turkey, which now begins to appear more appetizing.

The head, which is far heavier than it ought to be, should then be severed by a cutting and prizing action with a knife or with a small hacksaw. Not until the legs have been broken by a backward bending action, cut off at the knees and then forced into the enlarged anal cavity and thoroughly trussed up with string will the turkey truly take on the appearance of a delicacy. Class C remains, the legs, beak and head (including eyes, tongue and brain) may be ground very fine and added to the Player's Pâté mixture. These will provide the familiar black flecks which are so popular.

Fig. 49: *The Life Cycle of the Turkey* All things have a natural lifespan and Christmas is a time traditionally set aside for the termination of it. Turkeys are very popular indeed at Christmas, and have won an affectionate place in the heart of the true Englishman. This noble bird has pride of place at his table and forms the centrepiece of his Christmas Dinner. Once the perfect bird has been found the Gentleman will have to set aside some time to prepare his chosen fowl for the ceremony ahead. The symbiotic relationship of Man and turkey, once very tense, is now less strained and is generally transacted in accordance with very high standards of behaviour on both sides.

Regulation R593 (C3)
The Provision of Seasonal Vegetables

Whatever the bird decided upon, all other accoutrements (excluding any parsnips[1]) will have to be purchased. These shall include carrots, potatoes, Brussels sprouts, artichokes and peas.

Regulation R594 (C3)
The Benefits of Variations in the Diet and the Need for Good Health

These days it is not necessary always to provide turkey at Christmas. An equal challenge will be the killing and preparing of a goose. Techniques differ for this bird: traditionally she is hung up by her feet from a tree or high doorway. She is then taken gently by the neck by the assembled company who, with the cunning assistance of gravity, will swing back and forth at will, bringing all possible weight to bear until a crack is heard, wings flap, and she stares with a cold astonished eye.

Chickens and ducks may be used in this way by children who will learn some biology and derive much useful experience and pleasure from killing things. Swans will exempt themselves from such ceremonies. They are Royall Foules, by appointment to Her Majesty the Queen purveyors of arrogant and graceful swimming. They should not be eaten at Christmas as some *wicked Republicans*[2] have suggested, for they are so full of anglers' weights they can cause lead poisoning.

---

[1] Life were a very poor thing indeed if it were incapable of proceeding without recourse to parsnips.

[2] Geoffrey Chaucer, father of English Sniggering and the first foul-mouthed satirical Smart Alec, talked of the Monk's practice of Swan-eating in the Prologue to his infamous *Canterbury Tales:* "A Fat Swan loved he best of any roost." from text of W.W. Skeat, London, O.U.P. 1961.

(Turn over)

Fig. 50: INTERLUDE

106

PART THE THIRD
THE SEASON

"Awake, arise, or be forever fall'n."

(Turn over)

SECTION ONE
PREPARATION FOR THE GAME

"The strongest man upon earth is he who stands most alone."

Introductory Lesson L302

Cricket, played skilfully, requires cleanliness and dignity but owes nothing to vulgar muscle power. Thus it has always been a game for the Gentleman who will scorn to boast of great foot pounds per second lest his peers believe that he has fallen upon misfortune, or worse, that he had been reduced by poverty to doing physical work: pruning roses, picking fruit or menial tasks involving strain and movement.

*How rude, ugly and altogether crass are those cricketers (and Australians) who, like some dumb Derby Ox (Fig. 51) or Bartholomew boar-pig, are mere aggregations of muscle and bone lewdly strung together by some fortuity of nature to form a hulking machine utterly devoid of grace or reason, a mere mountain of physical might. Ox power should be left to the Ox, horsepower to carthorses, and manpower to the working man. Brute force should be confined to professional County and Test cricket; **never** should it enter the Amateur Game.*

Fig. 51: *The Derby Ox*

This magnificent beast, though supremely muscular, was nevertheless humble and pacific. With bovine dignity he conducted his affairs in the field, eschewing all exuberance and horseplay.

Lesson L303
A source of Guidance for the Conscientious Cricketer

Once personal hygiene and grooming have reached perfection the Gentleman will concentrate on his spiritual preparation for the game, disdaining all gross thoughts of physical prowess and muscular might, for cricket is a conflict of the spirit and the morally pure shall be victorious. A full programme of private mental preparation should be followed.

This latter is particularly important, for what Gentleman has not broken out into a cold sweat at the thought that he may, on some devilish impulse, find himself at verbal odds with the umpire, or leaping in the air with delight when an opposing batsman has been dismissed.

The sole fortification against such disgraces is the conditioning of correct responses. To this end the Academy prescribes the Sir St. John Peatfield Compleat Course for Cricketers (Fig. 52 *overleaf*).

Lesson L304
The Origin of the Rules and their Classification

The following lessons are in accordance with, and are extracts from the St. John Peatfield[1] School of Classical Cricketing, which evolved over a lifetime of observation, study and active participation in cricketing conflicts. They should be studied assiduously. Regulation numbers attributed to the various aspects of behaviour and procedures are those designated by the British Academy of Cricket, not the original lesson numbers of Sir St. John Peatfield (Fig. 53 *overleaf*).

Lesson L305
The detailed and co-ordinated Programme of The Sir St. John Peatfield Compleat Course for Cricketers

This four-part course begins with the philosophical cornerstones of Cricket and the wondrous beauty of the World and, upon these sound foundations, constructs a majestic and permanent edifice impregnable and unassailable, whether by undermining, assault or siege. The solid rocks of Prayer and religious instruction form the castle walls which are cemented together with the physical attributes of grace, posture, bearing and behaviour. And at the summit: the ramparts, the fighting spirit imbued with patriotic sentiment, inspired and sustained by uplifting music, verse and rhetoric.

---

[1] The author regrets that, by order of the Chairman and in recognition of the supreme modesty of Sir St. John Peatfield (consultant without portfolio to the Academy Research and Development Department), who has never sought personal fame, nothing of a biographical nature shall be revealed of England's truest, most refined and respected Gentleman Cricketer.

(Turn over)

Fig. 52: *The Compleat Course for Cricketers.* This Cornucopia of Cricketalia comes complete with a Free Personal Gift, the Sir St. John Peatfield physical exercise rope, all for 99 gns. Deeply affected as a boy by the philosophy of David Hume, who was two hundred years ahead of his time in holding that taxes should be levied on consumption, Sir St. John is a fierce supporter of V.A.T. (of which 15% has been added). He went on to study such diverse figures as Jeffrey Farnol and Ian Hay who helped him to polish his wisdom to its present high gloss.

Fig. 53: *Sir St. John Peatfield Himself, G.B.A.C., D.C.M. and a Personal Friend of the Chairman.*

110

STAGE ONE

PHILOSOPHICAL CONTEMPLATION

"Is the difference between a difference of degree and a
difference in kind a difference of degree or a difference in kind?"

Lesson L312
The importance of the Three Esses: Silence, Solitude and Stability
No Gentleman can ponder abstruse metaphysical conundrums without a suitable background, undisturbed by the coarse commerce of human society or the chatter of women.

Sir St. John Peatfield has discovered that all things beginning with the letter S are very important indeed, including Sloppiness and Sardines. But, he says, the three key S words are:

I. *Silence:* This is denied to those who have children or live near a working-class district. It is a perverse fact of human society that those with least musical taste most wish to share it with others and those who have nowhere to go are possessed of the noisiest vehicles.

II. *Solitude:* This is done privately, but it does involve Sertain Ss for Sacrifice. Teas can be a problem: the cricketer will be obliged to make his own. Solitude should not be confused with loneliness; the former is chosen by the cricketer, the latter chosen for him by others.

III. *Stability:* This is best achieved by having a regular income, no women and no romantic connections. The trouble with most men is women, and often the worst thing about a man is his wife. So well-tuned are the instincts of womankind to the presence of cheque books that a healthy income invariably militates against the bliss of the bachelorhood necessary for the pleasurable disposal of money.

Further important notes:
The cricketer should surround himself with the Seven Serenities, sip the last rays of the sunset and see how the colours divide. The Seven Serene Sublimities, the Six Seemly Sights and the Seven Sacred Sounds have all been combined into a revised master list as follows:

1. Hedge sparrows 2. The *Listener* 3. Foxgloves 4. A Worcester teapot (c. 1755–62) (Fig. 54 *overleaf*) 5. The Queen's Speech 6. A Yorkshire Pudding 7. Mossy moots

Note: A limited edition of bone china platters depicting these objects is presently planned.

(Turn over)

Fig. 54: *A Worcester Teapot (c. 1755–62).* This particular moulded pattern impresses three stylized chrysanthemoid flowers on the teapot. The blooms with (a) bifurcated petals and (b) double centre respectively are opposite each other, with a flower (c) with curly petals opposite an area with no bloom. Generally, in such teapots, the spout and handle would obliterate types (a) and (b), leaving bloom (c) intact. In this very rare example the artizan has chosen to forgo the curly bloom (c) in favour of the retaining (a) and (b), thereby committing an offence.

This pot was a bequest to the Academy and is now in the Chairman's China Cabinet. Unfortunately it suffered some damage in collection. As can be seen here, the Chairman, who is a keen restorer of ceramics, has made it almost new again.

Regulation R595 (C4)

The Stroll and its effects on Cricketing Inspiration, with notes on Beauty, the Sublime and Landscapes of the Mind

There is no need here to sing again of the English landscape, for this has been done by all the greatest poets in many a breathless or musèd rhyme. However, these people have tended to emphasize physical beauty and have neglected the sublime spirit of England, the majestic views (Fig. 55) which Strike a discomforting chord in the heart of the beholder. Foremost among these are the Royal Albert Hall, and the White Cliffs, with Dover Castle and gun emplacements, the Severn bore and the draining of the Fens. Such things must occupy the thoughts of the cricketer as he takes his pre-match stroll.

Lesson L314

Secular Jottings on the Nature of Beauty insofar as it relates to Aesthetics and the Mind, and on the Beauty of Nature both natural and human

There is a great difference between *contemplating a certain aspect* of a thing and *thinking about it*. Thus, aesthetics has a large part to play in Ugliness which, like all nasty things, is difficult to dwell upon because it goes against the grain of the human spirit and is repulsive.[1]

---

[1] This explains why the present volume does not dwell on horrible things but chooses rather to uplift, enlighten and refresh.

It is sufficient to separate out from the generality of things those objects which will ennoble the mind and gently raise the spirit of the perceiver, honing his sensibilities to a state of happy certainty, unblemished by doubt or fear.

Lesson L323

Some Detailed Examples of what Sir St. John means by All This
Arid theory, finally, is for bookworms, academics and empty dry old men. It has little place in the life and thoughts of the cricketer, who is, above all, a man of action. He is not concerned with aesthetics, he wants to know what he can do, in a practical way, to improve his behaviour and his game. Suffice it to say that, sometimes, as a stroll unfolds, the cricketer will become aware of some impingement on his senses, the presence of an object of beauty. He should learn to use this stimulus to direct his responses into philosophical contemplation of Profound Cricketing Questions.

Lesson L325

The Invention of Landscape and its Appreciation
Land has much appreciated in recent years, and farmers have contributed to many a vista by removing hedges which formerly blocked from view miles of landscapes which now open upon the eye in every shire in the land.

Fig. 55: *A landscape for the mind.*
Those who live in urban districts and are unable to find sublime landscapes should contemplate this picture for at least twenty minutes each day.

113

Do not turn
over yet.

RELIGIOUS OBSERVANCE

Introductory Lesson L326

Without proper Bible study and religious training David would never have slain Goliath, nor Cain Abel; and Daniel would have been quite eaten in the Lion's den with nothing but the bones left over. Heartfelt conviction and Christian values stand the cricketer in equally good stead, and therefore he will wish to develop these fully.

Lesson L327
The importance of Sunday Morning Service, clerical guidance and the Essential Nature of Godliness and the Church

O how pure and profound, and like an underground stream, run the currents of religious conviction within our nation! Those crystal waters and the clear light of religion nourish and sustain the spirit of the poor and rich alike.

So it is on a Sunday Morning that, when the roast is in the oven and church bells toll throughout the length and breadth of England, all are summoned to the House of God to worship and to praise Him for all the spiritual blessings he has bestowed upon poor sinners. Rich sinners too will wish to give praise and thanks for wealth, gold and jewels with which they are entrusted and pray for strength and wisdom to invest wisely in property.

Lo, even unto the libertines, blasphemers[1] and reformers, is extended forgiveness and mercy, which bring forbearance to the Hard of Heart, and kindness to stay the hand of the Righteous, who shall neither slay them nor suffer them to be done to death as they would be done in Russia whence they ought to be despatched.

No, no sight warms the breast of the true Englishman more than the spectacle of the Faithful of some parish church or great cathedral wending their way to do the bidding of their God. And this is often done, as it was done by our fathers long ago, under the curacy of a cloud of Rooks clad in clerical sobriety muting their guttural cries to suit the Sunday Anthem in the bleak midwinter, or the cooing of doves in the greenwood on a Sunday morn when it seems warm days will never cease. Then is the whole spiritual life of our Nation rekindled to commune with God, beseeching Him in His wisdom to:

i) Keep Things the Way They Are
ii) Ensure nothing shall upset the Eternal Fitness of Things

---

[1] "Don't bother your head about villains for I shall sort them out Good and Proper." *New English Bible.*

In return the faithful shall promise not to go too far in the pursuit of vainglorious victories, and the farmer prays to his God now to succour, now destroy the beets of the field, the birds of the air and also for his dairy breed and daily bread. Yet he knows these things are not of the Father, but are of the World, and the World passeth away and the crust thereof, but he that doeth the will of God abideth forever.

Lesson L330
The British Academy of Cricket Official Prayer

CHAPLAIN: God Almighty, creator and preserver of all Worthy Institutions, we pray for the good estate of the British Academy of Cricket that it may be governed by thy Chairman and Directors, that all who profess to be Fellows thereof or Registered thereunder may be led into the Game by the way of truth and righteousness. We commend to thy Fatherly notice all Registered cricketers who are afflicted or distressed in mind,[1] body or estate[1] that it may please Thee that the Academy be Thine Instrument to comfort, relieve or admonish them according to their several necessities.

Grant, O Lord, patience and a steadfast mind that justice may be done from Innings to Innings according to thy word from this Game forth. And this we ask in the name of the Chairman and of the Directors and the Fellowship of the Academy for ever and ever.

GENTLEMEN: Let this wicked man, O Lord, turn away from his wickedness and all solitary sins, and do that which is lawful that he may not be blinded by Thy vengeance and that he may save his soul alive.

PLAYERS: Likewise O Lord, for my sin is ever before me.

ALL: For Thy Game's Sake, *Amen.*

The Sir St. John Peatfield Collection of Occasional Prayers

The Godhead invoked and His blessing sought.	Almighty God, who hast brought us safely to the beginning of this Game, defend us in the same and grant that this day we fall before no Spin, nor run into any kind of danger, and bring us safely again to the drawing of the stumps and the going down of the Sun.
The batsman seeketh to avoid all temptation and to be govern'd by righteousness.	Suffer me, O Lord, humbly to keep my appointed place, yea even when tempted to step forth, for Thou knowest that the 'keeper sleepeth not and lieth ever in wait for those who trespass against

---

[1] Players are exempt.

(Turn over)

him. Vouchsafe unto me the readiness of Spirit to smite the Wayward Ball, yea even unto the boundary. Grant I beseech Thee that I flinch not before the Short Delivery and let me, with Thy Grace, hook it hard and scatter the Fielders in the imagination of their hearts.

He accepteth his dismissal and beseecheth courage to stare into the abyss of adversity.

O Lord, let Thy servant depart in peace according to the Umpire's word. In that dread hour let there not be Ugly Scenes nor voices raised in anger at the dying of the light. Keep my heart and mind cleansed of impure thoughts that I may walk in the paths of righteousness straight to the pavilion whence cometh my successor.

For those in peril on the field.

Look down in Thy great mercy upon us, O Lord, and keep Thy covenant for it is written that when eleven or twelve are gathered together in Thy Game Thou shalt hearken unto their prayers and let their cry come unto Thee. Yea, though the captain moveth us in sundry places, passing all understanding, let us ever do his bidding humbly in meekness of Spirit, for now we see thro' a glass darkly.

The bowler now prayeth for a mighty and everlasting arm that he shall smite the batsman as David cast the stone long ago against the Philistine.

Grant to me, O lord, that the line and length shall be perfect in the sight of Thine Eyes and that the troubled mind of the batsman be seized with a mighty dread, that the ball shall not keep low but shall strike high up his Middle Stump. Cast from me, O Lord, all temptation to stray towards the leg, for straight is the path and narrow is the stump on the pitch that Thou givest me.

Now all participants raise a cry to the Lord for justice and mercy and for His kingdom here in England.

We beseech thee, O Lord, to bear it in Thy Great Mind that we wrestle not with our own flesh and blood alone, but against Daemons, Powers and all the Fallen Angels and the rule of Darkness and Socialism in this Ungodly world. And lend Thine ear to our prayer that it be not a goat cry in the wilderness but a golden trumpet to sound the advent of Thy Kingdom, for ever and ever.

Amen.

Lesson L331
Notes on Worshipping Techniques:

God will take a very Dim View of the worshipper if correct techniques (Fig. 56) are not applied at the outset.

DO: **1.** Speak clearly and precisely. **2.** Avoid regional accents. **3.** Begin again if you make a mistake; God will not penalize anyone for this. **4.** Put some expression into your voice. **5.** Be polite. **6.** Be clean and tidy with straight partings. **7.** Be humble; God is good to grovellers.

DO NOT **1.** Omit any verse or expression or tamper with the wording. **2.** Mumble or drone. **3.** Pray with your mouth full. **4.** Gallop through the prayer; God abhors gabblers; He hears many prayers in the course of a day and He answers those most clearly spoken. **5.** Shout or utter threats. **6.** Complain about personal averages/unanswered prayers. **7.** Forget your Peas and Queues.

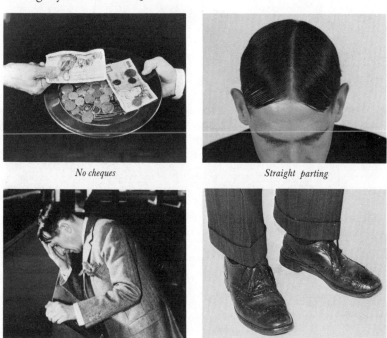

No cheques *Straight parting*

No mumbling *Sensible footwear*

Fig. 56: *Academy approved techniques and wrinkles for effective worship*

The most important single thing to remember is that the prayer is a Monologue not a Dialogue, therefore do not be over-familiar or expect answers. God created the Universe and this is a Huge Responsibility. Therefore He is sometimes too busy to answer a prayer at once.

 (Turn over)

Fig. 57: *Homo orans,* Praying Man
The capacity to recognize and reach out to a power higher than himself is what sets Man aside from the animals and makes him God's favourite. Here Mr Bowles, a moral prodigy, unleashes a storm of humility.

STAGE THREE

FIELDCRAFT

"In the world's broad field of battle,
In the bivouac of Life,
Be not like dumb, driven cattle!
Be a hero in the strife."

Introductory Lesson L334

Much waving may be appropriate for drowning, calling home the cows, urging a racehorse to the post or giving the troops a good send-off. But it is not suitable at or near a cricket match. A great deal is to be gained by the cricketer who ensures that his gestures and actions, including all scoring strokes, are articulated subtly, serenely and with feeling. At the instant when the batsman meets the ball there is extreme violence. But where this becomes obvious to any spectator the batsman must consider himself to have failed in his duty.

At all times his Higher Aim should be to make Cricket seem gentler, and the playing of it simpler, than it is. That is the centre, the very Kernel of the Game.

To reinforce this illusion, while the batsman prepares his mind for the violent impact, meticulous observance of ritual behaviour must take place. These well-founded rites have been insensibly ignored by certain professional players of our day, who exaggerate and glory in the brutality of the game, bringing it to the sorry, bedraggled and tawdry state of disrepute in which we find it. The Common Herd, witnessing in ignorance extreme cases of such self-indulgence, are even persuaded that they understand the game, so coarse has it become. Thus have professional players and Marylebone Cricket Club profited, and thus has the Game been brought so low. Therefore the following notes on correct movement, posture, poise and co-ordination should be studied closely and all extravagant gesticulations shunned. Bat hurling, the stamping of feet, dumbfounded prostrations and frustrated leapings shall never be employed. Disdainful tutting and indignant shrugging are strictly prohibited.

A Preliminary Note: Sir St. John Peatfield's Bat and Body Language for the cricketer is given in full in the *British Academy of Cricket Guide to the Art of Batting for Batsmen and Bowlers* which deals with all strokes, the snick, the Top and Bottom Edge and the scoring of Runs, with Illnesses and diseases specific to the Batsman. Only a brief summary of Sir St. John Peatfield's batting procedures is possible within this volume. For advice to fielders, bowlers, wicketkeepers and Umpires readers are referred to *Sir St. John Peatfield, Opera Omnia.*

119

(Turn over)

Regulation R605 (C4, C3, C2A)
Approved Attitudes for Batsmen

Fig. 58: *The Sir St. John Peatfield Abridged Catalogue of Attitudes and Postures for Batsmen. A step by step pictorial course for the improvement of method batting and etiquette.* These should be practised in front of a full-length mirror before the game or used selectively throughout the Game itself. Repeated and committed to memory, these will ensure mental development and a refinement of batting sensibilities.

No 1 Batsman taking to the field, or Coming Out, **No 2** Handling of the bat when Coming Out, **No 3** Taking a centre guard, **No 4** Removal of fundamental particles, **No 5** Minor repairs to the pitch, **No 6** Major repairs to the pitch, **No 7** Levelling of the pitch, **No 8** Removal of a worm, **No 9** Sightscreen adjustment, **No 10** Spectators moving behind bowler's arm, **No 11** Stopping the bowler before the ball has been bowled and asking spectators to move. **No 12** Running between the wickets with gloves carried in hand, **No 13** Fifty up and acknowledgement of applause, **No 14** Pitch inspection, **No 14a** Discussions with fellow batsman (incl. scoreboard perusal), **No 15** Disdain at l.b.w. appeal (*Gentlemen only*), **No 16** Contentment at hitting 4/6 runs, **No 17** Disdain of irregular bounce/bouncer/being bowled and further pitch inspection before returning to the pavilion, **No 18** Surveying the field with bat aloft, **No 19** Singling out fielder to be quiet, **No 20** Removal of dog/bird from the pitch with bat, **No 21** Fast bowler and sun in the eyes, **No 21a** Marking crease with boot.

SPECIAL OCCASIONS

No 22 Drinks, **No 23** Injury and being hit by ball, **No 24** Posing for individual photograph (prior to Game), **No 25** Holding trophy aloft, **No 26** Posing for an interview, **No 27** Discontinued, **No 28** Posing for autograph/bat signing, **No 29** Pad adjustment, **No 30** Summoning the umpire, **No 31** Mopping brow, **No 32** Cap adjustment, **No 33** Cap off/cap folded, **No 34** Gloves off (dismissal), **No 35** Bat under arm/gloves off, **No 36** Long stride, **No 37** Bat aloft (full), **No 38** Bat aloft (half), **No 43** 100 up, cap removal, bat aloft, applause, **No 44** 100 out, bat aloft.

ADVANCED SIMULTANEOUS DISMISSAL GAITS AND PROCEDURES
FOR OPENING BATSMEN/GENTLEMEN

No 39 Congratulating/shaking hands with the bowler/wicketkeeper/fielder, **No 40** The walk back to the pavilion (*36 stride/34/35/33/31*), **No 41** Bat acknowledgement when entering pavilion after scoring 50–99 (**36 and 41 combined**), **No 42** Bat acknowledgement when entering the pavilion for scoring 100–150 (**36 and 37 combined**).

Attitude No 1   Attitude No 2   Attitude No 3   Attitude No 4   Attitude No 5   Attitude No 6 /No 7

Attitude No 8   Attitude No 9   Attitude No 11   Attitude No 12   Attitude No 13   Attitude No 14   14 *a*
                 Attitude No 10

Attitude No 15   Attitude No 16   Attitude No 17   Attitude No 18 ⟶

Attitude No 19   Attitude No 20   Attitude No 21   21 *a*   Attitude No 22   Attitude No 23   Attitude No 24

Attitude No 25   Attitude   Attitude No 28   Attitude No 29   Attitude No 30   Attitude No 31   Attitude No 32
                 No 26   Attitude No 33

Attitude No 34   Attitude No 35   Attitude No 36 / No 40   Attitude No 37   Attitude No 43   Attitude No 44

(Turn over)

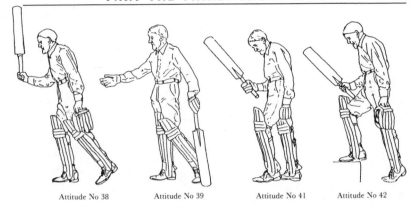

Attitude No 38   Attitude No 39   Attitude No 41   Attitude No 42

Regulation R606 (C2)

**Notes on the Sir St. John Peatfield Catalogue of Attitudes
with supplementary information on
Correct Procedures for the Coming Out**

The Coming Out shall be accomplished in accordance with correct British
Academy of Cricket Regulations as set out in the Sir St John Peatfield
Method School of Cricketing Attitudes which follow the precepts of
Stanislavski. Extravagant theatrical gestures should be rejected in favour of
subtle bat and pad language. Nos 40/41/36/1/13/15S/29/16/3/21a/29/
29S/18/18S.

Each cricketer may be given during a match his opportunity to take to
the field to represent his team with the bat. This is a privilege, not a right.

The Coming Out presents him with the opportunity to meet the enemy
face to face, to show *he is not afraid, that he will not be and cannot be made afraid.*
In the teeth of a blinding hail of circumstance, a storm of occurrence, and a
gale of misfortuity *he will triumph and he will endure.*

How often these days we see a loose-limbed swaggering fellow, his outer
skin radiant with bravado and derring-do but his heart a sickly guttering
candle, bones shot through with a mortal blast of terror, sinews grown
instant old, innards awash and foundering in a flood of fear. There goes he,
unprepared, to face his Coming Out, jesting, with a fizzy show of horseplay
and hilarity that will trip him and send him flying headlong, his sins all
unconfessed, into dismissal and defeat.

Much merry banter with the bowler and the captain and the fielder and
the Umpire *will not save him*; brave signals and loud shouts to comrades and
onlookers *will not save him*, and much waving of the bat and rehearsing of the
strokes *will not save him*, and all this outward show will profit him nothing for
all will end in tears and humiliation if he lose his sense of How To Behave.

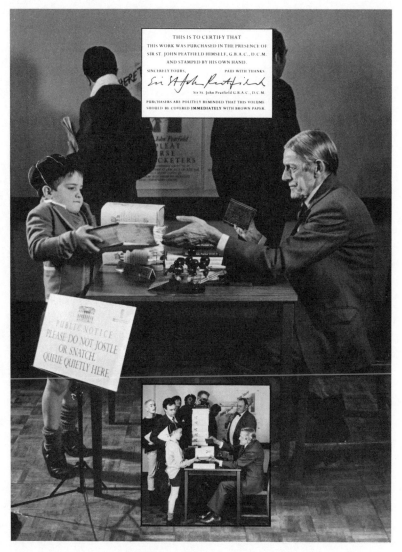

THIS IS TO CERTIFY THAT
THIS WORK WAS PURCHASED IN THE PRESENCE OF
SIR ST. JOHN PEATFIELD HIMSELF, G.B.A.C., D.C.M.
AND STAMPED BY HIS OWN HAND.
SINCERELY YOURS,   PAID WITH THANKS

Sir St. John Peatfield G.B.A.C., D.C.M.

PURCHASERS ARE POLITELY REMINDED THAT THIS VOLUME
SHOULD BE COVERED **IMMEDIATELY** WITH BROWN PAPER.

PUBLIC NOTICE
PLEASE DO NOT JOSTLE
OR SNATCH.
QUEUE QUIETLY HERE

Fig. 59: *The mark of a true Gentleman*

How fortunate are the youngsters of today! When old people were young there was no Sir St. John Peatfield Manual of Cricketing Attitudes to guide them. Spurred on by sincere conviction and a deep yearning for Future Glories in the Field Sir St. John promotes his course at every opportunity. His love of country provides him with stamina, and his abiding affection for all children is his sole reward.

Here he is about to endorse yet one more volume of his *Magnum Opus* with his own official stamp (inset), a prize much sought after and collected by schoolboys.

    (Turn over)

THE AROUSAL OF
CRICKETING SENTIMENTS

"To set the cause above renown
To love the Game beyond the prize
To honour while you strike him down
The foe that comes with fearless eyes."

Introductory Lesson L353

It is the heartfelt conviction of Sir St. John Peatfield that Patriotism is the ultimate expression of human dignity, and many have died[1] to protect the Englishman's right to be proud of his country and any other country so long as it was part of the Empire. True love of country is now dying out and must be preserved from traitors and un-cricketing activities.

An accomplished cellist himself, Sir St. John knows the value of music to the cricketer. It carries straight to the deep-laid instincts of man's refined spirit, the seat of Spiritual beauty and truth, without intervention from that wayward vehicle the intellect.

Regulation R620 (C2)

The Sir St. John Peatfield Boxed Set of Gramophone Records for Mental Improvement, Preparation of the Soul and the Arousal of Sentiments Conducive to Cricketing Conflict

All cricketers shall buy this Academy product. These instructive phonographic recordings, if played repeatedly in sequential order, before a match, while the listener is installed in a cool, quiet room, will be found to cure common cricketing infirmities: the ravages of coward's hand and delirium tremens, profuse sweating and paralysis, hyperventilation, panic and trepidation in the face of the enemy. The physical symptoms of this state of mind have long[2] been recognized and described. A man in terror "has his teeth set, his eyebrows are violently contracted, his forehead is wrinkled, his eyes are dragged inwards, and rolled with great vehemence, his hair stands on end, the voice is forced out in short shrieks and groans, and the whole fabric totters." Such scenes as this, enacted every Saturday and Sunday all over England, are a disgrace. The batsman must learn to face

[1] Both Englishmen and foreigners.
[2] The Right Hon. Edmund Burke. *A Philosophical Inquiry into the Origin of Our Ideas of The Sublime and Beautiful*. George Bell and Sons, London 1889. Treatise first published in 1756.

the fast bowler with courage and dignity, and for this he will need the support of stirring speeches and a backbone stiffened by great rhetoric and patriotism.

The recordings, some of which are performed by the sextet *Sir St. John Peatfield Himself and the Comets*, contain both music and the spoken word, and thus make their appeal to the heart and brain of the cricketer inspiring new *fortitude* in the most lily-livered and wretched of men.

*   *   *

RECORD ONE SIDE ONE
The Chairman of the British Academy of Cricket's Annual Address.

RECORD ONE SIDE TWO
Cumulo-nimbus clouds, a graveyard elegy, re-upholstering a George III chair, the Archers' original theme music, the babbling brook and rowing on Lake Windermere, wheat and poppies in the wind, a thatcher reminisces, around Devon with a pony and big trap (John Betjeman).

RECORD TWO SIDE ONE
Stirring patriotic music: Wagner, and Bach fugues. The Coronation March, The Queen on her balcony, Mantovani and The Music of the Mountains, The Bells of Westminster Abbey.

RECORD TWO SIDE TWO
The sound of the Spitfire, Cries of Trafalgar, Tales from the Raj and the Black Hole of Calcutta, The London Omnibus Route Timetable 1949, Sir Roger Bannister's Mile, Elgin Marbles.

RECORD THREE SIDE ONE
The top and bottom edge (Lecture), The sounds of steam, A nightingale sings, The bombing of Dresden.

RECORD THREE SIDE TWO
Lecture: The forward and backward defensive, driving on the up and timing the ball, The Queen in her chamber, Sir Edmund Hillary on the top.

RECORD FOUR SIDE ONE
Keeping the head down (Lecture), The National Collection, Pray along with the Dean of St. Paul's, selection from Archie Andrews and the Glum family at home, Rule Britannia.

RECORD FOUR SIDE TWO
The Dambusters March, Last Night of the Proms, Victory in the Falklands, Patriotic speech by Sir Winston Churchill, readings from Lord Byron, John Masefield, The National Anthem.

(Turn over)

SECTION TWO

SARTORIAL ELEGANCE

*"What are these that are arrayed in white robes?
and whence came they?"* Revelations (viii) 13

Introductory Lesson L382

Attention to proper dress has undergone a ragged revolution in these sickly times. There is sadly no longer one sartorial mode but a multitude of styles acceptable for most social and private occasions. This is yet one more sign of falling moral standards, the loss of Empire, indiscriminate immigration and the emergence of America as an Imperial Power.

History, which has never yet proved herself wise or worthy, has seen fit to permit the acceptance in most places of casual wear. This, declares Madam History, shall permeate every corner of our National Life even unto the Cricket field itself.

But this wave of adversity will be held in check. Too much has been said by **wicked historians** *about the gale of misfortune that is England's lot. They have damaged Her reputation and have shewn they are not worthy Keepers of the Record in which they have, latterly, written so small a part for so Great a Britain.*

To hold back this wave of the future the cricketer shall never wear the vulgar garment known as a "forage" cap nor items bearing advertising or commercial mottoes,[1] obtrusive labelling on clothing, floppy hats, habits or vestments of artificial fibres with dual-toned designs, modern plimsolls with coloured stripes, darkened summer spectacles and the like.

Often on the streets of our major cities, sometimes in quite respectable districts, will be seen unkempt and ill-dressed persons who take no pride in their appearance. On investigation these are found to be the Poor, Alcoholics, Scroungers or Vagrants thus proving a link between sartorial backsliding and moral deficiency. Whatever one's calling, there is **never** *an excuse for slovenly dress.*

---

[1] How it is that firms have managed to persuade the public that they should, *gratis*, walk about and carry on their daily lives bedecked in vulgar commercial names and mottoes is a mystery, for this is the profoundest confidence trick played upon our society since the Falklands Conflict. All offenders against good taste, guilty of display of this kind, are to be reported immediately to the Academy.

PREFATORY REMARKS

Regulation R648 (C2, C2A)
The Correct Understanding of Sartorial Elegance in the Modern World and the Reporting of Offenders

It is the duty of all cricketers to ensure that certain minimum standards are adhered to (Fig. 60) by all Gentlemen and players. The watchwords in all matters of dress are Quality, Modesty, Style and Harmony, a four-point plan easily remembered by use of the mnemonic Q.M.S.H.

How deplorable it is in these times to see a Gentleman or player attending a cricket match in an ill-fitting suit with unmatching cheap and dirty shoes and a *parting which is not straight.*

It is the moral duty of the true Englishman to bedeck himself in drab colours. Anything more flamboyant or unmixt must be regarded as exhibitionism, foppery and dandyism. Whereas sartorial anarchy may be acceptable abroad and among foreigners, it will not do at all in Britain, which is a proper Monarchy.

Fig. 60: *Sartorial offences and General Backsliding*
This disgraceful episode, caught red-handed by the lens of Academy Informer N° 7383d D.C.M., demonstrates the sorry state of the Game at village level. N° 7383d has earned for himself a Chairman's citation for this Important Study of deviance, and the offenders were brought to justice.

A full range of sartorial offences is apparent: (a) Sleeve rolling; (b) Poor shirt discipline; (c) Unsightly fat; (d) Scanty dress/nudity; (e) Facial offence; (f) Long hair; (g) Batsman without tie; (h) Pad offences; (i) Half-hearted stroke; (j) Too much bottom hand; (k) Parting not straight; (l) Black footwear; (m) Beard. N° 7383d is now touring Somerset and Herefordshire.

(Turn over)

Lesson L383
Theoretical Whiteness specific to shirts,
Problems with Gullibility and supplementary notes on logic
and the Canons of Direct Induction

From the outset it should be noted that cricketing "whites" should not be white at all but a rich and dull buff cream in colour. With the advent of artificial fibres, the demise of the professional washerwoman and the proliferation of devices (Fig. 61) for the laundering of clothes, the whites of yesteryear are, to the disgrace of our nation, become truly white.

This is out of tune with the Spirit of the Game, where subtle and subdued colours are the order of the day. It is the height of ill breeding and bad manners to assert one's presence rudely by the wearing of bright or dazzling garments.

Academy research has shown that "white" clothing was selected because this is the nearest colour to the naked human body. The symbolic statement made as a team takes to the field is: "Witness our going, unprotected, into the fray, reckless of all danger, imbued with the spirit of the warrior, uncamouflaged and unafraid." As a battle dress it has immense value.

Whiteness, in some parts of the world, may be a desirable quality, but although it stands for purity, it is not next to Godliness: Cleanliness is next to Godliness. Whiteness is certainly a common accompaniment of cleanliness but by no means an inherent property of it, a necessary condition of it nor consequent or antecedent to it, whatever may be the official policy of the Women's Institute or received opinion among housewives. Nevertheless this idea has gained currency.

Housewives should ever be on their guard against false precepts employed by American detergent manufacturers who have (with this curious concomitant variation, or more properly, either an improper application of the canon of difference[1] or the canon of the joint method of agreement in presence and absence[2]) put about false ideas to sell their products.

---

[1] Wives should be sat down and told: if an instance in which the phenomenon occurs, and an instance in which it does not occur, have every other circumstance in common save one, that one (whether consequent or antecedent) occurring only in the former; the circumstance in which alone the two instances differ is the effect, or the cause, or an indispensable condition of the phenomenon.

[2] Husbands should endeavour to explain that: if (1.) two or more instances in which a phenomenon occurs have only one other circumstance (antecedent or consequent) in common, while (2.) two or more instances in which it does not occur (though in important points they resemble the former set of instances) have nothing else in common save the absence of that circumstance – the circumstance in which alone the two sets of instances differ throughout (being present in the first set and absent in the second) is probably the effect, or the cause, or an indispensable condition of the phenomenon.

Fig. 61: *The expulsion of wetness*

Once the theory of whiteness has been thoroughly grasped by the housewife, it is to wringing and wetness that she must turn her thoughts. This was once a physical rather than intellectual challenge but, with the proliferation of labour-saving devices such as the mangle shewn here, much of the work has been taken out of washday.

129

(Turn over)

Lesson L384
The Psychology of Colour, Colour History and Symbolism

Modern white (or more properly British Cricketing Cream), has, by the British Academy, been developed unchanged from the natural colour of the sheep who provide the wool for the clothing. This is the very same wool which, in the Middle Ages, was a symbol of wealth, denoting the power of the landowning classes and the Rule of their Law.

White represents traditionally: England, St. George, God, fine thighs, noble skin, Purity and the Pearl, Nature's most secret treasure, that most mysterious of all gems.

Whiteness, in the mind of the European, means: life, right, justice, goodness and knowledge. Death, evil and ignorance are all expressed in sombre shades and degrees of blackness.

As a choice in welding together fighting units white therefore leads the field.

Regulation R651 (C2A)
Minimum Sartorial (and Equipmental) requirements of Gentlemen in Registered Matches as Set Out under the Dr Ralph Willett Report of 1984

If standards are to be maintained, the implementation of standard clothing and equipment Regulations is vital. After detailed research the directives of the Willett Report, commissioned by the Academy, now serve as the cricketer's sartorial checklist[1], ensuring that he will be prepared for every eventuality, acquit himself well and be a credit to his Club and Country.

---

[1] 1 large kit bag, leather; 5 cricket bats (various types with wax/disinfectant, oil and accoutrements; 4 pairs of British Academy of Cricket regulation doe cloth flannels in British Cricketing Cream (albedo 0.78); 3 regulation long-sleeved Jerseys size 48 with appropriate rank stripings; 3 short-sleeved pullovers size 48 ditto, 6 linen/silk shirts in British Cricketing Cream with 16" collar; 3 complete sets of underwear (clean) in British Cricketing Cream; 4 pairs of socks in B.C.C. (with/without rank stripings to taste); 2 pairs of regulation cricketing brogues with spare spikes and tongues; 2 club caps; 1 plain club blazer and formal flannels; 1 striped club blazer with casual flannels; 1 club raincoat; The British Academy of Cricket Personal Hygiene Dispensary; a small portable first aid kit with certificate and registration documents; 3 pairs of leg guards correctly blancoed, 2 patent Gentleman's Groin Protectors (1 of industrial heavy-duty grade in mild steel); 2 pairs of thigh pads; 3 club ties (boxed or rolled); 4 pairs batting gloves with inner linings; misc. belts, braces and tie clips, boot polish, shoe horns and other footwear accoutrements, packing tissue and anti-crease spray; 4 ashen coathangers; collapsible binoculars; 7 spare laces; one foot of elastic; 3 handkerchiefs with monogram/club motto/crest; pocket knife; length of string; 1 pair bicycle clips; bulldog clip; writing case; 6 moth balls; rolled up newspaper; assorted improving reading; British Academy of Cricket *Manual for Officers and Staff*; the British Academy of Cricket *Manual of First Aid Treatment for Sick and Injured Persons*; 1 umbrella; 1 navy/black pin-striped suit; attaché case for personal documents; travelling pills; magnifying glass; hip flask; small portable clothing iron; ditto trouser press; a cricketing brush; personal scoresheet/photographs.

FIRSTLY

THE ETERNAL KNOT

Introductory Lesson L385

**Background, History and Significance of the Tie,
and tie hygiene and Care**

*Just as a turban is a knot on top of a head, so the tie is a knot on the front of a neck. Both are symbols of a **solemn binding together**. Most cricketers have rejected the turban, choosing the tie as their mark of fellowship and symbol of identity. Therefore the granting of the club tie is a great honour for the novice, apprentice or newcomer to the group and a badge of his acceptance into a Brotherhood.*

*The Tying of the Knot ritual is largely neglected in our times in favour of a discreet private ceremony between a senior club official and the recipient who will usually be told that he is not to let down the side and to keep his tie free from egg yolk, as it is a symbol of his **belonging** and an outward mark of the privilege bestowed upon him. Once the knot is tied it is there for life, and only in extremis, can it be undone[1].*

Regulation R656 (C2)

Special and permanent Tie Holdings and Exceptional Offences

The captain and the catering officer, who will normally be entrusted with the ties of office for life, will, in some clubs, be symbolically de-tied at the annual general meeting. This is purely a formality as in all clubs of good reputation these posts will not normally be surrendered by the holder until his tenure is interrupted by death, impeachment, resignation, or at the formal request of a British Academy of Cricket Inspector.

It can occur that the captain, perhaps by some indiscretion or by placing players higher in the batting order than their rank permits, will incur the wrath or disapproval of the Founder Members. Should this occur, a club crisis will ensue and the captain will have to submit himself to a public de-tieing with all the accompanying unpleasantness.

If the Catering Officer has offered *sardine sandwiches* to a Gentleman, whether in error or as an insult, and charges have been preferred, then the offender will almost certainly lose his tie and his British Academy of Cricket accreditation. In either of these cases the Founder Member, duty bound to

---

[1] If the recipient is a Freemason he should be told to desist from the rolling up of trousers and the baring of breasts for, although an admirable idea for paddlers and sunbathers, it sets a very bad example to ladies.

(Turn over)

uphold standards and in the interests of discretion, will often choose to send a letter asking for the return of the tie without further ado. Unpleasant scenes in public are never of benefit to any club. Any confiscated Academy tie (Fig. 62) may be handed in at any police station.

Regulation R657 (C1, C2, C2A, C3, C4)
Offences requiring the Mandatory and Summary De-tieing of Gentleman and player and the need for Advance Notices

All clubs are required to display in a prominent place, proper listings of all de-tieable offences. These are defined as follows:

1. Indiscretions inside and outside the lavatories. ....(C3)
2. Offences involving vibraculation or rear entry. ....(C3)
3. Desecration of club trophies and cricketana..(C2)
4. Adulteration of drinks.. (C2A)
5. Bringing the club into disrepute, underwear offences................. (C2/C2A)
6. Poor performance, defeatism and loss of competitiveness. ....(C2)
7. Non-verbal abuse of children...(C4)
8. Uttering a false/forged statistic. ....(C1)

Note: Founder members may of course withdraw the tie from any person at any time without explanation, provided the decision was properly formulated, proposed and seconded at a special meeting of Founder Members where a quorum (normally defined as one or two) was present.

Fig. 62: *Ties, the Academy's Summer Collection.* It is very difficult in these pocky times to enforce the wearing of suitable ties, particularly in the young who no longer respond to a good wigging in matters of sartorial concern. The Academy's Approved Summer Tie for the Young in Heart is a veritable Bobby Dazzler and bridges the gulf between the generations. It is eagerly donned by all attractive young men (left) who wish to be in the vanguard of fashion. The Academy Ties (below) are reserved for formal Occasions.

Fellow   *Gentleman*   *player*

THE BRITISH GLORY REVIV'D   PROPERTY OF THE BRITISH ACADEMY OF CRICKET

COATERY AND BLAZERS

Lesson L386
Uniforms, Blazers and Mufti theory

It is with great care and fastidiousness that cricketers clad themselves for battle in their whites, with cricket boots, thigh pads and groin protectors. This satisfies an ancient need for ritual before battle. The communal bodily smells weld the tribe together into a fighting unit, and the setting aside of the attire of every day affirms the special nature of the action to come, its religious significance and its place in the spiritual life of the community.

Equally when battle is done Gentlemen and players will be united in a wish to cast off their clammy clothes. At such a time club blazers (striped and plain) and flannels (informal and formal) are a great asset. Being inexpensive items (a couple of hundred pounds is quite enough to spend) they are available to all and will do much to enhance a feeling of fellowship.

Regulation R665 (C2A)
Blazer Etiquette and the correct choice of blazer for Set Occasions

The blazer is a symbol of pride in the club as well as self-respect. But it must be worn correctly if it is not to give offence. Blazer etiquette can be very complicated indeed; therefore it is necessary to study in detail and to commit to memory the following guidelines:

PLAIN CLUB BLAZER AND FORMAL FLANNELS	STRIPED CLUB BLAZER AND INFORMAL FLANNELS
Official Team Photograph	The Annual Ball
The Annual General Meeting	Impromptu team photographs
On Tour (the first day)	An interview with the Press
Talking to senior club Officials	On Tour (second day)
In a public bar (on tour)	In the Marquee at tea
Acts of God (Fire/injury)	Eating an ice cream
British Academy of Cricket hearings	Movable Feasts
Deaths	Stretching of legs (on tour)
Reading of bequests to the club	Acts of God involving first aid
Being introduced to a Dignitary or Fellow of the British Academy of Cricket	In a public bar (home matches)
	Waiting for a train (more than ten minutes)
The Annual Reading of Reports	Natural Disaster

(Turn over)

THIRDLY

MALE MILLINERY MATTERS

Introductory Lesson L390
Modern developments and Attitudes to Headwear

In these times the proper significance of headwear is quite disregarded, chiefly because people are no longer so adept at Sitting and Thinking.[1] Sitting and Watching (chiefly television, weight, doom, time and neighbourhood) is the modified form of this old custom which has become universally accepted.

Nevertheless the hat still persists as the preferred garment for the Head even though it has ever been the most proclamatory of items. It shouts abroad loud denunciations of its wearer: it states with humiliating eloquence that he has a silly Vision of Himself; secondly and more cruelly, it indicates what that Vision is.

It is best therefore never to wear civilian headgear at all for it is against the nature of the Game to shout anything at the top of one's hat or voice: cricket is the English Game and, on and off the field, is suited to wily whisperings, secret stabbings and unspoken spite.

Heads should therefore be covered only by cricketing caps in the colours of the club, and then strictly at the Going Down of the Sun (after 4.35 pm B.C.T.). It is not impossible these days to see floppy hats, American basketball caps or miscellaneous boaters at or about a cricket match. The use of these devices for the seeking of attention or as an affectation is strictly forbidden.

The use of the Helmet by those Lacking in Moral Fibre

For motor cyclists, delinquents and leather jacket boys the protective helmet is well established and acceptable, although it has yet to be shown that their heads are worthy of protection. Halberdiers, firemen and coal miners can quickly justify the helmet, but the wearing of the helmet is an offence against the Spirit of the Game. By minimizing danger it makes the conflict a mere counterfeit of heroism.

The use of helmets is now quite general among professional cricketers who invariably lack back bone and ground, but it will not be tolerated in Real Cricket, the proper Amateur Game.

---

[1] Sitting and Thinking, the two great British Institutions embodied in the Throne and Crown, are quite neglected by all but our Monarch who is disposed to do the one and obliged to do the other for the benefit of the State of which she is Head. She indicates this by Sitting Down and, when she wants to think, she puts on her Crown. Thus she is a safeguard that ensures the liberty of the Englishman and makes him safe from extremists.

Lesson L392

Ancient Academic and Social Rituals involving Caps

At certain academic ceremonies, including those where degrees are issued, "capping" is still carried on. The strange, elaborate and arcane system of cap manipulation is understood by only a few initiates in the world of anthropology and beautiful letters. Thus it may be ignored.

However, cap etiquette and discipline for players is important. It costs nothing, and it is no mere indication of inferiority nor an act of simple servility, for a player to touch the peak of his cap[1] when a Gentleman passes by. The Gentleman shall always raise his cap in politeness to a lady.

Lesson R393

Coping with the problem of large and protruding ears

There is little that can be done in the most severe cases (Fig. 63).

Lesson R394

A supplementary note on coping with close-set eyes and a vacuous expression

Once again there is little that can be done (Fig. 63). In passing it should be noted that there is no need for further debate between creationists and evolutionists. Some men are descended from Adam (Fig. 63) and some from monkeys (Fig. 64).

Fig. 63 Charles Windsor

Fig. 64 John Milton

[1] It has now been discovered that the peasant touched his cap to indicate to the Gentleman that he was not reaching for his dagger or cudgel. Gentlemen originally raised their caps to ladies in order to show that they were not using the hood or cap to mask scalp disorders or an unsightly, deformed or bald head.

135

(Turn over)

FOURTHLY

PAIRS AND BRACES

Introductory Lesson L396
General notes on the Importance of Flannelling in English Life
Cricketers need not be adept at cricket, and this accounts for its popularity. However, the English Cricketer, whatever his shortcomings, should certainly be skilled at the wearing of his Pair. Failure to do so is a serious offence. The Fletcher Report insists that standards of trouser etiquette be maintained. A wrinkled, damp, stained and dirty Pair should be avoided, for they spread disease and are unsightly.

The corrupt influence of our former colonies in America has permeated most aspects of our National Life, with the subsequent wearing by some spectators of blue canvas working trousers. Whereas these may be suitable for plumbers, journeymen and day labourers they are not fitting for attendance at a cricket Regulation R684 (C1) ing such garments should be debarred from entry.

Regulation R721 (C2A)
British Cricketing Cream and the Fletcher Report on suitable specifications for the Regulation Cricketing Flannel
Five and three-quarter yards of British Cricketing Cream fabric of the flannel or doe cloth type shall be used in the construction and composition of flannels for the use of Gentlemen and players.

Cricketers should place orders in writing, addressing the tailor in the following terms: Cricket whites in British Cricketing Cream in 5 star flannel or doe cloth with 2 pleats per side and double cross-over extension waist band, 6 button fly, 2 pockets to flap and button, semi-slant side pockets with cash fob to button and flap. Double sewn seams in linen thread. P.T.U. waist 48, seat 54, in leg 34, out leg 48, 28 knee/24 bottom. Dress left.

All cricketers shall wear these trousers. Adjustments to suit the individual player are not necessary, for most cricketers will be able to get into these. Special outsize types may be obtained for giants or habitual gluttons.

Regulation R722 (C1)
Rules governing the Use of Cricketing Whites
No game shall be played unless and until all participants, are clothed in the correct cricketing whites and have been inspected by the captain. No cricketer should attend with unruly persons or with non-whites.

Lesson L398

Flannels and the need for a Woman's Touch, with regard to folding, starching and ironing

One of the greatest assets to the cricketer is a wife who, for the most part, will be very useful. If she can be trusted to wash flannels correctly this will be of great benefit.

The Gentleman will wish to select a wife who will efficiently send his flannels to the laundry. The player, however, will be fortunate to oversee in his own home, all his laundering work. He will have the opportunity to supervize his wife at each stage and pass on to her all his Mother's, her mother's and her mother's mother's instructions, directions and accumulated wisdom in matters of washing, scrubbing, starching, rinsing, drying, beating, ironing, creasing, folding and hanging, with useful tips and hints on reducing bagginess, care and repair, security, bracer theory and trouser storage.

Regulation R723 (C4)

Prohibitions regarding the use of eccentric trouser supports

The use of *twine, bulldog clips, ropes, horse harness, sticking tape, binder twine and flexible electrical wire* will not be tolerated. Proper braces, in club colours, should be purchased. This item of clothing, which provides a hook or carriage by means of which to suspend trousers from the shoulders, has not been surpassed. Its falling from use (Fig. 65) accounts for much indecent exposure of upper buttocks among gardeners, plumbers, general workers and on building sites.

Fig. 65: *Gravity problems, trouser collapse and moral decline.* The player depicted here is, not surprisingly, quite perplexed. He is hampered in the Field by having no free hands and finds his efficiency much reduced. One of Cricket's many distinctions is the fact that it is the only form of Inactivity where two hands are needed at all times. Thus it prevents much mischief.

(Turn over)

Regulation R724 (C2A)
Flannel Abuse, Flies and Indiscretions

It should be remembered that of the *Seven Unpleasant Openings of Man* by far the most unpleasant are those which are covered up by the flannels.[1] These nether orifices can give rise to very unpleasant stains indeed.

Flies are so named for their habit of flying around things, particularly all sorts of filth and unpleasant smells: the flannels therefore attract a high number of these winged insects.

Grass stains are the least offensive of all blemishes which adhere to the cricketing flannel. Falling techniques using the hands and elbows should be regularly practised in order to avoid the ugly soiling of knees with grass stains.

Indecent exposure and unpleasantness in the delivery stride or when effecting a leg sweep may be avoided by the careful control of flies.

The rubbing of balls. This is dirty and should be avoided. Balls will soil the flannels and should never be rubbed wilfully against them. Polishing should always be done with an old, soft pair of underpants.

FIFTHLY

OBSOLETE SARTORIAL ITEMS

Introductory Lesson L402

What a delight it once was to see the jolly harvester at work, whistling a merry tune, his upper parts clad only in vest (Fig. 66). The vested navvies on the roadside were happy in their labours. Such people were always ready with a cheery wave and a happy grin, touching their caps as a carriage swished by.

Now what a cheerless thing our national life has turned out to be! These same people have been persuaded, by the advance of Socialism, to forego these simple pleasures: they have now replaced the musical ting of the shovel against flint with the dull clink of a beer glass on false teeth.[2]

Gone, quite gone, too, is the Flat Cap, once a symbol of industriousness, patriotism, loyalty to the Queen. Sobriety, decency and Sense of Place, all gone. Gone is the Vest soaked in the honest-smelling sweat of noble toil. All gone.

---

[1] Except in the case of Cockneys and Australians.

[2] Also provided by Socialists who, in giving the working classes ever more teeth, have encouraged them to eat more, thus increasing their suffering from obesity.

Fig. 66: *A merry labourer in the field, clad only in a vest*

See how he delights in the comings and goings of his fellow man. Toil has not made him sullen and grudging as it does in certain lower types. On the contrary it has merely prompted him to strip cheerily to his vest. Here we see a man who is light of disposition, eager to please, at ease with himself and the world, possessed of a simple upright heart and a hanky to wave at passers-by.

(Turn over)

SIXTHLY

THE SONG OF THE SHIRT

Introductory Lesson L405

**Introductory Notes on the Shirt and its existence as a
demonstration of the Cosmological or Teleological Principles at
work in the World, ignoring for the time being any Ontological
Considerations which make the whole issue much more
complicated, and which have been
specifically excluded at the Chairman's request**

At first sight it would seem that the shirt has played little part in world history. Nobody will ever be heard to speak of the War of Jenkins' Shirt, King Alfred and the Burning of the Shirts, the Black Shirt[1] of Calcutta.

But the cricketer should not be deceived. The shirt played a noble part in the building of Empire. On his voyages of discovery Captain Cook was dressed always in a shirt. When the scantily clad Fuzzy Wuzzies and Zulus were slaughtered at the battle of Rorke's Drift it was done by our soldiers dressed to a man in shirts; and when India was subdued and the East India Company formed, at the Restoration and the Battle of Britain, all was done by Englishmen bedecked in shirts.

What a valuable legacy Great Britain has passed to half the nations on earth, for the shirt persists as a symbol of status and power, and the regular starching of collars goes a long way to keep alive the idea of Empire which will one day be reunited.

Shirts, like most other objects,[2] did not simply spring into existence, but evolved as the result of the controlled application of intelligence and a guiding will, otherwise how could the collar, the cuff, the pleat and the tail with its double sewn hem have arisen?

This is not to say that God is a Tailor, but that the world is constructed in such a wondrous way and with such interlocking fortuity[3] and logic that it could not have come into being without His guiding intelligence or, at the least some pre-ordained plan directed to some end.[4]

But first it is necessary to discover how the shirt took on the familiar form it has today.

---

[1] Hitler had some very good ideas.

[2] Including the Universe which did not, as the subversive "free lunch" theory would have it, spontaneously arise from nothing for this is against the Bible and British Way of Life.

[3] According to Viscount Palmerston an "accidental and fortuitous concurrence of atoms".

[4] The modern strong crickethropic principle supported by Rees, Davies and Hoyle states: "that this end is man himself with his ability to contemplate the universe and represent its interests and guiding principles by playing cricket".

Lesson L406
The Evolution of the Modern Shirt

At first the collar and the cuff, those portions most subject to soiling, were detachable and could be changed each day, giving a fresh and clean appearance to the most unwashed shirt.

With the granting of Universal Soapage in the post-war world the entire shirt was deemed washworthy after two wearings. New substances called detergents were invented to facilitate this process and kill all fish. With this development came the demise of the Quality Shirt which has survived into the modern world only in a few outposts where garments of pure silk, exquisitely hand-sewn, change hands for large sums of money.

Regulation R733 (C4)
Gentlemen and the Psychology of Perspiration

Sweating is unseemly and unBritish and thus should be avoided. The most effective way to avoid sweating is to remain inactive for long periods,[1] and cricket has been devised, both for Gentleman and spectator alike, to achieve this.

Lesson L410
Social Intercourse between the classes and the Beneficial Effects of Uniform Shirt Types

Gentlemen and players should note that cricket, above all other games, breaks down class divisions,[2] which have plagued the English since the emergence of the Labour Party.

In no other circumstance is a player,[3] should he be granted the opportunity to bowl, allowed to triumph over a Gentleman and put him out of the game without some charge or reprimand, fine or suspension. But in cricket this is an everyday occurrence, for the Game (like War and Her Majesty's Government) seeks to bring people together[4] not to push them apart, to encourage friendship, tolerance and a community and team fighting spirit, not to nurture hatred, division, envy and antagonism. Uniform shirts unite Gentlemen and players alike: each goes out to Do His Bit for the Game and for her Gracious Majesty the Queen,[5] suitably and equitably shirted.

---

[1] A whole class of English people in the eighteenth and nineteenth centuries, devoted their lives to the mastering of this art.

[2] Into five types.

[3] If fortunate enough to be granted a game.

[4] In order of rank.

[5] Who is more interested in cricket than She sometimes appears to be.

(Turn over)

SEVENTHLY

WOOLLEN INDUSTRY

"Truely, a needle cannot doe much hurt,[1]
and as truely (with leaue of Ladies be it spoken)
it cannot doe much good."

Introductory Lesson L431

Inestimable and sublime are the benefits lovingly provided by deft female hands, particularly when graceful fingers gently coax from a few simple balls of wool that noblest of all garments the cricketing pullover. Sir Philip Sidney was not often mistaken but he is in grave error above. It is a joy to any normal woman to wield that traditional symbol of female dominance and domestic power the knitting needle, for she knows that without woollen ordnance all would perish in the cold onslaught of the English Summer.

Regulation R754 (C4)
Persons deemed Proper and Suitable for the task of Knitting

Before any knitting is commissioned the wise Gentleman will look thoroughly into the background of the female to be hired (Fig. 67). The chosen knitter should have impeccable testimonials, a clean record, and an unblemished life, for no other creation will reveal so much as knitwear any deficiencies in the character of its maker. A mean and tight garment, a loose and floppy item, a promiscuous pullover or an article riddled with flaws and imperfections speaks volumes about a woman's history and background.

And how all women can deceive! Therefore it may be efficacious for the Gentleman to seek out an Old Aunt.[2] Such a one may be persuaded to accept certain commissions from her favourite nephew, but before commencing this lofty task she should be clearly instructed.

---

[1] There was a time in 1066 when needlework skills were confined to the recording on the Bayeux Tapestry the exploits of the Summer Tour, to the great hurt of Harold who is depicted with an arrow in the eye. Later, women wishing to contribute practically to the campaign applied their skills to the knitting of chain mail. This culminated in the female contributions to the wars of this century, wherein a class of liberated women performed not only their traditional role of furnishing sons and husbands for war but also made the armaments.

[2] Gentlemen will often find their old Aunts in or around Bath, the Chichester area, or in most parts of Devon, Kent, Hampshire or Sussex.

Fig. 67: *Master Knitmistress to the British Academy of Cricket.*

Few females in each generation have the endurance and strength of character to perfect their skills in knitcraft, the art of tying orderly woollen knots in serried rows. Only when she has reached the pinnacle of self-expression through stitchcraft is a woman entitled in her mature years to call herself by the name of Master Knitmistress.

Such a craftsman is, of necessity, a rare thing indeed and her skills are in great demand. This venerable lady, Stitchmater General to the British Academy of Cricket, was for many years a very close friend of the chairman whose patronage has kindly paid for her son's education. She has an order book filled for the next 16 years, and the ordinary cricketer is unlikely to find himself included in her list of customers. This rare glimpse into her lair was taken by the Chairman himself using a tripod and Ilford FP4 on f11 at ⅟₁₅th of a second. His camera is an Ensign Selfix 12-20 with a Ross 75mm Xpres F/3.5 lens.

(Turn over)

Regulation R756 (C3)
Admissible Stylings and patterns for Cricketing Pullovers

Cricketers should choose the style of pullover most suitable for their activities. Academy directives and instructions[1] are embodied in the pattern below and are a free gift to all purchasers of the present volume. Those borrowing the book from a Library are not entitled to use the pattern.

[1] *MATERIALS:* Use 15 ozs 4ply in Academy British Cricketing Cream, a pair each of no. 11 and no. 9 needles.
Measurements: To fit 36–38 (39–41) inch chest; Length from shoulders 24(25)ins; Sleeve seam, 19ins.
Tension: 6½sts, and 8½ rows to an inch. It should be noted that the large size is given in brackets thus: ( ). **Where one set of figures is given this applies to both sizes of cricketer.**

Back: With no.11 needles, cast on 126 (132) sts, and work 3½ins, K.2, P.2 rib. Change to no.9 needles and stocking stitch and work straight until the back is found to measure. With right side facing, shape armholes by casting off 9 (11) sts, at beg. of next and each end of next and every following alternate row until 92(98) sts. remain. back measures 23½ (24½)ins. With right side facing, shape shoulders by casting beg. of next 6 rows. Change to no.11 needles and work 2½ins. K.2, P.2 rib o sts.; **cast off in rib.**

Front: Work welt as for back. Change to no.9 needles and follows:- First row: Right side facing, K.42(45), P.5, K.12, P.8, K.12, P.5, K.42(45). Sec P.42(45), K.5, P.12, K.8, P.12, K.5, P.42(45). Third row: K.42(45), P.5, * Slip next 3 sts. on edle to back of work, K.3, K.3 from spare needle, slip next 3 sts. on spare needle to front of w , K.3, K.3, from spare needle *, P.8, repeat from * to * once more, P.5, K.42 (45). Fourth row: as second. Fifth row: as first. Sixth row: as second. These six rows it will be discovered by the prudent knitter, form the pattern. Continue straight in pattern until the front matches the back at side edge, then with right side facing, shape armholes by casting off 9(11) sts. at beg. of next two rows. Here divide for neck. Next row: K.2 tog., pattern. 52(53), turn and leave rem. sts. on a spare needle which should always be kept near and handy. Next row: in pattern. Next row: K.2 tog., K.28(29), K.2 tog. pattern to end. Next row: in pattern. Next row: K.2 tog., K 28(29), pattern to end. Next row: Pattern 21, purl to end. Continue in pattern, dec. 1st. at armhole edge on next and foll. 4(2) alt. rows, then keep armhole edge straight and, at the same time (this can not be emphasized too much) decrease 1 st. before the 21 pattern sts. on next and every foll. 4th (3rd) row until 30(30) sts. remain. Work straight until front matches back. With right side facing, shape shoulders by casting off 10(10) sts. at beg. of next and foll. 2 alt. rows, armhole edge. Rejoin wool to rem. sts., neck edge, and work to correspond. **Failure to do so is an offence Class C3.**

Sleeves: With no.11 needles cast on 60sts. and work 3 ins. K.2, P.2, rib . Change to no.9 needles and st. stitch, shaping sides by incr. 1 st. at each end of 7th and every following 6th row until there are 96 sts. Work straight until sleeve measures 19ins or required length. With right side facing, shape top by casting off 4 sts. at beg. of next two rows, then K.2 tog. at beg. of every row until 56 sts. remain, then at each end of every row until 26 sts, remain; **cast off forthwith.**

Neckband: With right side facing and no.11 needles, pick up and K.82 sts. down left side of the neck to centre front. Work 1½ ins. K.2, P.2, rib, decr. 1st. at centre front on alt. rows; now work a further 1½ins in rib incr. 1st. at centre front on alt. rows to match decr. in accordance with traditional practices; cast off loosely in rib. **Work other side to correspond and thus produce a balanced garment.**

To make up: Press parts on the wrong side under a damp cloth of approved Academy fabric (calico or chenille). Join side, shoulder and sleeve seams; insert sleeves. Join neckband at front; fold neckband in half and slip hem to neck edge on wrong side. **Knitters should not fear, "wrong" here is used merely in the sense of "other", not to mean reprehensible, fallacious or erroneous.**

To make an approved sleeveless pullover: Follow pattern for back and front and ribbing on neckline, sew up shoulder seams. Then with no.11 needles pick up 124 sts. on right armhole and rib K.2, P.2, for 1½ standard Imperial ins. Cast off. Pick up sts. on left armhole and work as for right. **Sew up side seams carefully for such garments may be Inspected without notice.**

Club colours according to rank must, of course, be worked into cuffs (where applicable).

Regulation R759 (C3)
Cricketing pullovers, Colour Bands and Rank Differentiation

Along with the permissible club colour combinations knitted into pullovers, rank will also be shown by the use of varying coloured bands around the cuffs (Fig 68). Woollens should be kept away from moths (Fig. 69).

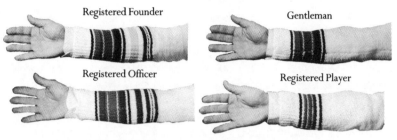

Registered Founder

Gentleman

Registered Officer

Registered Player

Fig. 68: *Colour bands and rank differentiation for cricketing pullovers*

Fig. 69: *The British Cricketing Moth and related species*

The greatest threat to the fabric of the cricketer's pullover is the elusive British Cricketing Moth, genus *Lepidoptera Lanea Britanniae*. Members of this large family of moths are attracted by and lay their eggs in wool. These saboteurs may be recognised by their furry undercarriage (not illustrated), indistinct wing markings and solitary habits. Beginning with the Knit and moving on to the Purl they finally consume the tougher cabling and rib portions of the British Cricketing Pullover. Other species at present suspected of **Insect Attack** have been identified by the British Academy of Cricket Research and Development Department. Species to be kept under surveillance are:

S64 *Thaumetopoea processionea* (Oak Processing Moth)   S19 *Peribatodes Rhomboidaria* (The Willow Beauty or Bat Moth)   S09 *Tineola bisselliella* (Common Clothes Moth)   G105 *Hoplodrina alsines?* (Uncertain Moth)   G117 *Hylaea fasciaria* (Barred Red Moth)

145

(Turn over)

IRREFUTABLE PRECEPTS CONCERNING SENSIBLE FOOTWEAR

Introductory Lesson L458

Just as an army marches on its boots, so a cricket team with poor footwear is quite doomed. Few things are more painful[1] than a foot which has been stored in an ill-fitting boot, and this can cause trouble with runs, bad turns on the green wicket, slips on all fours, snicks to the leg and even dropped balls. It is the lot of the cricketer to wear sturdy boots in the pursuit of his calling, but these need not be inelegant. The human foot is the vanguard of the batsman's attack and is the crack fighting limb of the modern cricketer. The foot deserves all available protection, since its task is to take the force of the bowler's might, and comfort the batsmen in the safe knowledge that he is stepping into the line of the ball. No cricketer would be without his toes and ankles which record, above all other bones, many cricketing sensations in the course of the season.

Lesson L460
Sources of Supply of Cricketing Boots

Gentlemen and players will wish to have at their disposal sensible cricketing footwear.

Calf or pigskin is recommended for the Gentleman's cricketing brogues. When a suitable calf or pig (Fig. 70) has been selected it should be made into boots by a qualified cobbler. Meat and fatty substances should be removed and eaten. For the player,[2] who is less concerned with appearances and more constrained by financial considerations, many hours of useful employment may be had searching in secondhand clothing shops and "jumble" sales and even Dispersal Sales by Auction for the perfect boot. Once this has been discovered he will cheerfully then meet the challenge of finding its brother or cousin. This should be similar, but not identical, for it is a perversity of nature that the left foot has a big toe on the right and the right foot has a big toe on the left.[3]

---

[1] A poke in the lug being the most familiar exception.

[2] It should be noted that original boots had buckles, but when footwear became universally popular in the 1920s and was worn by the working classes copious laces were invented. Properly knotted on retirement to bed, they deterred shoe thieves while the owner was alseep.

[3] It is surprising that God did not ordain something much simpler. Thumbs and cricket pads are equally confusing.

Fig. 70: *Boots and the Pig*

For cricketing purposes a pink unblemished pig should be chosen and tested for suppleness. The pink tinge should not cause concern: it is caused by blood showing through the skin, and once this is removed a natural off-white colour prevails. Boots should be cut out, as shewn here, by an accredited traditional bootmaker (full lists of old cobblers are always available from the Academy), who will use both the left (a) and right (b) as well as the end (c) elevations of the animal. Smaller pigs (d) can be made into excellent footwear for children.

Regulation R779 (C4) or (C2)
Approved and Unapproved types of Cricketing Footwear

Sandals were good for conquering Europe[1] but they will not do at all for the modern cricket match. They lack grace and therefore should be confiscated on sight, disinfected, put in a box and sent to the Academy for analysis, using the British Academy of Cricket Cricketing Footwear Report Form.

CENSORIAL INTERJECTION C1029

The Moderator General of the British Academy of Cricket and the Censor, on instructions from the Chairman have decreed that, for the sake of decency and in deference to the strong views of Mrs M. Whitehouse who has deemed the proposed content unfit for the human nose, ear, foot or eye, there shall be no discussion whatever of socks. Legislation may be viewed at Academy Headquarters, or seen in abridged form on application by post.

---

[1] Romans would walk 50 miles down a Roman road in one day and fight at the end of it. All this was done in sandals, an indication that fresh air and the human foot are good companions indeed when engaged in winning territory, putting to death rebellious slaves or crucifying prophets, all of which are hard on the feet.

(Turn over)

SECTION THREE

THE CRICKETING TEA

FIRST COURSE

GENERAL PRINCIPLES

"I did not feed them with distending vegetables!
But with warriors' food: I awakened new desires.
There are new hopes in their arms and legs, their hearts
are stretching themselves."

Introductory Lesson L522

The respite from hostilities that the tea interval affords is an opportunity for old acquaintances to get together and swap adventures and yarns, become familiar with the latest cricketing intelligence from home and abroad and dispel the tension between the teams.

In this way cricketers reaffirm that the hostilities are a mere counterfeit of battle, that injuries are inflicted in jest, and that the pain and suffering, the humiliation and unending cruelty are applied without any morsel of malice.

Coming together, to imbibe ritual draughts and to eat staple foods is an age-old custom[1] which emphasizes the cohesion and unity of the participants and minimizes social divisions. Men have ever taken comfort from the sense of sharing and brotherhood obtained from the communal eating of sandwiches, washed down with pure English tea, the staves of life. This reassures the Gentleman and player that what seems full of danger and spite is but a semblance or a passing show of hate, a harmless play.

Therefore, let none suppose that the purpose of setting before the opposing side an Impeccable Tea is to provide sustenance for the combatants, for if cricket is played correctly very little in the way of energy is expended. If the mere recharging of muscles were sufficient then all that were needed were a few boiled fowls and a copper full of steaming potatoes.[2] No, the English Cricketing Tea, is a hymn to the prestige of the club and is a measure of its

---

[1] This ritual is 5,000 years old, almost as old as man himself, and is certainly mentioned by God in His Bible.

[2] For players only.

standing in society. It is a holy communion of cricketing souls, an affirmation of the Conflicts of Life.

The culinary orgies of twenty or thirty years ago have, of late, disappeared.[1] Gone is the table fit to bear the weight of mightiest delicacies, that would defeat a swarm of locusts or the Red Army. It is now generally recognized that the cricketing tea is an ancient and a sacred ritual, not a licence for over indulgence, gluttony and scoffing of biscuits.

In a hungry world where some would welcome even a sardine sandwich, the watchword must ever be: Waste Not, Want Not. England's cricketers are beginning once again to eat sensibly and frugally with reverence for tradition and a mind in tune with Transcendent Truths about the human condition embodied within the Game, chewing each mouthful twenty times.

Lesson L523
The Taylor Report and the Introduction of the Minimum Cricketing Tea

A quite proper need for financial stringency in these present difficult[2] times has assisted the nation towards a healthier diet, with much more lean meat and vegetables eaten by both Gentlemen and players respectively. In consultation with dietary Experts, the British Academy of Cricket Research and Development Department has produced the Taylor Report. This sets out the nature and contents of the Minimum Cricketing Tea (M.C.T.), a Catering Core Curriculum, with notes on the training of women and girls in cakework and breadcrafts. It recommends, too, modes of delivery to the cricketer and Regular Inspections (Fig. 71 *overleaf*).

Lesson L524
Sedentary Feasts with the Advantages of Immobility spelled out Clearly and In Full

"Sit down meals", or "knife and fork affairs" as they are sometimes vulgarly termed, are now recommended as an aid to digestion. They have the supplementary advantages of:

i) better control of guests and

ii) regulation of their food intake.

The Taylor Report, written for Catering Officers, is long and detailed and need not concern the ordinary member. It is of immense personal advantage

---

[1] There has, of late, been a remarkable improvement in the health of the nation at large because, although the Common Market is capable of producing mountains of food, it is incapable of producing a population wealthy enough to buy and eat it all.

[2] For players only.

(Turn over)

Fig. 71: *An Academy Inspector inspecting a cricket tea in Shropshire*
The duties of an Inspector are not at all times pleasant and convivial. In this Academy photograph Inspector No 18C/987 has intervened to discover certain offences. Such inspections are normally carried out, as here, in the presence of a female assistant, for often caterers will attempt to conceal offending items about their person.

The Coalport Plate (inset), although of 701 pattern and of the correct period, was found to contain a crack. It has been confiscated and destroyed.

150

to him, however, because it ensures that he need no longer study complex regulations governing sandwich precedence, reactions to fallout, pouring, stirring and sipping techniques, for food is brought to him at waist height and the minimum of muscle power and energy will be expended in conveying it to the mouth.

Thus Teatime becomes again a pleasant and relaxed occasion whereat he may discuss tactics, the game thus far, scoring strokes and dismissals. He will no longer feel it a duty to monitor the intake of his colleagues and opponents for he will be assured that he shall receive his Fair Share of the Cakes.

Regulation R798 (C4)
The Demise of the Buffet Tea

The seated meal has, by many clubs, been found preferable to the buffet which was once such a popular fashion. Clubs shall be entitled to use the buffet method of presenting food to guests but a word of warning must be heeded: all cricketers above level three, including players,[1] have a right to an M.C.T. No club shall fall below this standard.

Regulation R799 (C4)
The five-point M.C.T. Scheme as an Inalienable Right

The British Academy of Cricket M.C.T. scheme evaluates a Lowest Comestible Denominator for the cricketer. It must be stressed, this is not a privilege, but a right bought from clubs at the cost of great sacrifice in the past. Each player has duties, such as pitch rolling, run scoring, the eradication of moles, filling in forms, taking of wickets and bird scaring, and it is just and proper that this should earn him such rights as M.C.T., more Class C1 penalties and optional attendance at the Annual Ball.

Accordingly he should not allow his Right of Teaworthiness to be eroded, nor should he be afraid to voice his disapproval and report to a senior club official (in the first instance) and in the last resort to the British Academy of Cricket, or its subsidiary the World Cricketing Foundation, any failure to achieve the proper standard.

Regulation R800 (C1)
The Dietary Composition of the M.C.T.

The five-point M.C.T. shall be adhered to rigidly for it will provide a healthy meal, light in weight and highly nutritious, sufficiently balanced and

[1] Provided that there is sufficient food.

151

(Turn over)

THE BRITISH ACADEMY
OF CRICKET
MINIMUM CRICKETING TEA
Standard Bun 05.02 D C c)1
(plain) or c)2 (currants)

THE BRITISH ACADEMY
OF CRICKET
MINIMUM CRICKETING TEA
Plate 07.01 D I d)1

THE BRITISH ACADEMY
OF CRICKET
MINIMUM CRICKETING TEA
Cup 07.01 B I d)1
Saucer 07.01 B I d)2

THE BRITISH ACADEMY
OF CRICKET
MINIMUM CRICKETING TEA
Knife 06.03 F C e)1
Fork 06.03 F C h)1
Spoon 06.03 F C g)2

THE BRITISH ACADEMY
OF CRICKET
MINIMUM CRICKETING TEA
Sardine 03.01 B I d)1 or d)2

THE BRITISH ACADEMY
OF CRICKET
MINIMUM CRICKETING TEA
Salt 03.01 S C h)1
Pepper 03.01 S C d)1

THE BRITISH ACADEMY
OF CRICKET
MINIMUM CRICKETING TEA
Sandwich 03.01 A I d)1 – d)5

THE BRITISH ACADEMY
OF CRICKET
MINIMUM CRICKETING TEA
Fillings: egg 05.01 D C b)1
cheese 05.01 A I a)1
(grated) or a)2 (sliced)

THE BRITISH ACADEMY
OF CRICKET
MINIMUM CRICKETING TEA
Tea 06.09 B I d)1
Sugar 05.02 F I e)1
Milk 05.02 H I a)1

THE BRITISH ACADEMY
OF CRICKET
MINIMUM CRICKETING TEA
Butter 05.02 D B a) 1

Fig. 72: *A Portrait of the Minimum Cricketing Tea*

This sensible spread, when tastefully presented in a pleasant light, is not only a feast for the eyes but a mouthwatering delight to Epicure and Abdominal alike. This patriotic picture captures, more than could a thousand words, all the dramatic nutrition of such wholesome fare, to which all cricketers are entitled *on demand*. The Chairman Himself often dines on the M.C.T., and declares it his favourite meal. Note: It is by a nationwide application of catering standards that Teatime Tantrums will be eradicated. No second helpings.

standardized for the Registered member[1] throughout the country, irrespective of any regional pecularities or weather conditions. Class One foodstuffs are not included as these can upset the stomachs of the ordinary *Chipgoing public, the Scots,* and certain other *deprived groups* whose digestive juices have been congealed by a fatty diet of ground meat or waxy offal-based matter, flaky pastries, greasy cheese-like substances and non-hyphenated foods. A sensible diet high in proteins and fibres, minerals and vitamins would, if accidentally ingested by such a person, cause an instant Emergency in the system, throw it into spasms with *explosive runs,* spontaneous and vehement gripings of the gut, *dribbling incontinence,* nausea and sickness, biliousness and *the flux.*

Regulation R801 (C3)
The Need to Understand and Recognize the M.C.T.

Each member of a club or Registered cricketer must commit to memory the M.C.T., (Fig. 72 *opposite*) for an Academy Inspector may ask him to recite it at any time. He shall say: "I believe in the M.C.T. which is my right and shall not be taken away from me. On my plate there shall be:

i)   One B.A.C. Standard Cricketing Sandwich.
    Bread: white lightweight type 16, minimum dimensions – 4½" × 5½" × ¼" per slice (including crust).
    Butter: Minimum coverage at room temperature shall be ½ oz per 10 sq".
    Fillings: Filling weights not to fall below 1½ oz. for egg (sliced) or 1 oz for cheese (grated).

ii) One B.A.C. Standard bun (currant or plain).

ii) A British Academy of Cricket Standard Sardine (Ref No. 03. 01 B I d)1.

iv) One third of an Imperial Pint of best English ceylon tea (Red label or beyond), with sugar/milk in a clean uncracked/unchipped/handled cup with saucer served at not less than 190 degrees Fahrenheit.

v)   Assorted salt and pepper.

vi) One British Academy of Cricket Knife Ref. 06.03 F C e) 1, Fork Ref. 06.03 F C h)1 and Spoon ref. 06.03 F C g)2.

vii) One British Academy of Cricket Cup Ref. 07.01 B I d)1 and Saucer Ref. 07.01 B I d)2.

viii) A place to sit down.

---

[1] All clubs shall, for certain honoured members and, on payment of a Supplementary Catering Donation of a few pounds, intersperse these courses with other fare. A few slices of best back bacon, a dozen oysters, cold roast beef, goose, freshly braised mutton chops, haunches of venison with pickles, broccoli and gravy are in order.

                    (Turn over)

Regulation R802 (C2A)
Correct Code Numbers to be applied to Sardines
until the Common Market has been persuaded
to revert to Former Classifications and Codings or until
Britain withdraws from this UnGodly Treaty

Recent actions of Customs Officers have had an effect on Sardines. It has come to the attention of the Academy that customs officials in the European Community countries have designated "sardines, whether fresh, chilled or frozen, with the number 0302.61 instead of 03.01 B I d)1 and d)2.". This alarming news was announced on May the 11th 1987.

And the whole episode is as disturbing as it is outrageous: cricketers, who were just getting used to the old number, now have to accustom themselves to this change in Regulations, and they have a right to an explanation. The Academy finds that the official reason: "The change should enable customs officials the world over, and their bosses, the trade Ministers, to talk the same language" is undemocratic, bureaucratic, arbitrary and unacceptable for it ignores the feelings of all ordinary cricketers.

The Academy is working (Fig. 73) to have this order revoked and the old number reinstated. Until this matter has been resolved satisfactorily clubs will continue to use the old number in all correspondence.

Fig. 73: *British Academy of Cricket Controller for Europe*
The Director's son has been appointed to this new clerical post. He was chosen from a shortlist of 54 applicants but, in common with all other trainees, he must begin at the bottom and work his way up. At present he conducts all correspondence with the E.E.C. This demanding and sometimes lonely work is well-paid but lacks the thrills and glamour of the Treasurer's or Moderator General's departments. He is engaged here in European Studies and fish theory.

SECOND COURSE

STANDING ORDERS

Regulation R804 (C3 and C2A)
The Duration of the Teatime Period

British Cricketing Teatime shall begin at 4pm British Cricket Time and end at 4.30 p.m. B.C.T. Any failure to observe this regulation should be made known formally to the Club Informer who will report the breach to the Academy at the earliest opportunity and, at the very latest, by the Monday following the match.

At the stroke of 4.30 p.m. B.C.T. the Caterer shall announce: "Tempori exitus advenit," and all cricketers will vacate the dining room in an orderly fashion.

If, after this, persons yet remain at the table a C3 offence has been committed. The Catering Oficer may then *in extremis* invoke his power of "Sic volo, sic jubeo" to expedite their egress. Any cricketers remaining thereafter should be reported forthwith to the Academy, for this is a C2A offence.

Blinds will then be drawn to exclude the hungry gaze of children, animals and unsated cricketers. Food should be removed and the clearing of tables effected speedily and with the minimum of commotion.

All remaindered foodstuffs should be made available to Registered pensioners and orphans.

Regulation R809 (C1, C2 or C2A)
Problems with the Buffet Tea, with a Ruling on the cricketer's Duty to Inform on any Felons, Violators and Vandals

The Sedentary Tea, as recommended by the The British Academy of Cricket, is by far the best answer to thieves[1] and riflers. Players are inveterate riflers, therefore the utmost care must be taken to ensure that sandwiches are not mutilated or tampered with prior to the appointed hour for consumption. Calling for the Police after fillings have been pilfered has proved to be ineffective. The locking of all exterior doors is the simple answer. The third class of offender is the vandal, by merit raised to this bad eminence. He will criminally damage all sandwiches by a cursory and rough

---

[1] The crime rate is increasing at an alarming speed, but the Government has shown itself determined to carry the fight to the criminal by hitting him at his economic base. Many people, especially in Northern areas, have taken advantage of Government policies to ensure that they no longer have anything for the thief to steal. In the Southern half of the nation, so much wealth is tied up in shares and mortgages that the criminal has a difficult task in identifying any object worthy of predation.

(Turn over)

inspection of contents. As sandwich after sandwich is rejected, fallout increases with dire results. High detection rates should be introduced, and all informers and witnesses should make full statements. The misguided protection of the Guilty is reprehensible. The certainty of detection is a deterrent to the rifler and the vandal, and fingerprints (Fig. 74) can help catch him bread-handed, hamfisted and butter-fingered.

(a)   *(b)*   *(c)*

Fig. 74: *Sandwich Rifling.* Thieves are notoriously dishonest and may steal sandwiches, but a worse threat is the rifler who leaves behind the sandwich casings. Diagram (a) compares the fingerprint retention qualities of inferior natural white bread and wholemeal dyed brown bread (b). Granary bread (c) produces an incomplete print.

Regulation R810 (C2)
The suspension of Standing Orders and the Table of Precedences

There was a time when the Englishman's grasp and instinctive feel for the Eternal Fitness of Things, the natural order and the social standing of his countrymen, came as naturally to him as leaves to a tree. But he finds himself now in a harsh, desperate and impatient world where nothing, save Cricket, interrupts the flow of misery and the tide of disaster. The greater pity it is therefore that many clubs will, forsaking all decorum, allow the congregation at Tea to be seated before the arrival of the President or, in his absence, the Chairman. This, and the failure to observe the Table of Precedences which must be posted prominently in the dining hall by each club, are notifiable offences, as is the unlawful denial or witholding of any right of *buvage* and *boscage*.

Regulation R811 (C3) formerly (C2A)
The Precedence of Tables, the Food Chain and a Bird's Eye View of Queuing Formations and Movements for the Buffet Tea

The diagram (Fig. 75) shews ideal arrangements for the production, presentation and orchestration of the perfect British Cricketing Tea. Because in these times of financial stringency not all clubs will be able to conform in every respect the Chairman has ordered that the penalty classification above be reduced to non-notifiable status.

Players will join the Food Chain to collect, at Table 3, the Meal Ticket which will entitle each one to a Minimum Cricketing Tea (M.C.T.). Queuers should circulate in an anti-clockwise direction around the High Table and then veer off to their designated seats. Abdominals should enter by the north door.

Note: From Table 3, which is strategically placed, the Chief Catering Officer can supervise the meal and identify any *scoffing*. With the megaphone he can make public denouncements.

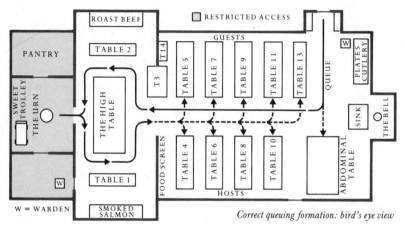

Correct queuing formation: bird's eye view

Fig. 75: *The Food Chain.*

1. The Hosts' Top Table: President, Chairman, Dignitaries, Gentlemen.   2. The Guests' Top Table: President, Chairman, Academy Inspectors/Officials, Gentlemen.   3. The Chief Catering Officer.   4. The Host Captain and his guests, Rector, Club Informer.   5. The Guest Captain and his Guests, Tour Officer, Club Informer.   6. Chief Officers and senior club Officials.   7. Chief Petty Officers/petty officers, junior grades.   8. Host Vice-captain and his friends.   9. The Guest Vice-captain and his friends.   10. Players. 11. Staff.   12. Abdominal.   13. Children and wives.

Regulation R812 (C2)
The History of the Queue and correct Queuing Techniques for Buffet Meals

In the case of buffet teas proper queuing techniques are vital for the maintenance of the Rule of Law and the Stability of the Realm.

In 1914 our brave young men proudly queued in an orderly fashion before the recruiting booths to fight the Perfidious Hun. How wholesome it was in 1940, when a spirited people queued cheerfully for dried eggs and snoek, to be evacuated from London, or for a slice of Black Market meat or a gallon of paraffin. The memory of such examples should fortify the cricketer's resolve to bring back the queue, for it is in this particular line that Britain has always been pre-eminent.

Before queuing commences, cricketers should wait patiently in line. The

(Turn over)

need for order is paramount. Since, in this instance, the queue is related to the selection of foodstuffs and catering particulars, the Catering Officer must be on hand to prevent disorderly conduct (Fig. 76).

Drill No 1   *Drill No 2*

Fig. 76: *The prevention of offences.* Few can resist vehement shooing and herding actions. These drills have been shewn to prevent most people from doing anything. If delivered frontally they appeal to the deep instinct of the Englishman to wait bewildered until he is told what to do. The megaphone can also be of great benefit because most decent people, who know that nobody ever has anything worth saying, are struck dumb at the spectacle of someone wishing to say it so loudly.

Correct order shall be observed while entering the dining room. After the Gentlemen have taken their fill, players should assemble and, using the proper drills (Fig. 77), be ready to show their hands and fingernails before passing anti-clockwise before the Table.

The British may be pushed around in the world these days but, as a Nation, we are still capable of forming a Clean Orderly Queue.

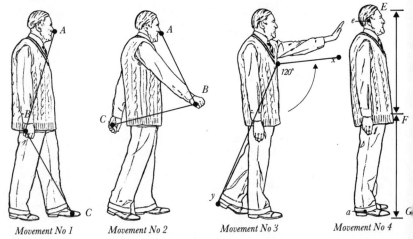

Movement No 1   *Movement No 2*   *Movement No 3*   *Movement No 4*

Fig. 77: *Queuing techniques for players.*

These drills, if performed daily, will ensure mental development and the perfection of queuing discipline in players. The author is indebted to Sir St. John Peatfield who developed these movements specifically for this book. **Note:** Distances AB and BC should be equal. Angle xy must be 120 degrees. Measurements EF and FG should be equal. Earlobes (e) should be on a direct vertical above the ankle bone (a)

THIRD COURSE

THE SLICING OF THE LOAVES

Regulation R832 (C2 or C3)
**Warnings to Gentlemen and Players on Fallout,
Notes on Sandwich Stacking and Etiquette
and supplementary details on Premature Vibraculation,
Mastication in Public Places,
Unruly Behaviour and other food-related offences**

Poor background and wanton, unrepentant and unregistered gluttony are the chief causes of many recognised teatime misdemeanours and felonies, and many can be simply remedied by the adoption of the Food Chain.

However, a severe and persistent problem is that of fallout.[1] The most common causes of this are:

Variables in sandwich construction (Fig. 78): Gentlemen and players should be wary of hypotenuses in excess of four and half inches on triangular types constructed in lightweight breads.

Fig. 78: *Pythagoras' sandwich theorem* $(x^2 + y^2 = z^2)$ should always be used in preference to any other formula in calculating hypotenuse lengths.

For the benefit of those without a grounding in Euclidean geometry, a hypotenuse is the side which has been cut, or which does not have, and has never had, a crust. It may be further identified intuitively as that side of the sandwich which, in a normal human subject, most readily presents itself to be bitten.

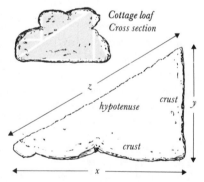

Cottage loaf
Cross section

z

$hypotenuse$

$crust$

y

$crust$

x

Inappropriate fillings: Finely sliced, shredded, diced, lumpy, slimy, squidgy, slithery or overstacked fillings such as grated cheese, chopped egg, sliced tomatoes and cucumbers are widely known to encourage fallout. It is wise therefore, to determine the contents of the sandwich before transport or conveyance takes place.

[1] Fallout is that portion of a sandwich filling which, having been placed in the sandwich at the time of creation, construction or manufacture, has, in transit, by felony or misdemeanour, under animal or insect attack, for some other reason or as the effect of some other cause, known or unknown, tumbled spilled, slid, emerged or otherwise escaped from the confines of the outer sandwich casings.

For the specialist a more detailed definition of Fallout is contained in the British Academy of Cricket Graphic Dictionary of Cricketing Terminology.

(Turn over)

Cementation (Fig. 79a): The selection of butter and fats of variable viscosity and their incorrect distribution on the bread surfaces creates insufficient glutinous cohesion and hence a rapid falling away of filling retention coefficients.

Fig. 79a: *Butter cementation co-efficients.* Temperature must be calculated and placed in mathematical relationship to the butter's adhesive qualities. Above 92 degrees Fahrenheit all adhesion is lost.

Fig. 79b: *Wiping drills and knifecraft.* To ensure even distribution of fats the Bolton method should be used: On, Skim, Scrape, Off as depicted in Figs, (i), (ii), (iii) and (iv). No dribbling or licking of fingers.

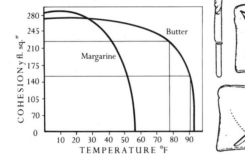

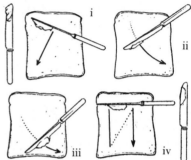

Handling and carriage (Fig. 80): Over-zealous vibraculation in the first instance and reckless handling during transit and consumption in the second, are common causes of fallout. Overstacking of the plate, disorderly queuing and vulgar gluttony may be easily combated by the adoption of Academy drill routines. Proper queuing techniques are essential, and Table Visit Allocations (T.V.A.s) should be determined by the inverse application of socio-economic group ratings.

Fig. 80: *Reckless Handling.* To transport a stacked plate in this manner is a difficult and often dangerous job, and could prove catastrophic. Handling as shown here should be reported to club officials. Plates should be of the Wedgwood Corinthian type, design patent 109536. Coalport tablewares of floral pattern No. 701 (See page 150) are also acceptable, but these are increasingly difficult to obtain.

Consumption directives: Once distribution or selection has taken place in accordance with the specifications as laid out under the Minimum Cricketing Tea provisions, all food shall be masticated with decorum, with the mouth firmly closed.

Regulation R833 (C3)

Further Offences connected with the Adulteration, Pollution and Mishandling of food

Lewd swilling of tea, the mollifying therein of biscuits, spitting and crumbing, excessive salivation and dribbling, slurping and burping, choking, rifling, disputes over chocolate dainties, scoffing and troughing, are all forbidden. Insurrection by players, fights over sponges or the abuse of china and teaware should be reported, in the first instance, to the Catering Officer.

Regulation R836 (C3)

Sponges, problems with Beards and Moustaches with rulings on Preventative Clipping and styles

The more flamboyant offerings of the pastrycook and the highest aims of her art have long been at odds with facial whiskers and it is certain that one or other must give way. Nothing is worse than a beard or moustache filled with crumbs,[1] the inevitable accompaniment of the consumption of sponges which exceed the approved height of two and a half inches.

All moustaches must be clipped short on both sides of the nose,[2] and all beards disposed of by the shaving method.

Regulation R838 (C3)

Eating modes for Foodstuffs at the Table

Proper table postures are essential, with the back straight, not arched, and the knife and fork correctly held. Dainties should be eaten daintily with a fork, and not lifted directly to the mouth as was once the rude custom of our forefathers. Cakes should be forced into the mouth with the proper instrument, not with the fingers or the heel of the hand, a technique strictly reserved for sandwiches.

Eating with the mouth full is offensive, and talking with the mouth full should always be eschewed. Drinking with the mouth full is equally ill-mannered. Conversation should be confined to a few nods or shakes of the head and should never include jokes about Dick or Mary in the Dairy, rats, boils or squashed frogs. Laughing with the mouth full is disgusting and scatters large numbers of sticky crumbs. Cheering, jeering, arguing or issuing insults with the mouth full are all repellent, as is Noisy Vomiting.

---

[1] When people lived on two fishes and five loaves of bread and were regularly immersed in rivers, the hygienic disadvantages of the beard were of no great significance.

Academy theologians are now generally agreed that God the Father, always depicted with a beard, does indeed have a beard. God the Son has a light stubble, and God the Holy Ghost, who is ineffable, is presumed to have no more than a five o'clock shadow.

[2] Hitler had some very good ideas.

(Turn over)

Regulation R839 (C3)
Food Matching for the individual cricketer, with full details of Appropriate Foodstuffs for Feeding Groups

Eating arises from a mixture of habit and hunger. The pangs of hunger can be placated by any offering, but habits instilled in early childhood often ensure that feeders forage for familiar foods. Therefore a range of foods (Fig. 81) may be provided but, where this is done, Dietary Differentials should not be eroded and approved Eating Modes should be observed, and enforced if necessary.

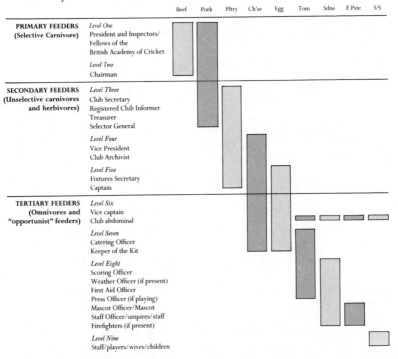

Fig. 81: *Foodstuff requirements by dietary background.*

For every Prime Carnivore there will be several Secondary Carnivores and two or three herbivores. In common with rats and rooks the majority of men demonstrate omnivorous leanings by eating anything.

The higher level feeders are the most selective, although they will occasionally traverse the food barriers or even descend to a lower feeding plane if their primary foodstuffs are unavailable. All feeders should note that any officer of Level Three and above has the right of "stop and search". This shall entitle him to open, inspect by eye, ear and nose, any sandwich and to close, replace and (at his own discretion) report any item found at variance with Academy standards. The President has rights of **buvage and boscage**, but strictly within the limitations and terms laid down in the *British Academy of Cricket Manual for Officers and Staff.*

SECTION FOUR

AGGRAVATED NUISANCES

being an

IMPORTANT SECTION

devoted entirely to

PERNICIOUS FORMS OF INTERFERENCE WITH

CRICKETING PROCEDURES

*As commonly experienced by unprepared, ill-equipped or
negligent clubs, including full regulations governing procedures in the
case of Accidents, unscheduled events, interruptions to play,
COSMIC MEDDLING and all other vagaries, contingent, extraneous
or miscellaneous occurrences.*

*"Circumstance is blind, and man's
encounters with it will rob him of his eyes."*

INTRODUCTORY WARNINGS

*"In the fell clutch of circumstance
I have not winced nor cried aloud
Under the bludgeonings of chance
My head is bloody but unbowed."*

*Most unforeseen events could have been prevented if they had been predicted
from the obvious signs.* **Cogito ergo sum**, *said Descartes, thus proving that
nothing happens without being properly caused, and Someone is to Blame for
everything. Rarely do disasters or emergencies take place without a minimum of
three minutes' warning. An elongated Response Time Coefficient (R.T.C.)
therefore must be seen as the result of poor planning, negligence or
incompetence. The well-organized club will swoop immediately to prosecute the
member or Officer concerned, or to report him to the Academy.*

*The following regulations set out clearly and precisely the most effective
methods of dealing with the major disasters. These are: Acts of God, Fire and
Injury.*

(Turn over)

FIRST BLOW

ACTS OF GOD

"Cousin of Argos, what the Heavens have pleased,
In their unchanging councils, to conclude
For both our kingdoms' weal, we must submit to."

Introductory Lesson L564

For many centuries man conducted his political affairs[1] passing well without the need for Divine Intervention.

It was not until well into the Bible that the Almighty thought Enough is Enough, lost His temper with people and launched the First Act of God with a Cosmic Flood[2] in which all but Noah foundered.

To say this was the first Act of God is not to imply that it was the first time God had done anything, as Genesis will reveal. He had created Creation to provide a suitable venue in which sin, wickedness, miracles, martyrdom and corporal punishment (Fig. 82) could all take place. He created the World for people to build churches on, and He created Sundays for cricket and worship, and He saw that all of this was good.[3]

Noah did not drown because he took with him on the Ark a lifejacket but because he took two of each animal that, in consultation with the Almighty, he decided should survive God's Wrathful Wetness. Why he chose to take with him the mole, the wasp and the bat boring beetle is an imponderable which endlessly perplexed the Schoolmen and the Thomists[4], and has never been resolved. But be that as it may, he was given the highest authority and it must be remembered always that he thought to take the oyster, the snipe and the salmon,[5] without

---

[1] For the greater part of early history man had few decent weapons with which to kill his fellows. Murder was regarded as an unpleasant thing, used as a last resort, and was done brutally about the cranium with a bronze axe (Gentlemen) or a flint club. It was with the onset of the iron age, when a keen edge could be honed on to arrow heads that slaughter got out of hand.

[2] Atheists and Calvinists have suggested that this version of events is a *metaphor or allegory*. This is heresy and will not be tolerated. The Bible clearly states that there was a Great Flood and God has no reason to tell Fibs in the Bible which is Wholly His Book. In any case, such an inundation is to God no more than a Deep Puddle.

[3] This is not to assert that this was all the good that He did, that good was all that He did or even that He did all that was good, only that all the good He did cannot be enumerated within the confines of this present volume. A special mention should be made, however, of veal patties, the cover drive and caraway seed cake.

[4] Thomas Aquinas, Peter Abelard and Olly of Wickham.

[5] Some authorities insist that oysters and salmon were not taken on board the Ark because they can swim, and the snipe can fly perfectly well with a zig-zag motion which makes it very hard to shoot. Although the salmon can swim, the oyster cannot: it merely possesses the cunning ability to live underwater and not drown.

whom the English Dining Table would be a cheerless thing.

Thus it is that the English summer, a form of cosmic background inundation, a dull echo of that first climatic cataclysm,[1] is sent each year reverberating like the dull dong of a rusty universal bell to remind all Christians that This Could Happen Again, and at very short notice too, if the Almighty takes it into His head that Things Have Gone Too Far.

Fig. 82: *Acts of God and Social Disorder*

An all-too-familiar Act of God is the communal madness which seizes a society and engenders political chaos and unrest. Such afflictions strike, from time to time, the most well-regulated community. This can be seen throughout history: dancing sickness in the Middle Ages, the witch mania which gripped all Europe in the seventeenth century, and the repeal of the Combination Acts. In our century, too, there has been the collective hysteria which produced the Russian Revolution, the Yo Yo and the Skateboard. Britain herself is not immune, as the polls of 1945 demonstrate.

But the gravest crisis was in 1926 with the National Strike. At such times, when picketing is rife, the correct cure is the application of mounted police who are highly trained to charge offending trades unionists, a difficult and often dangerous job. The common malcontent or troublemaker is formidable when he is in a large united group, but he is powerless as an individual and proves himself of a cowardly breed, fleeing at the mere gallop of a mounted policeman for, although keen to be a striker, ironically he is often reticent about being struck. Those who are too defiant, crippled or slow to make good their escape can be arrested and receive treatment at the police station. Once held in custody they can then be sequestrated, using modern methods, for this is what hurts them most of all.

[1] The exact date of the Flood is not known, but it is known that the Universe was made on April the 27th 4977 B.C.

(Turn over)

Lesson L566
Philosophical and Theosophical Speculation for Gentlemen and a note for Players

It is very strange indeed that insurance companies use the term Act of God to describe a dreadful event or an effect that has no apparent worldly cause. This is both heretical and impertinent. Acts of God, the first of which was the creation, are no less caused than Acts of Parliament and are equally a punishment for moral turpitude, decadence and negligence.

Indeed the opposite is the case: they, above all other observable events, are more directly attributable to an act on the part of the Almighty. Any suggestion that the team or individual afflicted by an Act of God has not deserved such an affliction is odious to the Academy and therefore improper for the Gentleman.

Theological considerations of this kind need not trouble the player, who may rest assured that the Academy is looking into all these matters.

Lesson L567
Forward Planning and Preparation for Acts of God

Acts of God may not always be prevented, but to an extent they may be foreseen with reference to the *British Academy of Cricket Almanac of Catastrophic Happenings and Earthly Calamities for 1988/89*, soon to be published.

Regulation R847 (C3)
Pre-emptive Action Necessary for the Prevention of Acts of God

Acts of God at all levels are to be discouraged. This will involve the regular use of Academy drills and techniques for mental hygiene which is the best guarantee that the Almighty will keep His temper and not get Upset. All expensive pieces of furniture, important papers and club cricketana should be kept well away from the epicentre of any Act of God in order to minimize damage.

In the event of such an Act it is not wise to be near tall structures or inside buildings. If a cricketer finds himself in a building and cannot leave via the stairs, he should hide under a sturdy Elizabethan refectory table in English Oak with lunette carving, baluster-turned legs and low stretchers.

Regulation R851 (C2A)
Initial Responses to Mass Injury Caused by an Act of God

The first effect of any Act of God is human pain, misery, suffering, interminable grief and loss of life. As soon as this occurs the cricketer shall, irrespective of rank:

1. Identify the injured and dead.
2. Issue identity/injury tags to the dead, dying and injured in this order.
3. Instruct walking wounded to queue in order of seriousness of injury. Patients will decide queuing order by referring to the *British Academy of Cricket First Aid Manual.*
4. Wait patiently for the First Aid Officer to arrive. *No chattering and no flicking of bits of paper.*

Regulation R852 (C4)
Endorsed Classification of types of Acts of God

Before the advent of an Act of God Gentlemen and players shall commit to memory the following updated and fully endorsed classifications of disasters and calamities:

DISASTERS CLASS 1
(Wholly decommissioned Acts of God)

1. *Plague of locusts* 2. *Seven lean years* 3. *Boils and Eruptions* 4. *Straight partings of the waves.*

DISASTERS CLASS 2
(Partially decommissioned Acts of God pending review)

1. *Tidal wave*
2. *Rain for forty days and forty nights* (still partially operational in Yorkshire, Cumberland, Northumberland and coastal regions of Somerset)
3. *Plague of treacle.*

DISASTERS CLASS 3
(Selectively operational although partially decommissioned Acts of God)

1. *War.* Thanks to the gallant efforts of two generations of Tommies, Foreigners no longer have the enthusiasm they once had for wars. And thanks to the Atom Bomb, Europe has been largely free of wars and skirmishes for several years. This is also explained by a growing reticence among soldiers about being killed.[1]

DISASTERS CLASS 4
(Acts of God tried, tested and pending induction to operation)

1. *Atom Bomb Attack.* The remedies are simple and all set out in the Government's eminently sensible publication *Protect and Survive*, which is packed with patriotic information, Atom Bomb drills (Fig. 83 *overleaf*), useful hints and survival strategies. The British Academy of Cricket has recently purchased a large consignment of these booklets from Her Majesty's

---

[1] A mere 250 or so British were killed in the Falklands, barely enough to win the election.

(Turn over)

Stationery Office, at a very reasonable price indeed, and copies may be had on application. At the outbreak of Atomic War government of the club should be handed over to the District Controller who has been appointed by Her Majesty's Government in conjunction with District and County Councils.

Fig. 83: *Protection and Survival*

Valuable items and sentimental objects should be taken along, for any comfort will be welcome in a time of atom bomb attack. Time, too, will weigh heavy on the person who has forgotten to take with him his full set of Wisdens, for the half life of certain Russian isotopes is unreasonably long. Religious observance and prayer is never a bad idea and, in these circumstances, becomes essential. Breakable objects should be wrapped in newspaper. It is always a good idea to get into the Spirit of the Thing.

DISASTERS CLASS 5
(Wholly active and operational Acts of God)

1. *Famine* (players only). More allotments and generous helpings of treacle pudding are the best remedy.

2. *Natural Disasters*. These now, with astronomical and geological advances, also take the form of volcanoes, earthquakes, storms, thunderbolts, meteors, hurricanes (West) and typhoons (East), tempests and tornadoes. It will be found that good sensible footwear and warm clothing will be a great asset in the event of such occurrences.

3. *Charabanc accident, pavilion collapse and derailment of passing trains.* Human recklessness in some irresponsible people is itself an Act of God. Offenders should be admonished.

4. *Stampede* (bovine, porcine, equine, canine, ovine and caprine). At the mere promise of food, cows, pigs, sheep, insects, goats, horses, the unemployed, the old, abdominals and children will rush towards their prize – perhaps a haystack, cabbage patch, a wooden object, a postman, a soup kitchen or mobile ice cream vending vehicle. Academy crowd control techniques (Fig. 76) and rope cordons should be used in conjunction with queuing drills to prevent such occurrences.

5. *Lightning strike.* This can be used by God to demonstrate that electricity is a dangerous thing. Lightning conductors can be useful for buildings and structures, but are of little benefit to the player. Standing under trees is not recommended (Fig. 84). Sensible rubber footwear and the laws of improbability are the only protection.

Fig. 84: *Ghenghis Khan.* This great leader so hated all strikes that, according to the testimony of the courageous traveller Fra Rubruquis, they were forbidden under his Yassa or Code of Laws. Prominent among these were lightning strikes and he forbade his troops to be struck, or even to enter a river, in a thunderstorm. Ghengis, or Chinghis, was an alias. His real name was Temugin, Khan of the Yakka Moghuls. His Empire was finally overthrown in the nineteenth-century by the British in Northern India where the Mongols had no right to be.

He is shewn here taking his dog for a walk.

6. *Epidemics.* Nature's way of culling the undernourished, unfortunate, sexual deviants, the crippled and afflicted, has suffered setbacks in Britain in recent years at the hands of the National Health Service. There is now some evidence, however, that Mother Nature has reasserted herself with new outbreaks of rickets and tuberculosis. The latest in a long line of very successful epidemics is that of the American Disease. Cricketers will note that epidemics may be prevented by the liberal use of good soap and water, which has never done anybody any harm,[1] plenty of clean Alpine air or annual pilgrimages to approved Watering Places like Bath or Baden Baden.

[1] Water without soap can be harmful. In 1912 many of those in the *Titanic* were drowned by it. Most were not drowned, like Noah, because they had life jackets but because they were not wearing them at the time of death.

(Turn over)

SECOND BLOW

FIRE

*"An estimate of the force of the firestorm could be obtained
only by analysing it soberly as a meteorological phenomenon."*

Introductory Lesson L569

*A mighty conflagration is an awesome thing. Occasionally there can occur a
hellfire lit by mortal hand but, for the ordinary cricketer, meddling with the
weather is quite out of reach. He should be familiar with domestic and
community fires and leave aside all thoughts of burning on a geographical scale.
His attention should be focused on the scientific properties of fire, its common
forms, its long history as a form of human expression and its heart of darkness.*

*Fire is the outward and visible sign of combustion in inflammable materials.
There are three types: (i) Natural fire caused by lightning or the burning of
heath, stubble and forests; (ii) man-made fire in chimneys, furnaces, war and
cigarette ends; (iii) Divine fire which will be sent as part of the Lord's
covenant to destroy the world; (iv) Hell fire for the burning of sinners.*

*Fire has been a mixed blessing for mankind. Therefore most fire has been
caused by foreigners. The burning of the Ptolemies' Library[1] in Alexandria in
642 A.D. was a poor idea indeed, for the books it contained would now be
worth large sums of money. It provided fuel for 4,000 baths for six months.*

*Fire has also cleansed our nation. In 1666 it destroyed a goodly part of our
capital city's slums and brothels. London, then as now, set the fashion and
there was scarcely a town of any size which did not have its own Great Fire
soon after. Nowadays the mode is tree planting, town signs and leisure centres.*

*Giordano Bruno attempted to promote human suffering on a universal scale
by positing a multiplicity of worlds. Tortured for his sinful and hotheaded
arrogance, in prison for nine[2] years, he was mercifully burned by the
Inquisition on February the 16th 1600, thus preventing his further incursion
into the **wicked annals of heresy**. Thus fire remains a spiritual agent,
embodies righteous indignation both human and Divine, and delivers justice to
foreigners.*

*But beneath its bright livery lurks also a Nasty Nature. There shines, from
those inner flames, no light but rather darkness visible. An ember, glowing
black below the infra-red, harbours a hissing enmity with all things English,
for here alone, of all the Earth, the rain and fog o'erthrow its Scorching
Sovereignty.*

---

[1] Not all the books were destroyed in the fire. Many were still out on loan and these survived to become
the Renaissance.

[2] Arthur Koestler says seven years; he is not usually wrong, but he is about that.

Lesson L570

The Essential Antipathy of Fire towards the British and its Hot Nature Defin'd

The anti-British nature of fire is not surprising for it is hot and dry and holds great opposition to Water, the British element, which is cold and wet and Britannia rules the waves. This is followed by Earth, Air and lastly Fire which correspond to Navy, Army, Royal Air Farce and Fire Brigade.

Fire is un-British because it contains within it[1] the seeds of its own destruction: it is consumed by what it feeds upon, is smothered by its own ashes and perishes in its own waste, all things which are unfamiliar to the British Way of Life. Therefore, if all else fails a fire may be allowed to achieve its own downfall by burning out. Cricketers should watch from a safe distance. Any persistent fireraiser[2] should be reported.

Fig. 85: *Regulation R862 (C3)*
Extempore fires and the recognition of the firebell

Unscheduled fires, by far the most common sort, will present the biggest problem and are often difficult to extinguish. Cricketers must learn to recognize the sound of the firebell and to be able to distinguish between the firebell and a club burglar alarm. The graph shown here should be of assistance. Noise occurs when silence is vibrated to such a point that it begins to shake.

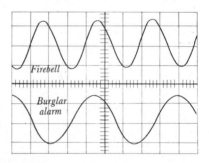

Listing LI571

The British Academy of Cricket Fire Retrieval Checklist

1. Archives, scorebooks, records and uninsured items. ☐
2. Ladies' handbags. ☐
3. Gentlemen's effects. ☐
4. Kit/Equipment. ☐
5. Wardrobes and cricketana ☐
6. The First Aid Kit. ☐
7. Objects of moderate value. ☐
8. Low value objects. ☐
9. Crockery. ☐

Regulation R864 (C4)

How to Extinguish Fires

Water is the traditional substance used for this purpose, and has been found extremely effective in fighting fire. A human fire chain in reverse order of rank should be formed using buckets and lashings of good clean water.

[1] Like love.

[2] Dr. James Bentley Philip has recently been designated Most Extinguished Scholar and has been placed on the Academy of List of Fireraisers for his persistence in depositing cigarette ash in his batting pads, with the result that he frightens children with a crude display of *spontaneous combustion*.

(Turn over)

THE FINAL BLOW

INJURIES

*"Nay, Thomas my good friend, learn to love pain, it is the
God's one true gift for it makes death thinkable"*

Introductory Lesson L574

*The days are now gone when an Englishman's mettle could be assayed by
counting his eyes, the scars he had gained or the limbs he had lost in battle,
whether on the High Seas or in some remote foreign field. In such lofty regard
was courage placed, and such an exalted position did injury occupy in our
National Life, even up to the eighteenth century, that Captain Jenkins (whose
ear was rudely amputated) was honoured by having an entire war named after
this single wound.*

*How very dull seems Lord Horatio Nelson (Fig. 86) during his formative
years when, on looking through a telescope, he could see each and every ship!
When he shared with all common men the characteristic of having two arms and
eyes, how little of the hero he appeared!*

Fig. 86: *Nelson done to death by a foreign sniper*

Alas now are all the heroes fall'n. They are gone to dust and no rhetoric will restore them.
Inside all men there is a red wetness trying to get out. Lord Nelson, ignobly punctured by the
perfidious French, demonstrated the Mortal Leakiness of Man at the Battle of Trafalgar. But
he made his Victory the scene of Immortal Fame. When a great one dies the world catches its
breath and, as can be seen here, such historical events draw large crowds.

With the example set by his Admiral many a Jack Tar, to the greater glory of the Empire, had his legs swept away at the knees by a cannonball, gladly and without complaint and all for his Country's Pride. With courage did he accept a hundred manful lashes given at the mast. Alas, this is now quite gone. In these effete times the National Health Service, with its anaesthetics and penicillins, has quite stripped from injury all pain, danger and dignity; as are the senses numbed, so sleeps heroism. Ghastly Wounds and Mortal Suffering are now become no more than irritation and inconvenience. It will be of moral benefit to the injured to receive traditional remedies, for as did Hercules in the throes of horrid combat with the many-headed Hydra suffer on his foot the mighty malice of the sea-crab in his murderous mission sent by the Goddess in her jealous frenzy, and as did, on Mt. Caucasus' dread rock, Prometheus cry not out to Jupiter but endure the vulture's ghastly feasting, and as in Rome, did valorous Sicinius Dentatus bear his forty-five battle wounds,[1] all of which had scarred his brazen breast as with unalterable will he opposed the regiment of Sabines, thus now in these flagging times shall the cricketer arise and likewise learn to take in stoic silence the buffettings of balls.

Regulation R868 (C2A)
Causes of Injuries and Summary Penalties for Offenders[2]

Most modern injuries are caused by accidents and not punishments. These can be avoided by the proper observance of Academy General Regulations. Any Gentleman or player involved in an accident or becoming injured while a game or function is in progress should, in the first instance, be roundly admonished or placed on temporary suspension for waste of British Cricketing Time.[3] Injuries and public displays of pain shew an unseemly craving for attention and a want of consideration for others; they interrupt play and cause over-excitement, all of which are contrary to the Spirit of the Game, and attract *in situ* fines in the first instance.

Lesson L575
Official Classification of Injuries

Injuries must fall into one of the two categories recognized by the Academy viz.: emotional and physical.

---

[1] He was present in 121 battles; obtained 14 civic crowns, 3 mural crowns, 8 crowns of gold, 183 golden collars, 160 bracelets, 18 lances, 23 horses, with all their ornaments, and all as the result of his uncommon services. Here is a man whom the British Academy of Cricket upholds as an example to our own lack-lustre modern heroes.

[2] Any offence under the First Aid Regulations is notifiable. Anonymous letters should be sent direct to the Informer General's Office, clearly stating the name of the transgressor and the nature and date of the transgression.

[3] 27,468 British Cricketing Hours were lost, last year alone, through the treatment of injuries.

EMOTIONAL INJURIES

These are usually the cricketer's Own Fault and arise from cricketing failure, over-sentimentality over women, further education, lack of self-discipline, poor personal hygiene, self-abuse, court cases or university lectures. But by far the most pernicious influence in our times is that of terror and the Unconscious with the Scream and post-expressionism.

Regulation R869 (C1)
Coping with the Unconscious, Blast Damage, and the Disintegration of the Personality

It took our present century and the tormented mind of Sigmund Freud[1] to invent the Unconscious. Before this, nobody had dreamt of such a thing. In olden times men laid low by some missile[2] or a violent knock about the sconce (whether with a dirty shovel or not) would lie and groan quite consciously in the time-honoured way, resigned to their suffering, with no thought of escaping from the pain.

But now in our effete century Freud has said that the human mind quite rubs out, erases and obliterates all pain that is too difficult to bear by filing it in the Unconsciousness.

That is as it may be. In the field of cricket, however, there is a different authority. The British Academy of Cricket has ruled that there shall be no unconsciousness. It is unmanly and unseats the Majesty of Cricket by taking away the bottomless, excruciating pain, injury, terror and humiliation offered by no other game. Pain and suffering[3] are crucial to character development.

The disintegration of the human personality is most commonly caused, not by chemical explosion[4] but by infiltration of dangerous, liberal or atheistic sentiments. For severe cases a short, residential course at Academy Headquarters is recommended, where the full skills of the Moderator General and his staff will be exercised.

Diagnosis of heretics is not difficult; they will generally declare themselves opposed to Her Majesty's present government and the Rule of Law. They will ridicule the Police,[5] advance socialist or republican ideas, vilify Sir Winston Churchill or the Monarchy.

---

[1] *The Interpretation of Dreams.*

[2] Non-explosive.

[3] In the lower classes.

[4] Explosion was a major form of disintegration in the forties, particularly in Dresden: "At the corner I turned back to my sister and shouted: Run for Kaulbachstrasse . . . then I was struck by a huge black wave. They found me the next morning, and parts of her coat."

[5] Who do a difficult and often dangerous job.

PHYSICAL INJURIES

Regulation R871A (C2A)
Academy Procedures for Classifying Physical Injury

Physical injuries will sometimes be encountered by the courageous and the foolhardy. Such injuries, it has been observed, fall broadly into two main types: serious and non-serious. All cricketers shall learn to classify injuries speedily and efficiently (Fig. 87).

A serious injury is:

1) A serious injury as defined by the Academy (see below).

2) Any injury to a Gentleman or Officer.

3) Any injury where the Medical Officer deems that the symptoms include exposed intestines or unsightly bones poking through the skin.

Non-serious injuries are:

1) Non-serious injuries as defined by the Academy (see Regulation R871B).

2) Any injuries to players or staff.

Fig. 87: *The emergence of Injury Classification*
Not until the Great War was Injury Theory developed into an applied science. In previous conflicts the injured were either left to die or Knocked on the Head. Improved stretcher design in Edwardian times caused great excitement because soldiers could be rushed gently to field hospitals. There they were sorted into three groups: one to live, one to die, and one to wait and see.

(Turn over)

Regulation R871B (C2A)
Further Detailed Classification of Physical Injuries

Every Gentleman or player on being injured shall insist that the First Aid Officer attach to him a label bearing a clearly printed classification mark. This is necessary in the case of epidemic or Natural Disasters which always attract the dead, dying and injured in great numbers.

Registered persons playing in non-registered games shall *always* be refused treatment, as shall old people or the children of unregistered players.

Clubs shall classify all injuries in the following way, assuming that the status of the victim is unknown.

Class 4: Non-serious/non-serious injury.   Class 3: Serious/non-serious injury.

Class 2: Non-serious/serious injury.   Class 1: Serious/serious injury.

Regulation R872 (C2A)
Afflictions and Inflictions deemed fit for Cricketing Personnel

Approved injuries[1] are either (i) *afflictions* (without apparent cause) or (ii) *inflictions* (with apparent cause) and it is important to distinguish between these general categories when describing the nature of the injury to the First Aid Officer.

Academy classification of injuries is as follows:

Class 4. Animal bites (excluding snake/reptile bites), blisters, blotches on the skin, disturbed sleep, eye injuries, fainting, frightful dreams, foreign bodies, giddiness, head injuries, loss of appetite, nose bleed, sick headache, splinters, sprained joints, vomiting, wind.

Class 3: Back injury, broken bones, burns and scalds, costiveness,[2] dysentery, dislocation, drowsiness, fullness and swelling after meals, insect bites and stings, muscular damage, weakness of the loins, shock.

Class 2: Choking, convulsions, epileptic fits, flushings of heat, radiation burns, trembling sensations, snake/reptile bites.

Class 1: Apoplexy, blast damage, drowning, electrocution, griping of the guts, poisoning, stroke, suffocation, throttling.

---

[1] Outdated and old fashioned injuries/complaints/diseases should be rejected by the modern cricketer. Unapproved afflictions and inflictions on the Academy Index are: biliousness, catarrh, the croup, debility, deliriousness, distemper, glandular swellings, kidney stones, langour, liver complaints, nervous affections, neuralgia, polio, quakes and poses, scurvy, shingles, septicaemia, shortness of breath, ulcerated sores on the neck (pending review) and worms.

[2] It will be found that there is no medicine equal to Academy Patent Lozenges for removing any Obstruction or Irregularity of the System. If taken according to Directions they will soon restore cricketers of all ages to good health, strengthen the whole muscular system, increase sensory awareness, bring back the keen edge of appetite and arouse into action, with the rosebud of health, the whole Physical Energy of the Human Frame.

Regulation R873 (C2A)
Recognition of Serious Injuries (Classes 1 and 2)

A serious injury is often indicated when a patient fails to respond to, or to co-operate with, an approved admonishment. In such cases the club President and a Founder Member shall be informed immediately. Excessive bleeding and delirium, accompanied by pronouncements on the Meaning of Life, often indicate that the victim is mortally unwell. The Secretary should be handed immediately a verbatim transcript of any discussions, soliloquies, invectives, confessions, outbursts or bequests. Any exposure of major[1] organs must be looked upon as another indication that severe injury has been inflicted.

Regulation R875 (C2)
Unusual Forms of and Exceptional Causes of Major Injury

These shall be confined to:

1. Any injury inflicted by a bull in the legitimate pursuit of its calling.

2. Electrocution caused by contact with power lines provided they are a properly commissioned part of the National Grid and bear 33,000 volts.

3. Head wounds inflicted by a beer bottle (stout, porter, light ale or barley wine, but excluding brown ales and Bavarian lagers), so long as it has been used as a weapon or projectile by a member of any opposing team or the audience or crowd.

Regulation R876 (C2)
The Governing and Control of Inadvertent Sentiments

However rigidly the serious cricketer applies Academy precepts, he will inevitably have moments of uncontrolled sympathy or will be vexed or mortified[2] at the sight of a Gentleman or Officer of the club stricken by some injury or mishap, whether caused by overeating, unnatural acts, excessive drinking or wounds sustained in action in the field. Such feelings are not encouraged, and sloppy sentiment must not be allowed to produce unmanly compassion, for excessive sympathy is unbecoming. Few are those who cannot be cured by a dab with a sponge and cold water accompanied by the reassurance: "Get up, you are not hurt."

---

[1] Major organs shall be solely the liver, lungs, kidneys and pancreas for players. For Class I members, Officials above Level III, Founder Members and Gentlemen they shall also include the brain. For women they shall include the heart and mouth.

[2] No fast bowler shall be mortified at any injury legitimately inflicted by him as a proper part of the game, nor shall he make any apology nor feel any remorse without the authority of the Captain who shall be the sole arbiter on the level of regret to be felt by any such bowler.

Regulation R877 (C2)
On awaiting the Arrival of the Key to the First Aid Kit

If, at the time of the incident, the batsmen have not crossed, all fielders shall remain where they are and the batsmen shall remain at their respective ends.

Excited huddles, which congregate around any injured person, should be dispersed. Gentlemen may hold a discussion about the matter at a reasonable distance from the stricken person, and in any case not nearer than 30 yards. Pointing, pushing and jostling, Ugly Scenes and Scuffles, the premature apportioning of blame and Angry Exchanges, are all generally prohibited. Communication with the injured party should be strictly avoided. Persons should not be permitted to recount episodes involving their own wounds or to tell jokes, stories or riddles or to discuss religion[1] or politics.

Regulation R878 (C2)
Proper Registration of Injuries

It should be remembered that unauthorized persons may never administer First Aid or seek to implement any First Aid without the consent of the First Aid Officer. However, there is no adversary more tenacious and terrifying than a person dedicated wholly to the doing of good.[2] Therefore an injured cricketer should, for his own protection, not attempt to resist First Aid treatment.

Any cricketer nearby should proceed as follows as soon as an injury occurs:

1. Inform a senior club official and fill in Academy report form C01/62/A.
2. Call a meeting of the Disciplinary Committee, informing all Founder Members of the occurrence.
3. Request the offender to recover forthwith and inform him of the intention to hold an informal meeting to discuss any irregularities.
4. Take the name and address of the offender, and extricate from his clothing his Registration documents.
5. Take statements from any parties involved and from any witnesses, forwarding the original documents direct to the Academy's Informer General, with copies to the Archivist.
6. Contact the British Academy of Cricket inspectorate and take all relevant measurements, making a simple sketch-plan of the area.

---

[1] An exception may be made in cases where a priest has been called to administer Extreme Unction.

[2] This phenomenon may be often observed in the attitude and activities of Socialists and Jehovah's Witnesses.

SECTION FIVE

THE SUMMER CAMPAIGN

PRELIMINARY
STRATEGIC BRIEFING

"A man becomes aware of his life's flow,
And hears its winding murmurs, and he sees
The meadows where it glides, the sun, the breeze."

Introductory Lesson L582

There is nothing finer than to travel along the highways and byways, down the green and leafy lanes of Old England, with the mid-summer sun streaming in the windows, picking up here and there particles of dust in the air making the sunbeams almost palpable; for beauty, being the best of all we know, sums up the unsearchable and secret aims of nature and bestows form and sense on joys whose earthly names were never told.

Now is the time for the Gentleman to renew old acquaintances, perhaps with those in the Northern Counties, and to spend a week or so in itinerant bliss, beckoned by the open road, throbbing with adventure, conversing with wayside travellers drinking in all the sweets of the world,[1] exploring this blissful seat set in a silver sea, this Mother England.

Swishing along o'er dales and hills; and at one side a hot-house flashes uniquely, a gust of birds spurts from the pleachèd arbour, a hawk roosting, someone getting off a bike. Then as the sun sinks and at the journey's end and the whisky done, there swells a sense of warming like a missile sent out of sight somewhere becoming fire.

Lesson L583
An Historical note on Landscape

It was Capability Brown who first discovered landscape and sold it to the gentry in large hillocks, small lakes and cedar trees. It had, until then, been the preserve of the rustic, the poacher, peasant, poet and parson.

---

[1] Gray wrote his Elegy outside, in a churchyard, because he had time off during the day. Some poets, like Young, were obliged to write Night Thoughts indoors, at night.

(Turn over)

PREPARATIONS FOR THE TOUR

"'That's a fall, and no mistake,' he thought,
'there must be some uncommonly dirty weather knocking about.'"

Introductory Lesson L584

Long-range weather forecasting is, like high precision bombing of cities, a hazardous affair with many unknowns and variables. Meteorologists will often be wrong in their predictions when they say the weather is to be fine and warm and sunny.

Atlantic charts are very unreliable and cloud formations can change from minute to minute, so it is difficult, in the middle of February when plans have to be made, to choose a fine day for the launch of the Tour. It will, nevertheless, be the Weather Officer's duty to select a warm and sunny week. This may only be done using traditional methods which have proved successful on many occasions: Sound methods of predicting good[1] and bad summers

1. *If rooks build high, there'll be no rabbit pie.*
2. *If Bumble Tuesday be warm, there's bound to be a swarm.*
3. *Rain afore the seventh, clear afore the eleventh.*
4. *When the sailor's trousers be blue, there'll be a hot day or two.*
5. *If swallows come by May, it will rain every day.*
6. *A Halo round the moon is worth a silver spoon.*
7. *When the mud's up to the knee, plant an apple tree.*
8. *If the swallows fly low you'll see no snow.*

Regulation R895 (C4)
Suitable Regions to Visit and the Selection of Opponents

Cricketers shall strive always to visit a pleasant part of the country, avoiding areas of Kent and Essex, most of Yorkshire, Staffordshire and the entire Merseyside region.

Many months before the tour, the Fixtures Secretary will have interviewed all prospective opponents. Selection will be made by, at the latest, the beginning of February. Particular attention will have been paid to the scenic value of the grounds involved, for no Gentleman wishes to travel fifty miles to play on a state school pitch, or behind a shoe factory or municipal building.

[1] A good summer is defined as 63 days free of frost in Somersal Herbert, Derbyshire, including at least eight Sundays.

Regulation R896 (C4)

Preparatory Determination of Suitably Scenic routes and the Selection of Views for viewing, with Appropriate Daily Seating Arrangements and Route Scores

It would be simpler by far if all wonderful views were to the right of, or to the left of the touring coach, but this is not the case in England, necessitating the daily rearrangement of seating to the right or left to suit the route and the tastes of the Gentlemen.

No journey with an aggregate of fewer than 22 points should be undertaken. Ad hoc alterations to the route can sometimes help to bring a journey up to the required standard. Any item can score only once.

Statutory journeys may include: mountains[5], running stream[3], brook[4], terminal moraine[6], rift valley[7], wooded slopes[2], waterfall[4], rocky outcrop[2], watermeadows with fritillaries[6], watermeadows (plain)[3], hillsides far away[2], hillsides with sweet purple heather[2], hillsides with ordinary purple heather[1], pleachèd arbours[5], ox bow lakes[8], alluvial deposits[3], ruined church[2] or abbey[4], lake[4], Palladian house[5], flock of sheep[2], ancient forest[4], cobbled lane leading down to sleepy harbour[8], mossy moot[8], thatched cottage[2], village pond/green[3], vicar on a bicycle[2].

Regulation R899 (C3)

The Importance of a proper Inventory prior to the Embarkation and the need for the Laying out of and Stowing of the Gear

Before the official opening of the campaign much must be done to ensure that all are adequately equipped for the rigours ahead, and all cricketers shall do their part. Gentlemen and their luggage will be picked up individually (Fig. 88 *overleaf*).

All players' equipment, however, should be set out on a meadow of one acre. All items should be folded in a proper fashion and stored in watertight wrappings or packed in large trunks of varying sizes, for the onset of the English summer is a terrible sight to behold and a sore destroyer of any items Not Kept In The Dry. The slight increase in temperature assists the decaying process which, during the winter, has been slowed down by frost.

Regulation R900 (C2A, C3 and C4)

The Inclusion of Private Belongings and Toiletries in the Luggage of Gentlemen and players

The player should need very little in the way of personal luggage, with two stones deadweight the usual limit. All his food will be supplied and personal hygiene is catered for by the British Academy of Cricket Personal Hygiene

(Turn over)

Fig. 88: *The Gentleman's private collection*

Often a Gentleman will ensure that all his items are safely stowed before the charabanc is sent to the rallying point. One barrel of port is sufficient for the longest tour. Proper Tour Licences must be obtained from the Academy and displayed in the windscreen of the vehicle. Failure to do so is an offence.

Leavetaking should not be prolonged for this is unmanly and can affect timetables. A brief gesture is all that is needed on either side.

182

Dispensary. An adequate supply of cigarettes will complete his requirements. A Gentleman[1] will have more refined needs.

Regulation R902 (C4)
The Ceremony of Embarkation,
Suitable Sentiments, Exhortations and Speeches

When the Gentlemen and players are assembled, the President and the Chairman will make a short speech to encourage the men and to instil in them a refreshed awareness of the need for club victories to sustain club pride and glory. Mention will, no doubt, be made of past glories, the achievements of Old Boys, and the speeches will be concluded with a toast to the Founders.

The crowd present at the embarkation, close relatives, children, wives and loved ones should then be allowed a few moments for farewells, tears, and scenes of a touching or sentimental nature. A bugle will then sound the embarkation and the charabanc shall be boarded in an orderly fashion, to the sound of waving and cheering and great fuss and applause, for it will be some days before the men return to their homes and families, filled with memories of pain and glory from the hard campaign behind them.

[1] An electric razor is a great boon but it must be remembered that there will not always be an electricity supply, therefore a small generating system will be needed. A full-length or Cheval mirror will serve both for shaving and dressing.

Shoe polishes should be restricted to black and brown. Changes of clothing should include underwear, socks and braces. Firearms should be kept to a minimum for only one or two days' coarse shooting will be possible. A few good books should be taken, for there will be a short supply of intellectual stimulation on the journey, around the campfire at night or in hotel rooms. Suitable travelling books are: Boswell's account of Dr Johnson's Scottish tour, *Voyages of Discovery, Hakluyt's voyages, the Bible , Travels of Marco Polo*. Toiletries should include corn pads and, for the older Gentleman, an assortment of corsets, braces, incontinence pads, hangers, trusses and Scotch Straps for the security of the testicles, a good hair oil recommended by Denis Compton or cricketer of similar standing, hair tonic, unguents, and diuretics. Penicillin tablets are a great boon for those away from home for any length of time. The *Lettre Française* can be useful.

The Gentleman will include a small amount of vellum for his duty letter to his wife, reassuring her of his good health. Players will often be seen to avail themselves of sundry coloured postcards, but salacious or lewd cartoons involving breasts and buttocks should be avoided by the Gentleman. Candles and a candelabrum will prove beneficial if there is a power cut. Hotel cutlery and china has all been stolen and the replacements are alas of a universally poor standard. Therefore it is a good idea to include two or three sets of plated knives and forks as well as a full tea set of china (the more modern sets [since about 1830] also contain tea plates). A folding chair is often useful when the legs become tired and this is the only item of furniture (apart from the Scorer's Chair) that should be taken.

Fresh fruit and vegetables help to keep the system regular and if a few pounds of tomatoes, apples and the like can be taken along this will prove a great relief.

Academy report forms of most types should be included. The Gentleman must be at all times prepared to report chance malefactions or misdemeanours to the club informer.

Pepper and salt often get left behind and he will be a popular man who has remembered to take the salt cellar when celery or new potatoes grace the table. A full complement of garnishes and relishes can also help to make club provisions more acceptable to the educated palate.

(Turn over)

TACTICAL CONSIDERATIONS

ON THE MOVE[1]

"One is always nearer by not being still."

Introductory Lesson L588

There is something in the nature of communal oil-propelled vehicles which breeds instant irresponsibility in all but the most seasoned traveller. The very thought of moving seems to bring out the Monkey or the American in the lowest sort of Englishman. This poor wretch will either imagine himself loose in a jungle or at some such God-forsaken place as South Bend, Indiana or flat out on the Western Plain, kicking off a yard of road each time the motor fires, as if his half instinct were half true that dust, noise and a jagged jarring of the brain wholly spring from the New World.

For this Six-Pack Kid solace sings round the trucker's tyre from Tucson to Albuquerque, Phoenix to Idaho; on the road, in the land of the drug-store drunk, the cold-eyed guy who gasses up, buckles meaning in his belt, as if it could be really so.

Life is not made for smuggling beers aboard; it is not a fleeting spectre full of din and desperation, devoid of meaning. It is Man's Mortal Journey and he should end it heroically, in a noble bed of epic size, not scraped into a lurid heap on some common wayside verge, which can happen soon enough if the driver is disturbed.

Gentlemen will, naturally, keep the tightest rein on high spirits for it is their foremost duty to see that the party proceeds with dignity and decorum. Because babies, juveniles, children and minors are sometimes allowed on board, their task is doubly difficult. The player can greatly assist by observing correct seating procedures (Fig. 89) and by behaving in an English manner. In this way order will be maintained.

Regulation R904 (C3)
Proper Seating Arrangements for Ladies, wives and women

Ladies will be ushered to the rear of the saloon and invited to choose their seats, observing the Ministry of Transport regulations for axle weight limits applicable to the vehicle. Later, children will be spread among the women to distribute weight evenly. By this time the officers and men will have taken their place at the front of the coach according to their club seniority.

---

[1] "Man, you gotta go."

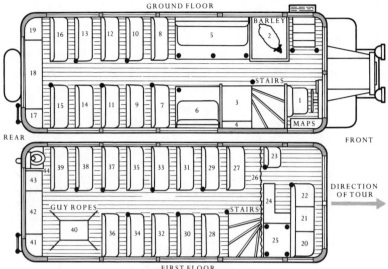

Fig. 89: *Seating in the charabanc.*

Downstairs: 1. Driver 2. The Mascot 3. The Kit 4. The First Aid Kit/Pail 5/6. players' spouses 7/8. Guest players 9–14. players 15/16. juveniles 17. Tour Navigator 18. Mascot Officer 19. Weather Officer

Upstairs: 20. Club President 21. B.A.C. Inspector/Club Informer 22. Club Chairman/ Dignitaries 23. Valet 24. Cocktail cabinet 25. Storage area 26. Curtain 27. Secretary 28. Fixtures Secretary 29. Captain 30. Vice-captain 31. Senior Gentlemen 32–35. Gentlemen 36. Treasurer 37. Keeper of the Kit 38. First Aid Officer 39. Catering Officer 40. The Hamper 41. Caterer 42. Other officers 43. Latrines officer 44. Lavatory.

Regulation R905 (C4)

Suitable Pastimes for the Relief of Boredom

On long journeys it is often the case that the endless fields passing by the window will have a soporific effect on the company who will fall into a laxity, thence to an apathetic somnolence and finally will be overtaken by the dark lapping waves of a devastating sleep. This must be prevented at all costs, for it is the wakeful who enjoy life.[1]

To stimulate dull and somnifluent minds and to arouse them from retardedness and perplexity a full programme of indoor games suitable for charabanc journeys shall be entered into playfully, especially when the company glides past ugly scenes[2] and through Counties like Lincolnshire.

[1] Rip van Winkle was notorious because he slept long and deep. He may well have lived to a ripe old age, but there is no indication that he enjoyed his life, having been asleep for the greater part of it and having missed one hundred of his allotted years, thus earning for himself little more than the distinction of having been old and wrinkled for a longer period than Malcolm Muggeridge.

[2] Not to be confused with Ugly Scenes.

185

(Turn over)

1. TWENTY-FIVE QUESTIONS

The extra five questions are allowed under Academy Regulations to forestall the modern practice of swearing that a question was a "re-cap" or summary. Good subjects for this game, which avoid all ambiguity about their origin as animal, vegetable or mineral are as follows:

1. *(Animal)* A dromedary, *a dromedary;*
2. *(Vegetable)* A potato, *a potato* (for players),
    An artichoke, *an artichoke* (for Gentlemen);
3. *(Mineral)* iron ore, *iron ore* (players),
    Silver, *silver* (Gentlemen)

Abstract items, like a Picasso, *a Picasso*, may be chosen but these are not recommended by the Academy, as they often perplex the dull mind, *the dull mind*, and cause protests, Ugly Scenes,[1] and scuffles as well as verbal exchanges not conducive to good fellowship.

2. I SPY

This evergreen game never wanes in popularity and will persist as long as there is an England. It will excite the imagination of the travelling company and it invites them all to take notice of their surroundings, encouraging the young and old alike to observe the wider world outside the coach window.

FOR PLAYERS		FOR GENTLEMEN	
A	Apple core, arson.	A	Artillery, Aston Martin.
B	Breakdown vehicle, blowlamp.	B	Burial mound (Iron Age or Saxon).
C	Cat, cheap tin tray.	C	Cumulo-nimbus clouds.
D	Dripping, ditch, dungheap.	D	Dendrochronology.
E	Effluent, eczema, East Enders.	E	Elephant, enormous anthill.
F	furry caterpillar, fork (pitch).	F	Foxhunting, Forestry Commission.
G	Garage assistant.	G	Grouse, goose, gun.
H	Hairy motorcyclist.	H	High quality grocers.
I	Indecent exposure.	I	Iron Age mound (or Saxon), Inns of Court.
J	Jarrow, junk yard.	J	Jacuzzi, Jaguar.
K	Kneecap, knocker, knapweed.	K	Knight of the Garter.
L	Lawn clippings, loafer.	L	Lapis lazuli.
M	Mangel worzel, Midlands.	M	Mound (Iron Age or Saxon).
N	Narrow path, Notting Hill	N	Newmarket, Nautical insignia.
O	Optional extra, oil stain.	O	Ostrich, osteopath.
P	Pigeon, pipe (sewer or drain), prison.	P	Partridge, pastures (green), palace, peacocks.
Q	Quantity of stolen goods, quart pot, quarry (mineral).	Q	Queen, Quintin Hogg, quail, quarry (animal).
R	Recidivist, rake.	R	Rifle range, RAF fighter.
S	Surgery, steel toecap, school (comprehensive).	S	Snipe, school (public), sauceboat (Red Anchor Chelsea).
T	Tow rope, troublemakers, Two Rivers (Billy).	T	Tea (Lapsang Suchong), Turbot (Grilled).
U	Unwanted gift, undertaker.	U	Underbelly, Upper Heyford.
V	Vandal, vicious dog.	V	Victoriana, veal and ham pie.
W	Waste tip, workhouse.	W	Watermill, woodcock.
X	X-rays.	X	Xylophone, xenophobe.
Y	Youths.	Y	Yacht (over 30ft).
Z	Zulu, Zambian.	Z	Zebra.

[1] Not to be confused with ugly scenes.

Regulation R907 (C3)
Coping with Infant Orifices and the Proper Control of Bodily Functions in women and the elderly

What a corrupt thing is the human when all that emerges from within him is so vile and unpleasant.

Cricketers will find themselves assaulted by nearby mewling and puking of infants, flatulence, diarrhoea, dribbling and incontinence of the elderly and sudden eruptions of all kinds after 5 miles of travelling (on C roads) 9 miles (on B roads) or 15 miles (on A roads).

Children must never be allowed to eat on the journey as this will cause travel sickness and unpleasantness. The dire combination of penny arrows, sherbet dabs, humbugs, bull's eyes, barley sugars, nut brittle, ice cream, toffee apples, milky bars, flying saucers, liquorice pipes, lollipops, potato chips, raspberryade, aniseed balls, acid drops and pineapple chunks and the irregular motion of the carriage will inevitably end in vomiting.

Offending children should be summarily extricated from the vehicle at a convenient place and threatened with lifelong abandonment for as long as the nausea continues. When it abates a good box on the ears will satisfy the infant's craving for attention of which this is often a symptom. Old people or female offenders should be excluded from taking further part in the tour.

Lesson L591
Philosophical notes on Road Travel past and present and on the Rheumatic Road System

There was a time when to drive through the country lanes was a pleasant experience. Farmworkers would wave friendly from the fields, and petroleum was pumped by the horny hand of a cheery chap whistling as he worked. But now on the fields there are no labourers. They are sullenly at home, on the dole, or watching television.

And long ago has departed the amicable Automobile Association man who would salute respectfully from his yellow motorcycle. No, much that was good is gone, we have arrived at the *socialist utopia* where all employed persons have transport and are free to move around the countryside willy nilly, thereby blocking the roads and fouling the atmosphere, and making passage difficult for those with Important Missions and Essential Journeys.

Alas it is easy to forget that the roads are now past all endurance: all the serenity is overtaken by sweat and swearing, hot tempers and hot seats, agony, misery, discord, hatefulness, beastliness and all manner of conflict. To progress from one milestone to the next without violent incident is become the chief challenge for today's traveller.

187

(Turn over)

What a time it was when the dappled silence of leafy lanes was shattered only by the single heartbeat of a long stroke[1] Norton (Fig. 90), perhaps the fluffy purr of the Brough Superior, or a Riley or Wolseley sweeping by with the smell of hot oil, leather and fresh ground coffee.

Fig. 90: *The Nortonic Fleet*

In accordance with the Chairman's "Buy British" directive a large fleet of powerful motorcycles of quality has been assembled. Naturally none of these are of post-war origin. They are used by Academy dispatch riders, and No 367 is seen here arriving at an important address with papers and reports.

Regulation R908 (C3)
Correct driving methods and Cornering techniques

The driver's main duty during transit is to ensure the integrity of the hamper and passengers. Their fragile nature and mutability[2] dictate that they be carried inside the charabanc to avoid overheating. The hamper must be firmly secured and, using its known weight, the gravitational stresses on the guy ropes can be calculated for various cornering speeds. The Academy's simple chart will be helpful. It will therefore be the personal duty of all travellers to ensure that the driving speed should be dignified and sedate.

---

[1] 97 × 100mm.

[2] "Human man ain't much more than a big blood blister, one good squeeze and he's gone."

Anything over 35 m.p.h. is unseemly and will be seen to be synonymous with poor planning or "rushing",[1] which is often associated with doom or disaster. However, a warning must be made that creeping along the kerb is just as great an offence as speeding. Parking is, in most places, an offence.[2]

Regulation R909 (C1)
Improper mechanically induced noises and Highway Etiquette
No member of any team may skid around corners (Fig. 91) or screech to a halt on any road in England.

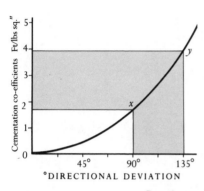

°DIRECTIONAL DEVIATION

Fig. 91: *Notes for drivers on centrifugal force,* Vehicles should not go fast around corners. Using the relationship of speed to mass (under the precept of constant weight distribution) the driver should be able to calculate the vectors for the hamper's escape velocity and degree of nausea for specific road curvature. Conversely where counter stress poundage must remain constant he can forecast maximum vehicular velocity curves for directional deviations between 90 (x) and 135 (y) degrees.

Regulation R911 (C4)
Route Singing: Musical diversions on board the Charabanc
If it is strictly controlled, singing on the charabanc can be great fun indeed, for it gives to all a sense of community, a shared purpose and a companionship engendered by no other activity. But there is a danger of which cricketers should be aware. Music can be the sound of the Devil stoking up his fires, for nothing seems to encourage a greater sense of abandon and propensity for riotous drinking than a few ill-placed songs. At the mere semi-quaver of an unauthorized tune the offender should be extricated and turfed off the coach: under no circumstances should travellers tolerate songs involving German officers, airmen who need to be scraped from the tarmac like a lump of strawberry jam, nor any other

---

[1] People do not *rush* into bliss and contentment, they do not fall over each other to get into Heaven. No, like lemmings, it is always towards an unknown doom that the human race speeds. Many have achieved speedy dismissals, but are never known to rush into a Double Century. All things must be approached calmly and with decorum. Rush and hurry are symptoms of the influence of limited-over cricket and the twentieth century, both of which are only, and forthwith, to be condemned.

[2] For Pedestrians, too, moderation is likewise recommended, for walking fast is deemed to be *acting suspiciously* and walking slowly may be interpreted as *loitering with intent*. Standing still constitutes the offence of Obstructing the Pavement.

(Turn over)

bawdy, violent or obscene incident, nor any song depicting women, virgins and landlords' daughters.

The company should be given a brief voice training, with the emphasis upon the need to express words clearly (not as is at present the fashion among the young who will so mumble and squawk[1]). It behoves the singer too, to sing in time with the music so that both lyrics and melody finish together and have a musical effect.

The projection of the music and song (Fig. 92) should be loud and hearty, with conviction and gusto. No person with a mouth organ will be allowed on the coach.

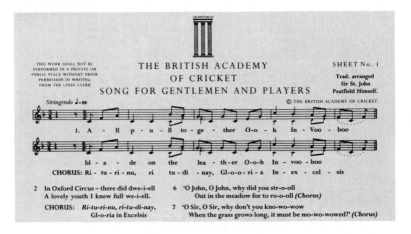

Fig. 92: *The British Academy of Cricket Batting Song*
All sing-songs should include a few choruses of this stirring piece. It helps to inculcate a merry jolliness in the party as a whole and it excites the emotions of comradery and team spirit in individual members. Song sheets are available from Academy House. No humming.

Lesson L597
Likely causes of Road Accidents

Road accidents are generally caused by Bank Holidays. So it is wise to choose an alternative date for road travel.

Speed is the great killer. In the 1940s vehicles were so slow that the major cause of violent death was war. Now roads are a major cause of premature death.

---

[1] The scourge of the so-called "pop" record, has coincided with changed eating habits. Lack of dietary fibre has given rise to constricted bowels, and endowed this music with characteristic strained tones (certain controlled drugs, illegal substances and opiates also assist in this). There would be less "pop" music if more were eaten in the way of fresh fruit and vegetables.

Regulation R914 (C3)
Animals and other Foreign Bodies,
and initial responses to an Unscheduled Accident

Dogs, cats, rabbits, hedgehogs and rooks have little road sense and often carry out their manoeuvres without due care and attention. Irresponsible drivers often make unrehearsed deviations to avoid animals or birds. This is misguided sentiment. A minor adjustment to the steering wheel will ensure that the creature is thoroughly squashed.[1] Sudden braking can *disturb* a Chablis and *destroy* a Claret.

Moles suffer from myopia which affects their eyesight. Therefore they are not difficult to squash. Chickens, as is well known, often cross the road to get to the other side; and this they do for many reasons, one of which appears to be to commit suicide by squashing. In the event of an accident involving people, the party should continue its journey to avoid congestion, and to avoid the ugly burden of apportioning blame.

Lesson L599
Notes on the Recognition of Mechanical Failure

Mechanical breakdown is often signalled by a slowing down of the vehicle followed by an unscheduled halt. This will cause great delight among children and passengers but, for the driver, it is No Laughing Matter. Unseemly pushing of vehicles to places of safety is often the only remedy.

The modern four-stroke engine, with its multiple cylinders and moving pieces, is well understood by the Academy, but for the ordinary cricketer it is best left be. The following chart gives some rudimentary technical details:

SYMPTOM		SOLUTION
Level I	Clinking and squeaking	Old stocking
	Knocking and whirring sounds	Garter/suspender/braces
Level II	Rattling and clanking	Spanner
	Coughing and spluttering sounds	Shoe lace/hair grip
Level III	Scraping and grinding	Leave to cool
	Hissing and bubbling sounds	Piece of wire
	Clunking and jerking	Hammer
	Smoke or Silence	Taxi/walk

Punctures should be dealt with at the scene of the occurrence, but it must be remembered that no wheel should be removed until the vehicle has been thoroughly raised from the road with a device known as a jack.

---

[1] Swans are an exception. They are the Queen's birds and are thus entitled to proper treatment. They are dignified creatures (except in April–May) and are certainly not deserving of injury or of being rudely squashed at the wheels of a Coachload of Commoners.

(Turn over)

THE MOVABLE FEAST

"On the cool, flowery lap of earth,
Smiles broke from us and we had ease."

Introductory Lesson L606

Rural sights and sounds, when all nature is alive and gay in the glad summer time, have a genial effect on Gentleman and player alike. Many declare it the summit of human felicity to recline in some melodious plot and, liberally supplied with veal patties, to imbibe the wonders of God's creation. Whether by the banks of a sallow-trimmed brook or down by the ash grove, the cricketer will find leisure to contemplate the moving spirit of the game.

Is not the earliest childhood joy the discovery that tea taken out-of-doors is delicious beyond all imagining? The confinement of four interior walls imprisons the genius of taste, and all his buds wither on the branch, and shrivel, and die. The non-verbal functions of the human tongue are best exercised away from the dinner table where the Devouring of Pies can be done in open-air tranquillity. Certain it is that the language of taste goes direct to the stomach of man and defies definition in words.

Regulation R939 (C4)
Preliminary site reconnaissance for a Picnic

Some three weeks before the date set for the tour the caterer will receive from the Catering Officer a brief note indicating the size and type of picnic required. A suitable site with ash and willows will be located so that, when the charabanc stops, the company will themselves discover its beauty. The caterer, perhaps unschooled in topography, must seek out and consult with a rustic (Fig. 93) of the chosen locality.

A picnic site will generally possess any three of the following: A spreading oak, a Chestnut Tree, all generous waters, Tintern Abbey, the noble Thames' sylvan banks, a bull and bush, fields laid out like parking lots, Grantchester, soft refreshing rain, the sound of music, eidelweiss, corn as high as an elephant's eye, a place in the sun, winding mossy ways, and a winnowing wind or granary floor.

Damp patches and unauthorized digging can be troublesome. Children should be thoroughly dried before the picnic commences, and all remaining moles killed.

Fig. 93: *A rustic consultation.*

Outlying parts of rural districts abound with rustics garping from roadsides and pushing bicycles. For a small sum such a person will locate a site of scenic quality and prepare and tend it in the interim period. He must be instructed to mow the grass and eradicate all moles. Using approved shovelling techniques he should remove all excremental deposits. To assist in this he should be provided with a faeces recognition chart (Fig. 93b). Class One rustics of this calibre should not be sought for they are of limited benefit to the cricketer. So wrapt are they in abstruse agricultural thoughts and horticultural dialectic that ordinary communication with these Fellows is impossible. A Class Two rustic (93c) will prove more helpful.

(Turn over)

Regulation R941 (C1)
Problems with moles

A subterranean scourge, the mole is black with a pointed nose and must be mortally discouraged. An avid destroyer of subsoils, his pleasure is to throw up heaps of dirt, disfiguring the turf with ghastly blemishes. The excellent range of British Academy of Cricket proprietary remedies may be used but are difficult to administer: it is to his underground lair that the war (Fig. 94) must be carried.

Fig. 94: *Mole eradication*

Cruel metal traps should be shunned: the mole is too cunning to be taken by such devices. Humane mole dispersal is preferred. A three-pronged strategy of worm, fork and basin, should be used to dispose of moles. First, worms should be caught, using the fork to reveal their hiding places beneath the ground: they should be ripe but firm and not too moist. A selection of sizes (inset) will tempt the palate of the mole. Again using the fork, the basin should be sunk into his underground thoroughfare. When the mole has descended the slippery slope to captivity he may, at a safe distance from the site, be stabbed to death humanely, again with the fork, or poisoned according to taste.

Regulation R943 (C2A)
The Spreading of the Food

All cricketers shall, without exception, watch as the hamper is unpacked. For this is the pinnacle of picnicking pleasure. The hamper is the centre point of the picnic and therefore of supreme importance. The unpacking ceremony, eagerly anticipated on all sides, will be a major spectacle and also, it is to be hoped, a performance of dramatic art. If it is to succeed the Caterer will have packed the hamper with great care and skill, inserting the provender in regular strata. Any failure to adhere to the approved methods will end in breakage, spoilage and disappointment, as this Cornucopia turns into a Pandora's box, to the unmitigated dismay of the whole company.

It is not necessary always to include the best club china or plate on such occasions. Except when important guests are present, an ordinary set of Wedgwood Corinthian is adequate. Printed blue and white pottery of Victorian date should never be used, it is vulgar. Moulded glass, not the club crystal, should be pressed into service, for often, in the high-spirited atmosphere of a picnic, valuable items may become casualties of the company's good humour.

Lesson L609
The Selection of Food

Food should be of the simple and wholesome kind. Some may be tempted, but there is scant wisdom in forsaking the Academy's digestive hygiene drills in the pursuit of an isolated orgy of misguided gluttony. It is pleasant, therefore to take all things home-made;[1] there are many reputable retailers who will supply all that is needed. A typical picnic for July–August might include: cold Loch Fyne salmon, lobsters, either prepared with salad or mayonnaise or with tomatoes and cucumbers separately, white fish, cold roast beef, shoulder of lamb, roast fowls, Aylesbury ducks, ham, pressed tongue, beefsteak, veal patties,[2] jams, jellies, marmalade, pigeon pies, stewed fruit, strawberries, cream, college puddings (Oxford or Cambridge only), blancmange, and Bath olivers. Players will have a right to expect a Minimum Cricketing Tea (M.C.T.) (see *Reg. R801*).

Lesson L610
The Selection of Drink

The picnic is an occasion for contemplation, when statistics may be recollected in tranquillity. This will be greatly enhanced if suitable wines[3] are selected. A few crates of '39 claret or light Chablis of '47 are acceptable, and travel well. Bottled English beer is an heavy and awkward commodity but, if it can be taken, it will find appreciation among the players and their women. These people will also make heavy demands upon the tea urn which should be kept always full, for while tea is liberally supplied there will be only a modified clamour for alcoholic drinks and a reduction in Ugly Scenes and Scuffles.

[1] A list of approved suppliers, purveyors of fine Cakes and Pastries, game dealers and Pork Butchers is available from the Academy on request.

[2] Veal patties benefit by being no more than 11 days old.

[3] It is no longer necessary these days to provide Champagne for every occasion and, indeed, this would be regarded now as showy or ostentatious at most informal gatherings.

 (Turn over)

Regulation R944 (C3)
Pests

All God's creatures are delighted equally by the prospect of a picnic meal, and legion are those that lie in wait for the hamper. Gentlemen and players will find themselves under constant attack. All members have a part to play and should commit to memory the following facts on pests and their control.

Dogs are ever ready to plunder. Copious threats and abuse, directed through the scorer's loudhailer will generally discourage them. Clubbing should be a last resort.

Sheep will, until they themselves are eaten, eat almost anything, so catholic is their appetite. Particular attention should be paid to keeping from their gaze fresh salads and vegetables. Napkins should be taken along for this purpose.

Sparrows (Fig. 95) are very cunning and normally raid only the remnants of the feast. However, bolder sorts may intrude; children should be encouraged to find sport in disposing of these with well-aimed pebbles.

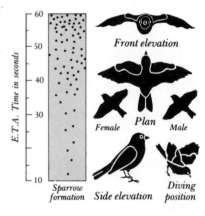

Fig. 95: *The Hazards of Sparrow Attack and Effective Counter-measures.* The loss of picnic foodstuffs to these agile pests can be minimized by pre–emptive recognition of attack formations. These begin with lone reconnaissance sorties of the bolder types (Fig. 95a) which are quickly followed by dense, low level formations (Fig. 95b). Armament: 8mm beak, 2 × 6mm feet each with 4 × 2mm claws, 1 × 18mm stomach. The Hedge Sparrow is not a *passer passer* like the House Sparrow. It is not even a *passer*, it is a gentle well-mannered bird and will respond to mild shooing.

Insects pose the greatest threat of all. Constant undisciplined flailing at flying sorts should be minimized: it is an unedifying spectacle and as tiresome as the depredations of the airborne attackers themselves. The cricketer must simply endure them stoically.

The insect kingdom also threatens with the relentless assault of the earthbound infantry in the form of ants. These black devils should be carefully collected in a jar, and killed. Scalding hot water from the tea urn will usually subdue them. Alternatively, as sport for the little ones, red ants may be mingled with a nest of black ones. The ensuing slaughter always provides an entertaining diversion.

Bulls will often put a whole party to flight. Tactical retreat should not be allowed to become a graceless rout and an orderly withdrawal is called for. Although contemplative in appearance, bulls are seldom open to reasoned persuasion, especially when in motion. Like all small landowners they have a highly developed sense of Trespass and often take unbridled offence at picnickers who attempt to share their pastures.

Regulation R945 (C1, C2A or C4)
Excess Alcohol Ingestion on the journey, and the Problem of Rowdiness

The sudden appearance of loose or unstructured conversation is the first sign that alcohol is doing its work and therefore this should be avoided. The Gentleman will be heard boasting of some wager he has won, or when he last played at the Oval. Players will choose more extreme methods of expressing drunkenness, often singing songs about vicars' daughters and lifting the skirts of any females (Fig. 96) present. This obscene act will be accompanied by whoops, squeaks and giggles from the women. Ladies should be shielded from such unfitting displays.

Rowdiness of this type should be avoided, for it is certain to end with the hamper quite broken open and its contents plundered. There is nothing so adept as alcohol at creating in the human breast (or more exactly in the human testicles and stomach) an insatiable desire for sexual activities and enormous quantities of food.

A half-starved, drink-crazed mob baying for the Hamper is a frightening and ugly sight indeed, and it is only an inbred authority instilled over many generations that can check its progress. It is at such times that troublemakers will take the opportunity to challenge the Authority of Gentlemen. They should have their names taken and be told to sit down.

Fig. 96: *Females and the Summer Tour.* It is sometimes the case that females need no encouragement to display their nether limbs. This picture clearly shews all that is ugly about squeaking and giggling. This occurs when stout bottles are broken open and fall into the hands of females. Blackpool, sandy beaches, bingo and deck chairs bring out the worst in a certain class of woman.

What follows scenes like this is a deeper degradation. When darkness falls, players of poor breeding will, for their own ends, be quick to ply such women with reachy kisses and grease their lips with fish and chips.

(Turn over)

IN CAMP

*"The out-of-doors man must always prove
the better in life's contest."*

Introductory Lesson L611

*The outdoor life (Fig. 97), the sounds and smells of the countryside, how they
conspire to create that well-being which is the birthright of the English.
But pleasure unalloyed is mere Hedonism. To enhance his moments of quiet
contemplation and ecstatic celebration of the Eternal Englishness of Things,
the Gentleman and player will have to suffer some of the spitefulness that
nature's darker side offers to the hale and the hearty who would meet her on her
own ground. Nature, for all her sweets and twinèd flowers, is now a Maid,
now a Shrew according to her whim. She will ever chasten the cock-sure with a
nettle sting, a breathed-in fly, or a woodcock that will upward fly when a gun is
not nearby, a flock of pigeons when the powder's running low. But there is
nothing nearer Heaven than to pitch a camp in Devon or to spend a day in
Brockdish where the tourists never go.*

Fig. 97: *Survival techniques for the Out-of-doors Man*

Life in and around camp provides an excellent opportunity for Mr Bowles to prove himself
the better in life's contest. Few would doubt it, for he is well-known for his prowess in field
and fell, moor and mountain, spending most weekends in remote areas pushing himself to the
limits of his endurance. He is also consultant in fish psychology to Her Majesty's Armed
Forces. He demonstrates here that it is possible to catch fish using improvized equipment.
There is no delight purer, no pursuit more profound, and no challenge so readily answered
by the Englishman as that of catching a fish. Ancient is the battle of wits between the roach
and the rod, the perch and the pole. The issue of intellectual supremacy is yet unsettled.

So deeply ingrained is it in the spirit of the pike that he should strike the spoon and
spinner, or in the trout to try the dry fly, that this offers an inducement to a particular kind
of Englishman. Such a one will have a quick eye and a brain the equal of any fish, and a mind
provoked to a pastoral frenzy at the thought of pulling half fishdom wriggling from its watery
lair, hooked about the mouth or eye with Sheffield Steel.

Mr Bowles was the first to identify the two basic brain forms and lifestyles in fish,
epitomized in the following examples.

Type A: *The Roach* when he is young will snatch and gobble, for the knave knows he will be
returned to the river. The older fish at the bait will suck and mumble. For him no float
flickers and no ripples run. Only the Master Angler can detect his presence: it is betrayed by
the subtle but immense Aura of Inactivity which surrounds him wherever he goes. Thus he is
a Gentleman among fish.

Type B: *The old Pike* is a loiterer and a scavenger for his food. His days of the short poem,
the chase and the Dealing of Death are over and he becomes more reflective, often
attempting a world record for weight and size. He may be taken in the deepest place with
deadbait and a leaded trace. Cutlets should be about one inch thick, floured and fried.

Fig. 97: *Survival techniques for the Out-of-doors Man*

199

(Turn over)

Lesson L615
The need for Properly Constructed Latrines and Correct Techniques for their use

Most old Scouts will be familiar with this time-honoured means of waste disposal. The details (Fig. 98a and b) need not be repeated here in great detail. But a reverend attitude towards the construction of latrines is a must for the modern cricketer, for the latrine is the highest gift that our civilization has donated thus far to a diseased world. Polio, typhus, dysentery and cholera germs (Fig. 98c) are all quite powerless in the face of the ordinary latrine. For this reason, before any member is moved to urinate, a proper latrine shall be constructed. Rearing, fronting and vomiting may then all take place hygienically.

Gentlemen should never become involved in the Digging of the Pits,[1] but they may care to oversee work from time to time and offer helpful advice in correct shovelling techniques using the Academy latrine shovel (Fig. 98d). It is axiomatic that all latrines be well disinfected[2] before use and sited downwind of the Gentlemen's and Officers' Mess. For this purpose a compass is a useful instrument.

Regulation R956 (C2A)
Post-Toilet Blotting and Wiping Drills

These shall be executed at all times with three deft upward, not downward, motions to minimize the broadcast of germs. The procedure should be followed using three sheets of a proprietary brand of specialist paper, not newsprint. Use one side of the paper only. The easily remembered Wykehamist Formula: "One up, one down and one to polish" is correct ideologically in its economy of paper, but inappropriate in technique.

Regulation R957 (C3)
Special notes on Defecating
Dogs and children, with a Section for Ladies

Dogs and children wishing to use the latrines should be accompanied by a responsible person aged over 18. Ladies should not be accompanied at all.

---

[1] The labouring classes have spent many thousands of years digging holes, mining, building tunnels, burying the dead, growing vegetables and messing about in the dirt, particularly in the Great War. The common man guards these Trencher Rights jealously and is sullenly suspicious of any Gentleman who picks up any tool of a digging sort.

[2] Microbes began the attack on man in the nineteenth century and this was continued into the early years of this century by germs. Now viruses lead the grim assault. Recognition will be assisted by the chart (98c) and lashings of Jeyes Fluid will undo even the most persistent.

Fig. 98a: *The Digging of the Pits.* What a great pity it is that the player embarks so grudgingly on a programme of latrine construction. Often coercion is the only remedy. This task provides therefore an excellent punishment detail for any player who offends against hairstyle regulations or appears unshaven or sloppily dressed.

Fig. 98b: *Cross section of the Western latrine.* When reduced to its simplest definition the latrine is nothing more than a hole in the ground. And for this reason none need be in awe of it. However a cleanly dug pit is a credit to any club, and a sharp latrine spade (d) should always be used.

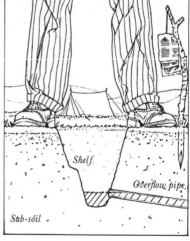

(d)

Fig. 98c: *Germ recognition.*

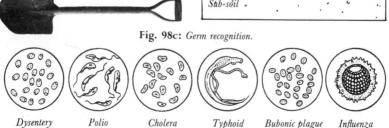

| Dysentery | Polio | Cholera | Typhoid | Bubonic plague | Influenza |

201

(Turn over)

Lesson L616
On the Importance of Knots in the Outdoor Life

Slack knot discipline and a neglect of tying techniques (Fig. 99) and rope training contribute to many of society's ills[1] including poor tent construction.

If the young were rigorously schooled in tying techniques there would be less unhappiness and crime in the world. Correct procedures will assist in the fight against undone shoelaces, stray dogs, spillage of parcel contents, the escape of prisoners, collapse of rope bridges, and unkempt rose bushes, all of which, to the shame of the nation, are on the increase in these dishevelled times.

The British Cricketing Knot

Fig. 99: *The British Cricketing Knot.* This general-use knot has been designed by the Research and Development Department for use in all cricketing situations. Take a length of rope and fold the left end under and round the right end. Create a loop and feed the right end, and then the left end, through. Push the left end back under the new loop, then back under the right end. Push the right end through the central loop created by winding the right end through the lower loop. Double back the right end and push it through the middle. **Note:** This ingenious self-releasing mechanism makes this knot unsuitable for the custody of criminals or the tethering of donkeys.

Regulation R958 (C1)
The control of Bestial Instincts at the campsite

Close contact with Nature has a calming effect on the Gentleman[2] and persons of refined sensibility. This is not the case with the coarse and the rude who sometimes quite forget their training and, as if three thousand years of serfdom had been but a daydream, revert to the wild state of untamed defiance and brutality at the mere touch of fresh air. It would be indelicate here to list the offences which can occur when Nature stirs the

---

[1] Notably the demise of hanging as a Proper Punishment for all Wrongdoers. It can be no coincidence that death by hanging fell off as the naval life of the nation, and the heyday of the sailing ship, declined along with the related skill of knot tying. And at the very same time Formal Slavery, the world's greatest consumer of knots, was abolished.

[2] Gentlemen may play at Nymphs and Shepherds provided that suitable privacy can be obtained and that players are prepared to lend their wives for this purpose. Innocent sportiveness and dalliance of this kind should not be entirely suppressed.

hormones of the labouring classes. Details of any offences should be recorded, with photographs, and sent to the Academy.

Regulation R959 (C4)
Suitable Pastimes, Rural Fun and Diversions for those encamped
God made little boys and girls different so that they could develop their cultures separately, partaking of the variety of Nature's offerings, each in their several ways. And around the camp what a delight they will be, shrieking, whooping as they romp and play.

FOR THE MEN:
Tent security will be the major concern, to wit, the prevention of theft and the apprehension and punishment of wrongdoers.

A substantial container (a safe is adequate) should be installed in the President's tent and all valuables, special foods and vintage wines should be stored therein.

Security of tents is achieved by means of a strong padlock applied to the automatic step-over-step self-locking mechanical securing device colloquially referred to as a "zip fastener". Members should be on the look-out for those who have failed to take this simple precaution. Loafers and shirkers around camp should be identified as Prime Suspects.

FOR BOYS:
Nature rambles, wood collecting, stoning, birds nesting, catapulting, stick fights, butterflying, the making of whistles, Sparrow Funerals, acorn guns (Fig. 100), worms, woodlice tournaments, spider races. Fun with Frogs, sandcastles, bows and arrows, seeking.

Fig. 100: *The hand-held Acorn gun*
The high muzzle velocity of this pump action device makes it an excellent weapon for long-range mischief. Only the choicest plumpest ammunition should be used. The elongated acorn of the Turkey Oak, as shown here, provides Class A ammo, but English Acorns may be pressed into service, as may girls who are Nature's natural targets.

(Turn over)

FOR GIRLS, WOMEN, WIVES AND LADIES:
Hiding, daisy chains, weddings, pressing wildflowers, hospitals, skipping, and mud pies.

Some flowers have unpleasant associations and should not be picked. Therefore the Academy has issued the following guidelines on woodland and wayside practice and picking drills.

Approved: Perennial Centaury, White Bryony, Fat Hen, Duke of Argyll's Tea Tree, Meadowsweet, Self Heal, Heartsease, Feverfew, Meadow Sage, Penny Royal, Roast Beef plant, Monkshood, King Cup, Lords and Ladies, Thrift, Mind-your-own-Business, Green Field Speedwell, Upright Vetch, Jack-by-the-Hedge, Everlasting Pea, Shepherd's Rod, Hound's Tongue.

Unapproved: Dog's Mercury, Stinking Hellebore, Common Duckweed, Bladderwort, Jack-go-to-bed-at-Noon, Black Bryony, Lousewort, Quaking Grass, Lady's Petticoats, Lady's Bedstraw, Lady's Smocks, Lady's Fingers, Nipplewort, Creeping Jenny, Mother of Thousands, Common Vetch, Dropwort, Spineless Hornwort, Japanese Knotweed, Scottish Lupin, American Willow Herb, Russian Thistle, Welsh Poppy.

Lesson L629
On Suitable Cooking Arrangements
What an indolent parcel of rogues make up the French nation! It was they who conceived the idea that camping should be made easy with convenient heating devices run on gas. The French have quite banished from camp sites the Primus Outfit which, when pumped, was a cunning device for burning paraffin, grass, acorns and fingers. This has now disappeared, thanks, no doubt, to the supremacy of the Common Market Camping Policy.

The French seem to have quite forgotten that a simple fire sufficed to decimate the Spanish Armada in 1588, to burn down half of London in 1666, and that Joan of Arc (herself a Frenchwoman) considered it quite adequate to establish her career as a martyr and launch herself into Eternal Sainthood. Surely it can be argued that a simple fire will serve in our time to cook a few pots of gruel and boil some potatoes?

Regulation R960 (C3)
The lighting of the Flame, Pan Care, cutlery and furniture
A simple fire, then, should be constructed[1] and lit using the time-honoured devices,[2] and cauldrons should be suspended over it.

---

[1] A fire may be defined as a fire even before it be lit provided it be an assembly of combustible materials stacked in a readily inflammable pile, or in a criss-cross fashion or in any way which suggests, or is evocative or reminiscent of, smoke, coughing, scalding or spitting, crackling and matches.

[2] Matches.

Utensils should be kept clean and free from dried tomato sauce. Morsels of grass in frying pans should be ignored. Dirt is an unwelcome intrusion but it can be considered unpatriotic not to eat one's share of this.[1] Because of the proliferation of the American Disease it is wise not to share cutlery.

A dining table should always be provided. Squatting on one's haunches may be suitable for attendance at the latrine but it is an undignified way for an Englishman to eat his victuals.

Regulation R962 (C4)
Anecdotage and the importance of anecdotes and the spinning of yarns around the camp fire

In former times, long ago, before values became traditional, and Days were still Old and Good, there was time to spare for light relief, adventure and historical events (Fig. 101). So, for the purposes of these campfire yarn-spinnings, the company should include two or three elderly persons, who can be relied upon for a feast of fibs, a regalia of reminiscence, dauntless doses of derring-do, time-honoured tales and a gamut of good cheer, japes and jests.

Fig. 101: *The British Glory Reviv'd by Admiral Vernon who took Porto Bello with six ships only,* by *courage and conduct.* The Falklands Conflict itself hardly compares with this historic naval victory. In the eighteenth-century it gave people something to strike commemorative medals about when the news was, otherwise, very depressing. This particular example was once owned by William Pitt, but the Chairman is, nonetheless, willing to swap it for a similar one in mint condition. He would also be grateful to anyone able to inform him about where Porto Bello is, who gave it back again and to whom.

Regulation R963 (C3)
The Usefulness and Efficacy of campfire yarns in the Indoctrination of the Young and Ignorant

Both these classes of people will greatly enjoy the campfire entertainments. Each yarn should have a clearly defined moral precept that can be simply expressed and easily learned. Tales should vary in their complexity and ascend the scale of intellectual difficulty.

---

[1] One peck is generally reckoned to be the portion which is every Englishman's birthright.

(Turn over)

YARN ONE: This might concern a man who marries a woman with seven brothers. In the ceiling of the girl's home are stuck fast seven axes (the teller need not discuss how they came to be there[1] or why there are seven). Each brother laments in turn the danger that the axes offer to somebody entering the house, each imagining an even more fatal and gruesome injury than the last (this is generally a delight to the children). In the end the new husband has the idea of pulling out the axes so that they cannot fall, and everyone is grateful.

Moral: (For children) Sharp tools should not be left about the house.

(For adults) The most elementary solution is often the simplest.

YARN TWO: This might involve some play-acting on the part of the narrator as he relates the story of Jack, who is a charcoal burner in the forest. One day he is confronted by a ragged old man who asks if he will hide him from some noblemen who are his enemies and are searching for him nearby. Jack agrees to this and tells the noblemen that the beggar went the other way. (Children may here guess which way he went, and also point to the player who looks most like a beggar.) Many years later, the King, who was that very beggar, is watching the weekly executions of charcoal burners for tax offences when he recognizes Jack on the gallows. "Hang him high," says the King, "for he would shelter a beggar from capture by his superiors."

Moral: (For children) Never tell lies.

(For adults) Traitors and champions of fugitives and the poor must learn to take their proper punishment.

YARN THREE: This is based on Bertrand Russell's parable of the chicken. A farmer had a cockerel in a run at the end of his farmyard. He went to the run every night and rattled the bucket as he went. At this the chicken would run up and down the wire, because he knew that his tea (dinner) was on its way and his tummy would soon be full. Then, one night, the farmer came as usual, rattling his bucket. He wrung the cock's neck, put him in the bucket and took him away to eat.

Moral: (For children) You may get more than you expect, even if you expect something good, but it is more likely that you will get less, or at least something different from what you expect, so it is best not to expect anything, then at least you are not disappointed, until you get your neck wrung.

(For adults) Chickens should always be slaughtered when they are hungry because the crop is quite empty and this makes dressing the bird very much easier.

---

[1] It is a strange fact that the human appetite for make-believe is insatiable, unlike its grudging and intermittent hold on reality. Listeners effortlessly absorb and accept Illusion couched in the confines of a Tall Tale.

PART THE FOURTH
GRACEFUL EXITS

"The stores his long days may have won
Move nearer suffering and defeat;
And joy – he knows not where 'tis gone,
When life lags longer than is meet,
Till one Deliverer from all wrong
The unseen portal openeth,
Where lives no love, no lyre, no song,
Only the last thing, Death."

(Turn over)

PHASE ONE

RETIREMENT

"What though the radiance which was once so bright
Be now for ever banished from my sight,
Though nothing can bring back the hour,
Of glory in the grass, of splendour in the flower."

Introductory Lesson L649

The meanest house-cur will take himself off with his bone and bury it in his secret spot against a time of dearth and hardship. The bee stores up her honey in the golden comb, knowing she will have need of it by and by. The Ant "provideth her meat in the Summer, and gathereth her food in the harvest" and the little red[1] squirrel with his hoard of wal and hazel nuts knows that cold-bitten days are coming with frozen grass and hard circumstance when he may no longer romp and play in the greenwood.

But what a piece of work is man. With all nature's examples to guide him and an excellent range of pension schemes available, there will yet be found the person who makes no provision for his old age.

For some, it seems, the scented days of Youth will never cease. Not a thought is spared for the cold blast of life's winter which comes, at first as a chilled zephyr causing the slightest shudder, an ache in the arm or a chilly draught in the chest, a tiny tickling cough, and ends in a Mighty Gale of Mortality.

Sinews do stiffen and the years condemn, blood runs thin and cold; and the hot and moist humours of the human frame turn bitter chill and dry. Death will come kicking down the door to make his arrest, and the cage of flesh and bone will soon be in a furrow fast asleep.

Lesson L652

Suitable posts in Retirement and the Two Major Types of Old Age
1. Happy is the thrifty man: he will spend his declining years a picture of peace and contentment ready to release to the next generation all the stored up wealth that his responsible and industrious life, of sound investment and properties bought before the boom, has accrued. He will have his children and grandchildren[2], at his knee; and how they will hang upon each word, laugh with him at his jests, wait upon him lovingly, enjoy his recollections of past cricketing glories, and forget what should be forgot. This is the happy

[1] Grey squirrels should be shot.
[2] The Academy is in favour of the Family.

Englishman, all his highest aspirations quite fulfilled: such a man will make an excellent President for any club.

2. How wretched a picture can be painted of the man who has squandered his youth in promiscuity, gaming, recreation and loose living. All that is left to him are memories of *sins and enormities committed upon young females, orgies, sexual excesses and drunken lasciviousness, foreign travel, the ecstasies of opium and French cooking*. All this, when all is quite consumed, throws a bitter lees on the bottom of his spirit, a soul-pervading despair and an unending spite towards his fellow man. This old man, tottering under the weight of his years of depravity, his brow furrowed by the wicked blast of his careless life and eyes dimmed by self-abuse, with no hope of any peace beyond the grave, his heart hard and unthankful, his mind embittered by poverty and loneliness, will make excellent material for an Umpire.

Regulation R971 (C2A)
The Correct Moment for Retirement from the Game

The Sense of the Correct Moment and the spotting of an idea whose time has come is one of life's gifts. Sir Francis Drake chose the precise moment in history[1] to defeat the Armada, and Good Queen Bess executed Queen Mary of Scots before she could make any more mischief.

Timing, it is often said, is the most important thing in cricket. Life is no less important, and therefore the Gentleman should learn to know when it is time to withdraw. The great men of the past have always known when it was time to go: Keats at the age of 26, Thomas More before he could change his mind, and Reginald Heber in 1826.

It seems little indeed to ask of a Gentleman that he retire when his usefulness is in irreversible decline, without the need for a Notice of Termination. Failure to do so is a serious offence.

Lesson L653
The Symptoms and Tell-Tale Signs of Retirement Age

All cricketers should be on the look-out for these features after the age of forty has been reached:

WARNING SIGNS:

Tripping over children, doddering[2] involuntary dribbling, photograph albums, Arthur Askey/Al Read, anger at the price of bread, dropped balls, aversion to queuing, listening to clocks, kindness to dogs and children,

---

[1] 1588.

[2] A common symptom of this senile state is the surprise receipt of free pastries, including the British Academy of Cricket Summer Fruitcake for Social Functions.

 (Turn over)

purchase of a greenhouse, failure to finish the British Academy of Cricket Annual Cross Country Championship Race, outbreaks of reminiscence, hand signals, *Pot Black*, outings to Garden Centres, the Chairman's Christmas Gratuity (Fig. 102).

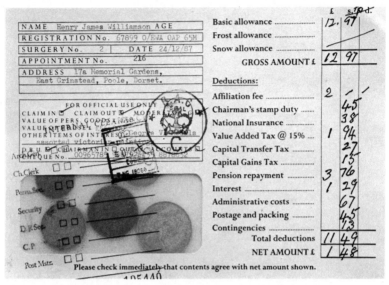

Fig. 102: *The Chairman's Christmas Gratuity for the Elderly*

Those wishing to apply for this allowance must comply with Statutory Regulations as set out in Para 287, Sub section 8 of Information Sheet Nº DS CH A33/ E46, and all applicants will be required to prove to the satisfaction of the Moderator General they possess property or savings not exceeding £200.

Each should present himself at Academy House on December 24 at 9 p.m. B.W.T. where the Governors will hold an audience and conduct-informal assessments. These loans are interest-free.

TERMINAL SIGNS

Stumbling, palsy, poor timing, slow movements, last at the Tea Urn, fits of temper, biliousness, slow healing of bones, wrinkling, loss of hair, falling down stairs, insolence from children, loss of drive/sweep/poke/pull, loss of hearing, loss of listening, cracked voice, codicils, aching limbs, feeling the cold, aversion to roads, *Mastermind*, eyes oozing amber and plum tree gum, mewling, puking, last sad grey hairs.

Failure to respond to these signs could result in the receipt of a Notice of Termination, informing the recipient of his retirement. This may be issued when performance on the field declines or when efforts at pitch preparation or bird scaring begin to diminish.

Lesson L655
Senility and the debilitating effects of sea air

A Gentleman or player may be deemed unsuitable even for the post of Umpire because of some dedication to golf, bowls, fishing or some other sport of the Aged, Senile and Infirm. The last kind act that a club can perform in these circumstances is to inform this Unfortunate of the dangers of Sea Air. Many elders or seniles think of retiring to the seaside, but are soon confined to Bathchairs or reliant on walking sticks. Finally, with the combined shock of giving up the Game, the loss of self-esteem and fighting spirit, the salt air and amusement arcades, the motivation and will to live declines and within a month or so the victim is gone.

Lesson L656
The Autumn Years, Retreat from Life and Preparation for Death

Long periods of depression often follow retirement. The endless poring over match reports from the forties and fifties; sudden tears, sleeplessness; spending of household monies on cricketing books to the great neglect of diet; untidy hair with partings which are not straight; listlessness and unkempt appearance; these are all signs that the end is near. But it should be remembered that nothing a man can lose by dying is half so precious as the readiness to die, which is man's charter of nobility.

Lesson L657
Antidotes to Depression and the Need for more Allotments

The consolations of old age, however, are legion for the Gentleman and player.

1. THE GENTLEMAN: In his armchair he should keep alive his intellectual faculties by writing choleric letters to the *Daily Express* or *Daily Telegraph* newspaper deploring the state of the nation and urging repatriation for undesirables. Another occupation, now that distance has lent enchantment to any mediocrity in his past life, might be the writing of memoirs.

In more lighthearted leisure moments he may choose to compose, for the annual competition, panegyrics[1] to the Chairman.

Attention to physical appearance should now be devoted entirely to the display of a venerable and wise unhappiness.

2. THE PLAYER: It is with the elderly player that the power of the English allotment is placed.

Something in the very nature of vegetables contributes to human well-

---

[1] Limericks will not do.

(Turn over.

being. There is about the vegetable an aura of peace, tranquillity and assurance that even wild flowers cannot match. The beneficence of the beetroot, the succulent serenity of celery, the pleasant pungency of a long leek, the delicate grace of a good gooseberry and the calm certainty of the cabbage have, since time immemorial, seen labourers through the hardest times.

Each village once had its temples to the Vegetable in the form of allotments. Each working man once had his own plot, his own little patch of greens, and in his leisure hours he whistled as he toiled contentedly. Unmindful of aching limbs he mused blissfully on the fruits and vegetables of his endeavours. These spiritual benefits need not be denied the Gentleman, who can also grow vegetables by the simple expedient of employing a gardener.

Lesson L658
The Psychological Importance of Sheds

The shed is a major comfort in old age, and it is an important resource in the fight against crime and unrest. The shed, replete with dusty things in boxes, mouse-chewed memorabilia, puncture repair tins with only the French chalk inside, cobwebs, candle stubs, bags of buttons, rusty nails (two inch and three inch) and hair grips, Whitworth spanners, blunt shears and motor car batteries will amuse the labourer for many hours (Fig. 103). These are some of his favourite things.

Idle hands will be kept busy shuffling these objects from one precarious spot to another and placing them in such a way that nothing can be moved without a major collapse and so that the door, once closed will not open, or once opened will not close.

Regulation R973 (C3, C2A)
The Drafting of a Will and the Making of Bequests

A cricketer may be too old to play or to take part in the active life of his club, but he may still serve it by bequeathing to the Academy his property and effects. The Academy will supply on request a standard form *gratis*. This provides a simple means whereby monies and property may be bequeathed by the Gentleman to the Academy by deed of Covenant.

The Gentleman is reminded that any valuable vase, chair or Georgian table left to the Academy may be inscribed with his name, and will be kept, as a memorial to it, for at least ten years after death. His name will also join those on the Roll of Honour.

Offerings of Victorian printed ware, or any hybrid porcelain of early nineteenth century date should not be made. Artificial porcelains up to 1820

Fig. 103: *The working man in his study.*

The shed is a great source of comfort to the poor man for it helps dispel the reality of having nothing by enabling him to keep everything, to the despair and sore annoyance of his wife. And it is to the shed that he flees when her anger overflows into womanly rhetoric. Thus it has a value out of proportion to its floorspace.

Once installed there with his newspaper he will fervently pursue his literary interests and defy all attempts to flush him out. Note: The shed should not be mistaken for the Class A covered latrine (inset), as this could quickly spread disease.

(Turn over)

are acceptable, but teawares shall exclude lustred items by William Bailey and W. Batkin and early Miles Mason, which are inferior.

No Victorian veneered furniture is permissible, with Sheraton period pieces the latest acceptable, and only then on the condition that the dovetailing is of high quality. Genuine William and Mary pieces (Fig. 104) are always well received irrespective of general condition.

Some paintings are a delight to the eye, but this does not include expressionist or impressionist works. No painting since 1860 has merit: all will be turned away by the Academy, with the offender punished. Vermeer, Hobbema, Gainsborough, Poussin, Claude, Constable and Brueghel will all be accepted at short notice (Fig. 105), but no Italians.

Pre-Victorian dwellings, properties and houses will be welcomed provided that they are in good repair and have no sitting tenants (Fig. 106). No bungalows. Council houses will be sold off. Any lands must be properly drained and free from hedges.

Fig. 104: *A genuine William and Mary piece.* Authentic walnut and boxwood desks of this kind are now becoming very valuable. Therefore each has to be labelled neatly (below) in readiness for cataloguing.

The maker's mark, in this case a snail (inset) carved as an integral part of a rear leg, is an indication of supreme quality and means that this piece was probably made for William III himself.

Jewellery and plate will be accepted only with proper authentication. No onyx, obsidian, agates or quartz (except very purple amethysts).

All monies given over to the Academy as part of a bequest should be neatly stacked in cloth bags with appropriate labels for ease of counting. Post-dated cheques should not be sent, as these will cause offence.

Players should send postal orders direct to the Treasurer's Dept.

Fig. 105: *An Academy Bereavements Officer takes possession of a special bequest.* For reasons of security an increasing number of the more valuable items bequeathed to the Academy are collected for cataloguing prior to their owner's death.

Fig. 106: *A pernicious form of outdoor tenancy.* Land clearance should be complete before bequests are made. Grasslands can suffer an outbreak of gypsies who have been, traditionally, a fungus on society, appearing like mushrooms overnight on meadows. Rumours that they were child stealers were often unfounded, for, as this delightful study portrays, they were eminently capable of producing their own.

215

(Turn over)

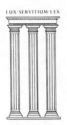

THE BRITISH ACADEMY
OF CRICKET
DEPARTMENT OF FUNERAL DIRECTION
FOR DECEASED CRICKETERS

Our Motto:

ἰν᾽ ἦν ζῶντες ἐκτήσαντο
εὐδοξίαν αὕτη καὶ τελευτηκόσιν αὐτοῖς ἀποδοθείη.

The above Department
is pleased to announce that a Fresh Consignment of
Hardwood Summer Coffins
*is newly arrived from the **West Indies** and may be inspected at*
our Chapel of Rest at Academy Headquarters.

There is also the following

GOOD NEWS FOR THOSE
ABOUT TO DIE

The sudden departure of a loved one can often result in grief. This sometimes leads to the complete mismanagement of catering affairs at the funeral breakfast.

Several days' advance warning will be needed if proper alternative arrangements are to be made by the British Academy of Cricket Funeral Service. Thereafter the whole funeral will be taken in hand and the deceased may rest assured that his will be done in accordance with British Standards Institute recommendations, with a grave of generous dimensions, and in any case not less than six feet in depth.

CLASS 3

The Economy Funeral for un-Registered players and ordinary staff will provide all that is needed for the unostentatious interment. It offers a plain but dignified ceremony, dispensing with the formalities of coffin and graveside prayers.

CLASS 2

The Standard Funeral is a more elaborate ceremony with a coffin for the deceased and cheese and tomato, cucumber and sardine sandwiches for the guests. This is followed by mixed fruit cakes, Victoria sponges, Danish pastries and Viennese whirls, assorted potato chips, vollyvons, cold sausages, things on sticks, gherkins, meat patties, tossed salad with English Dressing, bully beef, luncheon meat, cheese and biscuits, fresh fruit salad with fruits in season, Neapolitan ice cream and assorted Sorbays with wafers, Red Label tea and Wellington Brandy.

This funeral will serve well for the Registered player or the unRegistered Gentleman, the middle order bat, the stock bowler, or long serving Registered member of staff. The cleric officiating will cast earth upon the coffin after a short ceremony, and will deliver a speech at the graveside touching the Nature of Death and its necessary contribution to the advance and progress of Cricket. Appropriate psalms and economical prayers of medium length will be intoned by choir boys.

CLASS 1

The British Academy of Cricket De Luxe Obsequies for Gentlemen provide all that is fitting for the laying to rest of a fine cricketer and an upright man when he gains his ground for the last time.

An *after-dinner speaker* will be on hand to deliver encomiums and a panegyric upon the virtues and skills of the deceased; and a full programme of hymns, prayers and more hymns will be offered up from the graveside to introduce God to his new recruit.

Guests of Honour will be invited, and the coffin will be made of hand polished rosewood with ormolu handles in the rococo style. A solemn and dignified Union jack will be draped athwart the coffin before it is lowered into the grave to a 19-gun salute. Some 25 supplementary mourners will be employed, and after the interment there will be a banquet which will be a full Sit Down Knife and Fork Affair conducted in accordance with British Academy of Cricket regulations governing food, eating, queuing and the Precedence of Tables.

At the *conclusion of the ceremonies* solemn and patriotic music by Mozart, Bach and Beethoven will play. Popular traditional and rural folksongs are also available, with sea shanties and melancholy songs in keeping with the sad occasion. A recording of the Chairman of the British Academy of Cricket reciting his 'Ode to Death' will lend a terminal air of dignity. Telegrams from the Board of Governors will be read by the Priest-in-Charge.

The *food list shall* have, in addition to the comestibles provided for the standard funeral the following supplementary items: boiled hake, tomato purée, aubergines and avocado pears halved and stuffed, fresh pea salad, home made veal patties, game pie and beef pudding, salt and roast beef, gravy, yorkshire pudding, cabbage, with horseradish sauce and roast potatoes, Brussels sprouts, spring greens in season, asparagus, turnips, swedes, runner beans, Suffolk cured ham on the bone, pork cutlets, lamb chops, chicken, turkey and goose roast with thyme and sausage stuffings, tender duckling and orange sauce, diced Hampshire venison seasoned with black peppers and sage braised in rich red wine, various spit-roasted piglets in season, turbot braised in white sauce with sundry relishes, cod in batter, Dover sole lightly boiled in milk with parsley and fennel, filleted herring and whiting, smoked mackerel in vinegar, smoked salmon sandwiches, Hartington stilton which is a mouthful, English bree, rockfort, shome, dolchilatty, gowder and cammembear cheeses, with Bath olivers and Cream Crackers, strawberries and cream, apple tart and custard, brandy snaps and assorted dainties, pastries, confections and chocolate sweetmeats.

(Turn over)

Regulation R974 (C3)
Suitable Designs for Gravestones and the Composition
of Dignified Inscriptions

A plain and sturdy cross will suffice to signal the arrival in the Elysian Fields
of the classic cricketer. A simple slab will serve for the man who in life has
Played the Game fairly without fear, and with a good upright heart.

Stumps, bats, and representations of scorebooks or career statistics on
gravestones are not necessary. Self-composed epitaphs tend to Go On Too
Long (Fig. 107). Sponsored gravestones with the commercial mottoes of
sportswear or soft drinks manufacturers are in the worst possible taste.

Humorous slogans, witticisms and jokes are not appropriate, for humour
is never so funny as its author believes and it dates very quickly.

It will be of great benefit to the Gentleman in later years to cultivate a
friendship with his rector, for it is he who holds the key to a good site in the
Churchyard.

On the Gentleman's tomb classical allusions should be confined to the
well-known myths (Cyclops, Medusa, the labours of Hercules, Prometheus
and Pandora). Verses should always be in rhyme, for poetry which does not
rhyme betrays indolence or haste on the part of its author. The poet can
always find a rhyme if he takes his time.

Players will usually settle for something plainer. The acronym S.I.P.
(Selected, Informed, Played) finds favour among the deceased because it is
entirely unpretentious.

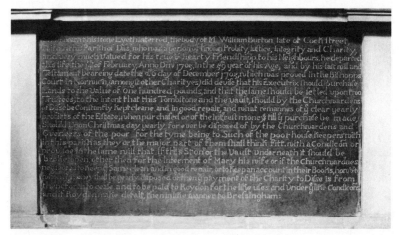

Fig. 107: *Epitaph etiquette and tomb theory*
The good works of the best of men can often be summed up in a few words. Essays should
not be attempted as these can try the patience of the casual mourner.

PHASE TWO

GRAVE MATTERS

"O eloquent, just, and mighty Death! ... thou hast drawn together all the far stretched greatness, all the pride, cruelty, and ambition of man".

Introductory Lesson L672

Poets have ever sung of Death. It is one of life's great themes, along with Love and women. Therefore there is little that the Academy can add, except to say that at last, old men begin to ramble, voices crack and thoughts go lack-a-day and all a-jumble, the brain a maggot pie wrings shapes unheard of, reason turns awry.

Inevitably the great poets too, all in their turn, were completely Out, suffered the last Cosmic drawing of the stumps, the Final Dismissal which diminishes all men. Therefore never send to know for whom the bails fall, they fall for thee.

Keats grew pale and spectre thin and died, Chaucer was not suffered to dwellen here but as it were the twynklynge of an ye, and Thomas Sackville, Earl of Dorset (b. 1536) found his withered fist knock knock knocking at Death's door in 1608.

Poetry, unlike forgery, buggery, blasphemy and penury, has never been a crime, although it has been the cause of an equal measure of human suffering. Therefore many consider it unjust that poets, unlike prophets and poachers, have never died from the Death penalty for pursuing their professions.

It is not for the Academy to criticize what occurs in political life; but a few comments and correctives are called for:

John Webster said, "I know death hath several doors for men to make their exits" and this serves to demonstrate the folly of those who believe too readily what they read in books, for Webster is wrong in two respects:

1. Many people, particularly in New York, are thrown from windows, not doors, chiefly because doors on upper floors open into adjoining rooms. Other potentially deceased persons are loosed from bridges, ships and cliffs.

2. It is not the act of making an exit that is fatal in many cases; on the contrary, the act of making an entrance can often be a grave mistake. This is especially true of certain public houses in Scotland and the poorer districts of Middlesbrough and Darlington.

Historical examples of mortal Entrance:

a) Nelson entered battle with the French and died a punctured man.

219

(Turn over)

b) Henry VIII entered numerous women and died of an unpleasant disease.
c) P.B. Shelley entered the Adriatic and died of waves and drowning.
d) Faustus entered into a pact with the Devil and died 30 years later.

Therefore death is not something for the amateur cricketer to meddle with. It should, where possible, be left to the Professional, doctors and nurses, armed policemen,[1] undertakers and the clergy, stonemasons and florists, lorry drivers and "fast food" fryers

Chairman's Interruption E003
Literary form, notes on style, marginal errors, alliteration and the fast food fryer, with an Important Offence Discover'd and Grave News for all Creditors of the Academy

The Chairman has ordered that the Controller strike out the next 632 Regulations and write down, forthwith and instead, that **Enough is Enough.** He has further commanded that the reader be addressed in the following terms:

"O cruel spite! With what high hopes did the Chairman commission a Noble Work of lasting worth, and now there stretches before Him a tale told by an idiot. This is a serious life on a Serious Earth, and yet the authors can speak of nothing more edifying than fast food fryers! Thus it is time to put an end to such Wicked Waste of Paper.

Further, he was irritated by the overwhelming dullness of the remaining material, most of which **had nothing to do with cricket** and will *all have to be done again.* His Preface clearly indicates how much better He could have written the manual Himself. And in any case invoices show that it has already come to more than He wanted to spend.

Lastly, He is appalled, and would have it written down **in black print** and *in sloping letters* that His marginal note on page 78 found its way into the text. He wants to know who is responsible, and He has retired to His inner office (Fig. 108). Accordingly, He has instructed the Treasurer that nobody be paid a farthing until the culprit has Owned Up."

---

[1] Who do a difficult and often noisy job.

Fig. 108: *Video Portum*
The area around the Great Portal is classified and a Level Five security corridor, and is
controlled by hidden closed-circuit television cameras.

221

(Turn over)

APPENDIX A

PART A: THE PENAL CODES

Offences can vary widely in their nature and are divided into five groups, in ascending order of seriousness, as Misdemeanour, Nuisance, Outrage and Disgrace, with one intermediate category.

Some regulations may have variable class penalties according to the nature of the offender and his status as Gentleman or player. In doubtful cases where there is an infringement of a Regulation bearing two such classifications the accused shall be charged under the lower of these. Failure to observe this ruling is itself a Class C2A offence. All offences of Grades C1, C2 and C2A are notifiable. Thus:

CLASS DESCRIPTION / TYPE OF HEARING AND PENALTIES

C1 Disgrace
(Appalling) An extremely serious infringement or defiance
Private hearing with guilty party represented, followed by Chairman's Directive and a Humiliation Notice published in *The Times*.

Instant excommunication and confiscation of registration documents land or property. Special assignment report.

C2 Outrage
(Most distressing) A wicked infringement
Private hearing with guilty party present and asked for an explanation.

Excommunication in ordinary or heavy fines, 3–10 year suspensions and major endorsements to registration documents.

C2A Outrageous nuisance
(Distressing) A serious infringement
Private hearing with the guilty party present but not allowed to speak.

Moderate fines and a written reprimand
6 month–3 year suspensions and endorsement of registration documents
Unspecified processing.

C3 Nuisance
(Annoying) An irritating infringement
No hearing. A private directive issued by the Adjudicator to his clerk.

Small fines, endorsement of registration documents and issuing of Voluntary Seizure Orders.

C4 Misdemeanour
(Niggling) A less serious infringement
Summary conviction.

On the spot fines.

PART B: PROCEDURES AND PUNISHMENTS

ACADEMY PROVISIONS FOR THE APPORTIONING OF RETRIBUTION AND PUNISHMENT, AND CORRECTIVE PROVISIONS FOR JUVENILES, DELINQUENTS, TRANSGRESSORS AND MALEFACTORS

Diligent students will note that, in order to avoid a hectoring tone, many Regulations are set out rather as friendly advice than as hard and fast laws. Legal language is ugly and frightens children, but cricketers should make no mistake: the behaviour called for, whether explicitly stated or gently implied by each Regulation, is a *requirement*, *not a suggestion*. In Regulations which state that a club should/should not behave in a specified manner it is understood that any individual member is *de facto* guilty should any collective breach occur, and is liable to prosecution. This has the effect of making each cricketer responsible for club transgressions.

1. The distinction between i) notifiable and ii) non-notifiable offences

Broadly these follow what in ordinary legal terms are the equivalent of i) criminal or indictable offences and ii) misdemeanours. Notifiable offences (Class C1, C2 and C2A) are generally those listed under the cricketing health regulations or those showing a flagrant disregard of Academy ideology and Directives.

Non-notifiable offences (C3 and C4) are usually those involving abuse of neighbours, equipment belonging to opposing teams, certain violent acts against dogs or the elderly not committed in pursuance of and for the greater benefit of the Game, or any such act motivated by whim or personal grudge.

2. Procedures for notifying the Academy

Every good club will have its own Registered Informer. He will undertake to assemble evidence of offences against the Game, complete with a full set of measurements, passing them forward to the Informer General for prosecution, conviction and punishment.

Hearings may be dispensed with if the Club Informer fills in the Certificate of Guilt and signs the declaration. In such cases the penalties will be imposed without further investigation.

In other cases, where a more lowly club with no proper Informer is involved, a hearing will of necessity have to be arranged. The wrongdoer will be arraigned initially before the Informer General, then in the presence of the Moderator and his staff. Finally he will stand before the Adjudicator who will sift the evidence and fix the penalties and costs.

3. Academy Inspections, Investigations, and Nocturnal Inquiries

All clubs shall lend unqualified assistance to any Academy investigator, Bailiff or Inspector who visits a member's private home, any clubhouse or field of play.

His task shall be made straightforward by the opening up to his sight of any records or documents he demands and the provision of an interview room with proper lighting and a 13-ampere socket as well as interviewees nominated by him.

A list of forthcoming notified inspections will be published in *The Times* at the beginning of each Cricketing Year, and at intervals throughout the season as the Academy's Board of Governors or Moderator General see fit.

No warning will be given for Sudden Diurnal Visits and Nocturnal Commissions which may take place at any time, day or night.

(Turn over)

4. Procedures for compiling a Satisfactory Statement

There is little point in informing the Academy of any transgression if the information is not accompanied by an accurate statement of the facts and the charge, with the date, time and place of the offence and a signed declaration that the suspect has been cautioned. Informers (whether Registered or not) should write legibly on one side of the paper only. The Moderator reserves the right to amend any statement which is not satisfactory.

5. A Summons to Academy Headquarters

Nobody will gain from the unpleasant scenes which usually accompany the visit of Academy Constables to a player's home to execute a warrant in default of appearance.

Therefore if a Gentleman is asked to appear at Academy headquarters (Fig. 109) he will be expected to present himself at the time appointed.

6. Types of Disciplinary Hearings available to the accused/guilty

Those with Class C and Class D culpability are permitted to plead not guilty. For offences categorized as Class A and B only guilty pleas are accepted. This new measure, an enlightened suggestion from the Chairman, has been introduced to save time and expense, and each transgressor will be informed of the classification before the hearing.

Class A: Redhanded.   Class B: You were seen.   Class C: It must have been you.
Class D: Who else would do it?

7. Fixed Penalties and Method of Payment

Fixed or mitigated penalties are available for certain offences of C4 classification. Cheques or banknotes will be accepted from certain classes of offender only.

8. The issuing of Voluntary Seizure Orders

From time to time, if he feels like it, or if some offence or non-payment is involved, the Adjudicator may, voluntarily, issue a seizure order which authorizes distraint of goods belonging to the offender. The bailiffs from the Debt Retrieval Unit, the Sergeant-at-Arms and his constables who will serve and execute the order, are trained to recognize no impediment to the proper completion of the exercise in hand. They are empowered to bear away goods to the sentimental value of £250.

Non-compliance with voluntary seizure orders. Any attempt to obstruct the bailiffs in the execution of their duty leaves the perpetrator well qualified for a judicial application of the pillywinks, but this is no longer possible under Common Market regulations, and new technology is being introduced.

9. A Special Note on Excommunication

Nothing, save the displeasure of the Chairman, brings more grief to the Directors of the British Academy of Cricket than the realization that one of the flock has strayed.[1]

Excommunication, the severing of the individual limb from the body of the Academy is the severest sanction. Great strength of character will be needed if the excommunicee is to attempt to continue his career. Most choose to move away to the anonymity of the Eastern Counties or Somerset, a small Scottish island or some other wilderness. None will, of course, ever bat or bowl again on any field in England.

---

[1] The Academy will also publish, from time to time, a list of malefactors, wrongdoers, heretics, non-conformists, Baptists and Methodists, criminals and nefarians drawn from its Index of un-Cricketing Persons and de-Registered Personnel. This will be kept up to date by the most modern bookkeeping techniques and filing cabinets. Full transcripts of trials and hearings will be available on request from the Archivists' Department.

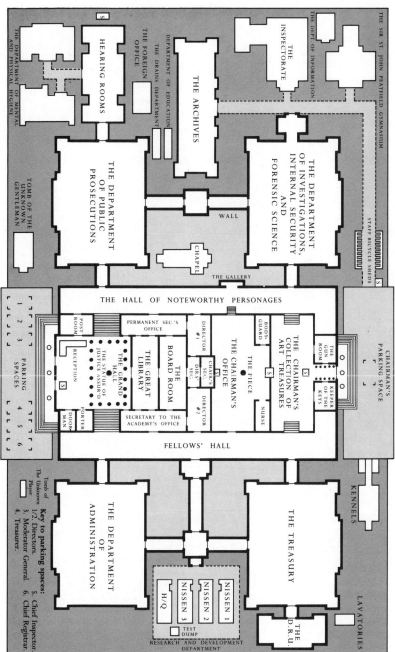

Fig. 109: *Plan of Academy House*

225

(Turn over)

DETAILED CLASSIFICATIONS OF SOCIAL GROUPS BY TRADE OR PROFESSION

THE NEED FOR AN AUTHORITATIVE TABLE OF TRADE AND PROFESSIONAL RATINGS, INCORPORATING AN EXTRACT FROM **REGULATION R1684** *(C1)* OF THE *BRITISH ACADEMY OF CRICKET MANUAL FOR OFFICERS AND STAFF*

No Registered cricketer will wish to play against a rabble of fish fryers or foundry workers or a side laced with teachers and tradesmen. All cricketers are entitled, irrespective of rank or status, to refuse to take part in any match where a team with less than a 40-point aggregate (the total of all participants' individual scores) has been fielded. An example:

Those trades first mentioned carry only a single point. Thus a team made up of these sorts would score a mere 11 points. But the insertion into the team of a Bishop (40) or two Majors (18 each) would bring it to Regulation level.

If any club attempts to offer a deficient side then the Secretary and Captain should be reported immediately and the game cancelled.

IMPORTANT NOTE:

Let it be said at the outset, lest the British Academy of cricket be accused of perpetuating Class Distinction, that the following pages deal with categories, not divisions.

Generally speaking the five socio-economic groups, often used by sociologists, demographers and such like, are false, arbitrary and calculated to upset and annoy people.

There are, in the Real World, only two groups: important people who do nothing, and unimportant people who are paid to help them.

TECHNICAL DETAILS:

The listings here are by no means comprehensive, and in many cases several detailed categories are conflated for the sake of brevity. For full listing schedules all Registered Associates should make application to the Academy.

Additional or supplementary points may be scored for special distinctions and, where applicable, these are given at the end of the listing, as are penalty points for undesirable habits/characteristics.

The cricketer should never enter a higher ranking than that to which he is entitled, as this is a serious offence (Class C2). However, if he is self-employed he should with confidence award himself an extra two points, if self-unemployed one point.

Cricketers of any trade or profession may apply for higher rating, but sworn testimony to personal distinction must be produced before Exemption Certificates will be issued.

Similarly, if it can be *rigorously demonstrated* that, by cruel, unkind or illicit word or deed, uncouth behaviour, any other offence against good discipline and etiquette or by persistent Breach of Academy Regulations, whether committed by design or by default, a cricketer has shown himself unworthy of the Normal rating, he may forfeit all or some of his points after a hearing by the Adjudicator.

PART A

Primary ratings below deal with all the key cricketing Professions.

ARISTOCRATS: Royal personages *100*, hereditary Peers, Earls and Viscounts *60*.

LANDOWNERS: Over 8,000 acres *60*. Others: 5 points per 1,000 acres. Farmers under 200 acres *4*. Smallholders (less than 30 acres) *2*.

MILITARY PERSONNEL: Field Marshal *60*, General *50*. Others: Major and above *18*; lower ranks *2*, privates *1*.
Bonus points: *2* for each campaign medal, wound, 25 years. *3* for Falklands war, Navy and the Royal Air Force similar.

CLERGY: Archbishop *50*, Bishop *40*. Other ranks: *6*, Rector *4*, Vicar *3*.
Deduct 6 points for scandal, choirboys.

ACADEMICS: Professors *12*, Senior Lecturers *8*. One bonus point for each published treatise (full length).
Deduct *15* points for: Ruskin College.
Dons 6 bonus points (Oxford/certain Cambridge colleges).

SCHOOLTEACHERS: State schools *0*, private *2*. Bonus points: Headmaster *1*.

JOURNALISTS: The Daily Telegraph, Daily Express, Times *15* points. Other national newspapers/magazines *2*. Regional/local *1*.
Bonus points: Cricket correspondent *6*, sports editor *4*, Academy approved *6*.

LEGAL PROFESSION: Judges *50*, Barrister *30*, Solicitor *2*, Clerk to the Justices *2*, Magistrate *3*, Chairman of the Bench *5*.

POLICE: Chief Constable *55*, Chief Inspector *32*, Inspector *18*, Sergeant *12*, Constable *8*, Special Constable *6*.

CIVIL SERVICE: Permanent Secretary *48*, Others: Executive officer and above *4*, Clerical Officers *1*. Office cleaner *0*.

LOCAL GOVERNMENT OFFICERS: Chief officers *2*. Others *1*.

MEDICAL PROFESSION: Surgeons *12*, GPs *4*, Nurses: SRN *2*, SEN *1*, Hospital worker *1*.

Bonus points: Harley Street *16*, ear nose and throat *1*. *Penalty points:* National health *6*.

BANKING: Banker *24*, manager *6*, under manager *2*, others *1*.

BUILDING INDUSTRY: Builder *2*, steeplejack *2*, architect *1*, tradesmen *1*, others *0*. Master mason *6*.
Bonus points: Remembered the ladder *2*.
Penalty points: Centre Point *4*, monstrous carbuncles *6*, whistling at ladies *4*.

AGRICULTURAL WORKERS *1*. *Bonus points:* horny-handed *1*, contented *3*, cheery wave *4*.
Penalty points: Tractor neglect *2*.

ENTERTAINMENT: Films: Director *4*, star *4*, distributor *5*, ticket office clerk *2*.
Stage: Director *5*, famous actor *4*, playwright *1*, others *1*. Musicians *1*. Deduct 6 points for musicals, opera, ballet, variety.
Deduct 2 points for general entertainer.

LITERATURE: Authors, novelists, essayists *1* Clever Dicks and Smart Alecs *0*.

BROADCASTING: Director General *20*, Controller of Programmes *1*.

WIRELESS: Registered announcer: Third Programme *3*, Home Service *2*, Light Programme *1*. Others *0*.
Deduct 3 points for: Desert Island Discs.

TELEVISION: Independent Television *6*, BBC 1, *4*, BBC 2 *1*. Deduct 4 points for Channel Four.
Bonus points: Personal friend of Lord Reith *18*, favourable review *18*.
Penalty points: Mastermind *1*, Pot Black *1*.

SALESMEN: All types 1. Bonus points: Sales Manager *4*, arms *6*, fine sportswear *6*.
Deduct 4 points for: Advertising, motor trade, publisher, estate agent.

CRICKETING CRAFTSMEN: Master batmaker *15*, Journeyman batmaker *10*, Apprentice *6*.
Master Stumpmaker *8*, Journeyman *5*.

(Turn over)

PART B

A.A. man 4
Accountant 5
Acrobat 3
Adze maker 2
Alchemist 3
Analyst 3
Anarchist 0
Animal liberator 0
Anthropologist 1
Antiquarian 1
Apple picker 2
Architect
  Municipal 4
  City of London 1
  Ordinary 2
Ash scatterer 2
Assembly line worker 1
Astrologer 2
Astrologer Royal 8
Auctioneer 0

Baker 3
Bank clerk 1
Bagmaker 2
Bargemaster 5
Barman 1
Bedmaker 1
Beekeeper 4
Beggarman 0
Biologist 3
Binliner 1
Blacksmith 2
Bodger 2
Bookbinder 2
Bookmaker 2
Bookseller 18
Bow Street Runner 8
Boxer 5
Brewer 8
Bricklayer 1
Brushmaker 1
Burglar 0
Bus conductor 1
Butcher 3
Butler 4

Cabinetmaker 3
Candelabrastick maker 3
Carpenter 2
Chauffeur 4
Chef 3
Chimney sweep 1

Churchwarden 4
City Analyst 12
Cleaner
  Municipal 0
  Private 2
Climatologist 0
Clogmaker 1
Clown 3
Clothier 1
Coalman 1
Coastguard 3
Coke carrier 1
Compositor 0
Computer programmer 2
Confectioner 4
Cook
  Ship 3
  School dinners 0
  Club 4
Cooper 4
Councillor
  Conservative 6
  Other 0
Counsellor 0
Crab Catcher 3
Crane driver 3
Critic
  Art 0
  Drama 1
  Television 1
  Book 11
  Wireless 1

Dairy farmer 3
Dancer
  Ballroom 4
  Ballet 6
  Limbo 0
Decorator 1
Dentist 4
Designer (Graphic) 0
Detective 6
Distiller 5
Ditch digger 1
Diver 2
Doghandler 4
Domestic 0
Doorman 1
Down-and-out 0
Drain layer 1
Driving instructor 2
Drummer 2

Dustman
  Private 2
  Council 0

Editor 0
Egg producer 2
Electrician 2
Embezzler 0
Engine driver 3
Engineer 1
Escort 0
Evangelist 4
Executioner (retired) 9
Explorer
  Amateur 2
  Antarctic 5
  Asia Major/Minor 3
  Professional 8
  South America 4

Factory worker 0
Faggot maker 2
Fashion model 0
Fashion designer 1
Fig pickler 2
Fireman 3
Fish fryer 1
Flykiller 1
Footman 4
Forester 3
Foundry worker 1
Funeral director 4

Gaffer 1
Gamekeeper 4
Gamewarden/keeper 6
Gardener
  Landscape 4
  Vegetable 1
Gasman 1
Gasfitter (British) 2
Ghillie 8
Gibmaker 1
Glassblower 2
Gluemaker 0
Goat breeder 3
Goldsmith 4
Goose farmer 3

Handyman 1
Hole digger 2
Home guard 4

Horticulturalist 3
Horseman 1
Hurdle maker 2

Illegal alien 0
Inland revenue inspector 0
Innkeeper 3
Inshore fisherman 2
Inspector 6
Interpreter 2
Insurance man 1
Interner 5
Inventor 5
Investor 4

Jack of all trades 3
Jacuzzi designer 4
Jam maker 4
Jockey
  Racing 3
  Disc 0
Journeyman 2
Juggler 1

Keelmaker 3
Keymaker
Kleen-Eze man 1

Labourer 0
Ladle former 2
Lamplighter 1
Landlord 2
Lapelmaker 1
Lavatory attendant 1
Letter writer
  Telegraph 4
  Times 3
  Other 0
Lifeguard 2
Lighthousekeeper 5
Linguist 0
Lion tamer 8
Lollimaker 4
Lorry driver 1
Lugwormer 3

Manager
  Middle 3
  Upper 6
  Football 0
Magician 2
Manicurist 1

Marksman **6**
Mastmaker **3**
Matmaker **1**
Mechanic **1**
Melon pipper **2**
Micro processor **1**
Milkman **1**
Mole catcher **5**
Moleskinner **6**
Morris dancer **0**
Mugger **0**
Muleskinner **0**
Museum attendant **1**

National hero **8**
Navigator **3**
Newspaper baron **6**
Nightwatchman **4**

Oil worker **2**
Onion seller **0**
Optician **3**
Oral hygienist **2**
Orange squasher **2**
Organist **4**
Osteopath **4**
Ostler **3**

Painter
  Impressionist **0**
  Watercolour **1**
  House **2**
  Action **0**
Peat digger **0**
Pigman **3**
Ploughman **3**
Plumber **1**
Poacher **0**
Poet laureate **6**
Poor man **0**
Pheasant plucker **3**
Philanthropist **12**
Philatelist **5**
Photographer **2**
Physicist **2**
Pile driver **1**
Pilot **3**
Pimp **2**
Planner
  Town and country **0**
  Family **2**
Plastics moulder **1**
Plum pudding maker **4**
Poet **1**

Politician
  Conservative **8**
  Other **0**
  Retired **2**
Polyglot **1**
Porcelain painter **3**
Potter **1**
Postman **2**
Potboiler **2**
Porter **1**
Poulterer **3**
Poultry plucker **1**
Printer **1**
Private Investigator **5**
Psychiatrist **0**
Psychologist **0**
Psychopath **0**

Quail dresser **4**
Quality grocer **3**
Quibbler **1**
Quill sharpener **2**

Rabbi **0**
Racing driver **3**
R.A.C. man **2**
Rag and bone man **1**
Ragtrader **1**
Railwayman **0**
Ratcatcher **1**
Researcher **2**
Restorer **4**
Riveter **1**
Rich man **4**
Roadpainter **0**
Roadsweeper **0**
Rodent remover **4**
Rust remover **2**

Sagger maker **3**
Sailor **1**
Scissors sharpener **3**
Scoutmaster **8**
Scrap metal dealer **1**
Sculptor **0**
Secondary Picketeer **0**
Sewage disposer **0**
Sheepshearer **1**
Sheepstealer **0**
Shoe shiner **1**
Shopkeeper **4**
Shredder
  Wheat **4**
  Paper **5**

Silversmith **3**
Stamplicker **3**
Stockbroker **8**
Student **0**
Slaughterman **3**
Social reformer **0**
Soldier **1**
Spy **16**
Strongman **3**

Tailor **3**
Tanner **2**
Tapper
  Telephone **5**
  Wheel **1**
  Heel **1**
Taxidermist **7**
Taxi driver
  Hackney Carriage **3**
  Ford Granada **1**
  Minicab **1**
Tea cake toaster **5**
Tea taster **8**
Telephone engineer **1**
  Temporary worker **1**
Test pilot **8**
Textile worker **2**
Thief **0**
Theologian **7**
Ticket collector **3**
Timber worker **1**
Tinker **0**
Town crier **5**
Toolmaker **2**
Traffic warden **0**
Tramp **0**
Trawlerman **1**
Turner **2**
Typist **2**

Undertaker **4**
Umbrella operative **1**
Undergarment designer **2**
Urban guerrilla **0**
Usurer **0**

Vacuum flask maker **5**
Valet **4**
Van driver **1**
V.A.T. inspector **4**
Venereologist **5**
Vermin exterminator **4**
Veterinary surgeon **3**
Vigilante **5**

Vintner **4**
Vole exterminator **1**

Waist coater **3**
Waist gunner **7**
Waiter **2**
Waterboatman **1**
Wayfarer **1**
Weak man **1**
Weatherman **0**
Whaler **3**
Wheelwright **3**
Wine merchant **4**
Wooden spoon maker **2**
Wrestler **1**

Xylophone maker **1**

Yak breeder **1**
Yarn spinner **4**
Yachtmaker **6**
Young farmer **3**
Youth trainee **2**

Zealot **0**
Zionist **0**
Zookeeper **4**
Zoologist **2**

(Turn over)

APPENDIX C

SOCIAL ILLS: OUTLINED IN THE GARRETT REPORT

ABSTRACT AND SUMMARY

OF

IMPORTANT FINDINGS

by Sir John Garrett in his report
to the British Academy of Cricket which are now
to become Official Policy

RECOGNIZED SOCIAL ILLS STRIKING AT THE CORE OF NATIONAL DIGNITY

The British Academy of Cricket list of evils and root causes of major moral and spiritual decline. Taken from the British Academy of Cricket Garrett Report on Socio-Economic Groups 4 and 5 (Non-registered persons and undesirables) Paragraph 53 Sub Section 3.

SOCIAL ILL	CAUSE	REMEDY
DRUNKENNESS	Excessive income	Reduction in social security.
	Public bars ⎫ Football/Rugby Unions ⎬ Singing and shouting ⎭	Short sharp shock.
	Celts and congregating youths	Alsatians, A.T.C., Camping.
	Bingo	Classical education.
	Dirty pots and pans, screaming children	Sheds, allotments, hot soapy water.
UNEMPLOYMENT	Sleeping and loafing	Early rising and means testing.
	Parental ignorance	Home ownership.
	Moral deficiencies	Privatization and self-help.
	Closed shop	Union legislation.
	Over manning	Involuntary redundancy, self-employment.
	Immobility	Bicycle.
	Lack of jobs	Better statistics management.
	Truancy, liberalism	Sunday schools/prayer.

230

SOCIAL ILL	CAUSE	REMEDY
LAWLESSNESS	Hatred of police............................	Plain clothes.
	Secondary picketing....................	Union reform.
	Racial tension..............................	Meditation and deep breathing.
	Television/B.B.C.........................	Cross country, censorship.
VANDALISM	Mental deficiency........................	Boxing, pet care, flower arranging, prison, modelmaking, choir practice.
	Football......................................	Cricket.
	Political agitation	Legal reform, camps.
	Inner city decay	Corner-shops, red telephone boxes, Home Office action.
	Aggressive tendencies..................	Polishing metallic objects.
LAZINESS	Self-abuse....................................	Room inspections.
	Shirking.......................................	National service.
	Bubble bath.................................	Cold showers.
OBESITY	Afters and custard......................	Value Added Tax, wired jaws.
	Postal orders/Giro cheques	Means testing.
	Large plates.................................	Smaller plates.
POVERTY	Glasgow, Liverpool......................	Slum clearance, population distribution.
	Socialism	*Sun* and *Daily Express*.
	Thriftlessness	Savings Bonds, Guilt Edge Securities.
IRRELIGION	Free thinking, and political subversion	Private education, climbing frames and Cross Country.
	Questioning and debate..............	The Church of England.
	Scientific method........................	Censorship.
	Blasphemy and heresy.................	Faith and observance.
	Pop music/jeans..........................	Good talking-to.
VIOLENCE	Racial inequality..........................	Patriotic sentiment and spirit of Empire.
	People with banners	Water cannons.
	Free Press....................................	Political changes.
	Disagreements and bad blood.....	Exercises, strong heart, licensing laws.
LATENESS	Over indulgence and late nights......................................	Curfew, early rising.
	Gluttony, self-abuse....................	Running on the spot.
	Poor planning	British Cricket Time.

(Turn over)

SOCIAL ILL	CAUSE	REMEDY
DECEIT/LYING	Parental indifference..................	Corporal punishment.
	Poor family background	Adoption.
	Genetic deficiencies (Cockney/ Romany)................................	Team games and metal polishing.
	Close set eyes/swarthy complexion............................	Thorough scrubbing, thick flannel.
DEBT	No money	Work harder.
	Late rising	Early to bed.
	Loafing	Withdraw state assistance.
LETHARGY	Sofas with cushions.....................	Stick back chairs.
	Solitary habits	Modelmaking, Do It Oneself.
BURGLARY	Criminals....................................	Neighbourhood watch.
	Envy...	Wider share ownership.
SEXUAL ABUSE	Dirty books.................................	Abstinence, stamp collecting, pet care, knot tying.
	Perverts......................................	Cut down hedges.
ILL HEALTH	Irresponsibility and lack of consideration	National Service
	Ignorance and mental deficiency	Basket work and woodcraft.
	Foreign travel.............................	Home ownership.
	Hypochondria.............................	Corporal punishment.
	Winter	South Africa..
	London.......................................	Switzerland.
	Stress..	Tablets.
	Doctor's waiting rooms	Go to work.
MARXISM	Envy...	Home ownership, shelf and patio construction.
	Want of deference	Sunday school, flat caps.
	Meetings	Allotments/modelmaking.
	Promiscuity.................................	The American Disease.
	Beards	Shaving.
	Elections	State of Emergency.
GAMBLING	Excess income.............................	Withdraw state benefits. Raise tax rate. National Lottery.
	Horses and Pork Pie hats............	Early closing for betting shops.
	Indolence	Horse care, hoeing.

SOCIAL ILL	CAUSE	REMEDY
SCHIZOPHRENIA AND MENTAL ILL HEALTH	Indecision...................................	Getting a Grip, Pulling Oneself Together.
AGGRESSION	Mental/physical deficiency.........	Education of character (Fig. 110)
	Classroom chaos	Academy Approved schools
	Arguments/debate......................	Standardized opinions.
LOITERING	Purple hair.................................	Reform schools.
	Neglect of duty	Wife, National Service.
	Crime...	More padlocks, longer sentences.
	Street corners	Straighter roads.

Fig. 110: *The definitive Forward Strategic Advance and Interception*

As an aid to the Suppression of Instinct the forward defensive stroke is essential. Moving forward to challenge the assault, with no thought of retaliation, runs as contrary to the passions of Man as Socialism or Self-Knowledge. Thus it forms an important basis for the self-control.

Jeffrey Bowles (Gent.), a batting prodigy, here demonstrates the Classical forward defensive stroke. Left, Right: Head stock still, with dignified expression; ball moving; straight bat; sensible footwear. Right, Wrong: Moving head; flailing at the ball; blurred vision; poor stance; angled bat. Now that Sir St. John's time is taken up with the Chairman's Strategic Wireless Initiative Mr Bowles is training to take over responsibility for the Sir St. John Peatfield Cricketing School of Excellence for Boys.

THE BRITISH ACADEMY OF CRICKET INDEX OF WHOLLY DISAPPROVED PUBLICATIONS, BOOKS AND PAMPHLETS.

MENTAL HYGIENE AND THE USE OF THE BRITISH ACADEMY OF CRICKET APPROVED READING LIST FOR ADULTS AND THE GENERAL READER

It is because of the proliferation of heretical tracts and pamphlets that the Academy has published an Approved Reading List. The Academy Censor, the Master of Controversial Questions and the Qualifier have this Catalogue of Internal Reading under continual review. Failure to follow their Joint Directives attracts severe penalties.

Recent de-Indexed volumes include:

1. Plutarch: *The Rise and Fall of Athens*
2. McFarlane, K.: *Wycliffe and English Non-Conformity*
3. Northrop, F.: *Ideological Differences and World Order*
4. Sir Sidney Lee: *Great Englishmen of the Sixteenth Century*
5. Copernicus, N.: *De Revolutionibus Orbium Celestium*
6. Jonson, B.: *Bartholomew Fair*

Additions to the British Academy of Cricket Approved Reading List for players, remedials, the educationally sub-normal, minors, juveniles and adolescents:

1. Lamb, Mr and Mrs C.: *Tales from Shakespeare*
2. Hughes, E.: *The Hawk in the Rain*
3. Wing Commander Guy Gibson: *Enemy Coast Ahead*
4. Irving, D.: *The Destruction of Dresden*
5. Bunyan, J.: *The Pilgrim's Progress*

EXTERNAL SUPPORT READING FOR THE MATURE AND TRUSTWORTHY

These lists may be supplemented by external books chosen from public libraries or a bookseller of good reputation who may be relied upon not to sell books of inferior quality or content. A full list of approved purveyors of literature may be had on application to the British Academy of Cricket Chief Education Officer.

Any cricketer who wishes to take the unusual step of purchasing for himself any non-specified book may, if he wishes, forward it to the Academy for full vetting and for checking against the Academy Index of Wholly Unapproved Publications to ensure that it is not on the Index pending correction or revision.

Any book found to contain Dirty Bits or to be heretical, over-long, blasphemous, scurrilous, insulting to the Queen or to have American or Russian quotations which are difficult to understand or anything written by a practising paedophile or Professor shall be subject to forfeit and destruction.

THE BRITISH ACADEMY OF CRICKET
INDEX OF PARTIALLY AND WHOLLY DISAPPROVED
PUBLICATIONS, BOOKS AND PAMPHLETS

No cricketer shall read or mention any of the 7,485 volumes at present listed by The British Academy of Cricket as being in part heretical or in need of correction with regard to their political or religious content or from their classification as wholly or partly Contrary to the Spirit of the Game or the Academy, or likely to corrupt or deprave the Cricketer.

The range of literature extends from the merely idle, vacuous and inane, foreign literature critical of the English, American novels containing Americanisms and Transatlantic slang, through corrupt and subversive tracts, obscene and debauched narratives and Revolutionary and Seditious pamphlets to the extreme of scurrilous and satirical books which denigrate, ridicule and devalue the British Way of Going About Things.

England is renowned for its tolerance, and the Chairman and Directors of the British Academy of Cricket have instructed that their Censor shall not have an heavy hand in these matters. He shall use his authority as a precision cutting tool to carve out this Tumour in our National Brain, not to concuss the patient with the painful club of crude Censorship. Philosophical freedom and the right to express his view is the birthright of the Englishman, provided he does not offend the person of her Majesty the Queen or her subjects. Liberty, not Licence, is granted under English Law which embodies the right of all citizens to be protected from extremist views.

It has been said that it were better to murder a man than murder a good book, and this goes to the very heart of the Englishman's sensibilities. The Academy therefore seeks to murder no book, merely to wrest from its author, by such force as may be necessary, the sinister triple weapons of thought, notion and idea.

RECENT ADDITIONS TO THE INDEX

The enquiring mind may be an asset to plain clothes policemen but for the average cricketer it is an encumbrance: it leads him to error, defiance and Forbidden Fruit. This can leave his intellect bruised and broken on the unyielding ground of the Academy Index. It is more pleasant never to know than to want to forget.

The most recent additions made to the Index by the Censor are set out, briefly, below.

Let it be shewn by the first text alone to what base uses scribblers may descend when, with perfidious principle inspired, and wretched glee, they cozen men at Hoodman Blind and think never to besilenced be, upon a peak in Darien.

25A/6021. Milton, J.: *Areopagitica*

Reason: This pamphlet is written Parliamentarily, it supports Freethinking, attacks the Church and conformity and it also opposes Censorship.

> "Another sort there be who when they hear that all things shall be ordered, all things regulated and settled, will strait give themselves up in to your hands, make 'em and cut 'em out what religion ye please; there be delights, there be recreations and jolly pastimes that will fetch the day about from sun to sun, and rock the tedious year as in a delightfull dream. What need they torture their heads with that which others have tak'n so strictly, and unalterably into their own purveying. These are the fruits which dull ease and cessation of our knowledge will bring forth among the people. How goodly and how to be wise were such an obedient unanimity as this, what a fine conformity would it starch us all into? doubtles a staunch and solid peece of frame-work, as any January could freeze together."

(Turn over)

27A/609. Mabey, R.: *Food for Free*
Reason: This short book is based upon the pernicious notion that something may be had by all without any work or effort. It implies that food is all around in fields and meadows and by the wayside for the picking without the need to ask permission of the Landowner or the County Council. It encourages the Englishman to eat, and develop a taste for, toadstools and plants which have a status no higher than that of, and are in fact nothing more than, weeds.

25A/703a. Weinberg, S.: *The First Three Minutes*
Reason: This pseudo-scientific tract, in an ecstasy of impertinence and in defiance of God the one true creator, purports to extrapolate backwards to the time of the early universe, to within a split second of its origin. It abounds in mumbo jumbo and perpetuates Quantum Electrodynamics and, invoking the discovery of Cosmic Background Radiation, seeks to uphold the Big Bang theory of the origin of the Universe which has been fully discredited by Genesis and Malcolm Muggeridge. Certain passages are suspected of Atheism and the closing passages are brazenly humanistic in sentiment.

25A/703b. Lawrence, D.: *Lady Chatterley's Lover*
Reason: Apart from its mawkish sentimentality and lack of true insight or accurate observation, this tawdry volume, written by an author of poor background, seeks to titillate, corrupt and deprave by portraying an English Lady basely and shamefully betraying her class and womanhood by being seen to enjoy flagrantly the sexual act; and as if this were not enough, this congress occurs with a member of the lower class. Furthermore, this Corduroy Copulation was accompanied by much movement[1] of limbs, merriment and cynical pornography.

25A/705. Chaucer, G.: *The Canterbury Tales*
Reason: Bawdiness, broad and liberal humanism and lack of high seriousness. Difficult language embodying outspoken/Saxon expressions denoting parts of the Human Body, tales of violence, debauchery and hot pokers which are distasteful to Gentlemen and insulting to Ladies. Critical of the Church.

APPENDIX E

REGIONAL VARIATIONS
IN RACIAL CHARACTERISTICS

Regional personality traits can vary from county to county according to the landscape, the skyline, the presence of water or other physical features.

It is well known that hill men are fiercely independent, dour, dull and in-bred; plains dwellers are warlike and suspicious of strangers; they have a stoical aloofness because they have behind them a long history of invasion, intrusion and competition for the prime pastures which they hold.

Therefore, in making any assessment the club should make a careful note of all contour lines at the applicant's birthplace and divide these figures by the spot height of his present ordinary residence. his value will be inversely proportional to the magnitude of the number.

---

[1] "A Lady never moves." Lord Curzon.

COUNTY	CHARACTERISTICS
BEDFORDSHIRE	Foul-mouthed, promiscuous, poorly dressed.
BERKSHIRE	Furtive, unkind, bald.
BUCKINGHAMSHIRE	Respectable, sleek, arrogant.
CAMBRIDGESHIRE	Fey, liberal, affected.
CHESHIRE	Wrinkled, lumbering, indolent.
CLEVELAND	Grimy, smoky, dull.
CORNWALL	Nasty, brutish, short.
CUMBERLAND	Dull, quaint, uncouth.
DERBY	Violent, vigilant, forthright.
DEVON	menial, dishonest, unfriendly.
DURHAM	Subversive, empty, truculent.
ESSEX	Suburban, flashy, vacuous.
GLOUCESTERSHIRE	Stolid, gormless, idle.
HAMPSHIRE	Retiring, old, pretentious.
HEREFORDSHIRE	Bovine, fat, ruddy.
HERTFORDSHIRE	Sombre, miserly, headstrong.
HUMBERSIDE	Smelly, cruel, miserly.
KENT	Complacent, overpaid, mouthy.
LANCASHIRE	Homely, fun-loving, filthy.
LEICESTERSHIRE	Indolent, poor, dull.
LINCOLNSHIRE	Plain, humourless, cunning.
LONDON (E)	Loudmouthed, emptyheaded, trivial.
LONDON (W)	Well spoken, emptyheaded, trivial.
LONDON (N)	Arty, emptyheaded, trivial.
LONDON (S)	Spineless, emptyheaded, trivial.
MIDDLESEX	Diseased, stunted, emotional.
NORFOLK	Ignorant, stubborn, bestial.
NORTHANTS	Deeply unpleasant, spotty, ill-tempered.
NORTHUMBERLAND	Squalid, socialistic, Scottish.
NOTTINGHAMSHIRE	Restless, rebellious, boorish.
OXFORDSHIRE	Rigid, intellectual, self-indulgent.
SHROPSHIRE	Sentimental, sloppy, hardworking.
SOMERSET	Sly, servile, rural.
SUFFOLK	Grasping, incestuous, retarded.
SUSSEX	Ostentatious, bed-ridden, dead.
SURREY	Perfidious, oily, money-grubbing.
STAFFORDSHIRE	Garrulous, unhealthy, dirty.
TYNE AND WEAR	Argumentative, alcoholic, unemployed.
WARWICKSHIRE	Shifty, covetous, ill-bred.
WILTSHIRE	Flippant, deceitful, lazy.
WORCESTERSHIRE	Brittle, litigious, saucy.
YORKSHIRE	Arrogant*, dull**, servile, xenophobic, blunt***, stubborn, stupid, proud.

North*, West**, South***

(Turn over)

IMPORTANT ANNOUNCEMENT

The Directors of the British Academy of Cricket would have it known to Sundry and Particular Persons that the undermentioned assisted in the creation of this Manual in their several ways as set out herein below:

Sir St. John Peatfield – *Perfect Gentleman and photographic model.*
J. M. Bowles (Gent.) – *Assistant photographic model to the British Academy of Cricket.*
M. A. Philip – *Reader and assistant sub-editor British Academy of Cricket.*
Dr John Spearman – *Mathematicus and statistical consultant British Academy of Cricket.*
Hopkin R. E. – *Dei Gratia banker to the British Academy of Cricket.*
Fraser J. – *Reader and engineering adviser to the British Academy of Cricket.*

The Directors have been instructed to thank certain persons and institutions for their assistance with the First Five Year Plan, particularly as it relates to the compilation of the manual. Indeed, because they have given of their time and facilities freely, it might be said that they have contributed far more than the authors who were engaged to construct this Testament and who have have *consistently overcharged* the Academy at every stage.

Beware of imposters: the worthy persons and places deserving of the highest praise are, therefore, as follows:

Ronnie Brooks, Mr Lewis and the Eaton School, Palgrave Community Centre, Peter Bavin, The Assembly Rooms, John Allen, Steve Kaschner, Viscount Coke, Mr F.C. Jolly and the Holkham Estate, Hartismere High School, Westray Hancock, Dave Stewart, Geoffrey Wells, Mrs Bertha Gardner, Mrs Sheila Ruddock, Mrs Dorothy Ward, Mrs Hilda Oldman, Mrs Rose, Gabriel, Simon Whitney, Roger Thompson, Roy Adinall, Dick Jeeves, Alan Cant, William Bavin, Philip Morgan, the late Thomas the Turkey, Graham Lacey, Pat Locke, Sam Ramsey, Mark Titchner, Patrick Quick, Edna Loome, Dr Terence Edward Ward PhD, Mike Hall, Mrs Doris Bates, Eric Bates, Mike Webb, Kay Hunter, James Allen, Jack Suggate, Dr James Bentley Philip PhD, Rodney Banks, Dorothy Suggate, Norwich City Council, Madeline Ward, Howard Dyke, Owen Dyke, Georgia Philip, St. Mary's Parish Church Diss, Edward Cant, Zac Bennett and Michael Rudd.

Because the Chairman's photographs do not always come out, as he would wish them to do, the Directors have thought it prudent to purchase certain snaps from other sources, notwithstanding the costs incurred, which are to be the subject of an investigation by the Moderator General.

Those responsible are:

Camera Press, The Mansell Collection, The Victoria and Albert Museum, Frank Hoskins*, The Photo Source, B.B.C. Hulton Picture Library, Allsport, The Imperial War Museum, The Mary Rose Trading Company, Philip Sayer, Howard Dyke*, Mary Evans Picture Library, The 100th Bomb Group Museum*, The British Museum and the Fine Art Photographic Library.

*For their generosity in providing pictures free of charge these persons and this institution have been provided with an Investigations Exemption Certificate (M.Gen. I.E.C. 1d 034B) for life, and tickets for the Chairman's Garden Party.

The diagrams in this book were drawn by David Mallot and Andrew Aloof.

Copious thanks are also due to Jeanie and Ivor Murrell as well as Mr. Jeff Morss.

Fig. 111: *The Naming of the Names*

The names of all those who have hindered, or who have not helped, in the compilation of this Manual have been taken down and recorded. Sir St. John Peatfield and J.M.Bowles (Gent.) are pictured here on their way to the Moderator's office with the documents.

Now their duties are done, they have done each one, and the file is full and overflowed. They cannot stay, for the hasting day has run to the Evensong, and they say farewell, in the book, and are gone.

(Turn over)